To Amy, Beth, Brenda, and
Lillian, my family, who
have helped make the
examined life worth living.

Explorations *in* Environmental Political Theory

Explorations *in* Environmental Political Theory

Thinking About What We Value

Joel Jay Kassiola, editor

M.E. Sharpe
Armonk, New York
London, England

Copyright © 2003 by M. E. Sharpe, Inc.

The author gratefully acknowledges these publishers and rights holders for permission to
reprint excerpts from the following works: Robert E. Goodin, *Green Political Theory*,
Cambridge, UK: Polity Press, 1999; Richard A. Slaughter, ed. *New Thinking for a New
Millennium* 1996, Chapter 10, Lester W. Milbrath, "Envisioning a Sustainable Society,"
pp. 185–197, London: Thomson Publishing.

Library of Congress Cataloging-in-Publication Data

Explorations in environmental political theory : thinking about what we value / edited by
Joel J. Kassiola.
    p. cm.
    Includes bibliographical references and index.
    ISBN 0-7656-1052-3 (alk. paper) — ISBN 0-7656-1053-1 (pbk: alk. paper)
    1. Political ecology. 2. Green movement. 3. Environmentalism—Political aspects.
    4. Sustainable development—Political aspects. I. Kassiola, Joel Jay, 1945–

JA75.8.E97 2003
320.5—DC21
                                                       2002066945

Printed in the United States of America

MV (c) 10 9 8 7 6 5 4 3 2 1
MV (p) 10 9 8 7 6 5 4 3 2 1

Contents

Explorations *in* Environmental Political Theory

Introduction and Overview
The Nature of Environmental Political Theory

Joel Jay Kassiola

> Environmental concerns [are] political concerns and . . . the best
> way to understand environmentalism [is] as a complex set of
> political ideas. . . . Environmentalism was . . . the first new and
> truly distinctive political ideology since socialism and as
> important as liberalism, conservatism, and socialism in their time.
> Moreover . . . environmentalism was different from any of the
> other ideologies in several important ways.
>
> —*Robert C. Paehlke*

Mission and Approach

The main point of this volume, and the central proposition that is shared
and defended by its contributors as expressed in the epigraph and essay
by Robert C. Paehlke, is that the fundamental issues raised by the global
environmental crisis facing humanity today are essentially political in
nature. Therefore, in the view of these authors, environmental issues
must involve political values. It is the overall goal of the authors to
rationally persuade the reader of the primary importance of political
theory—the systematic study of political values—to:

1. understand the political character of current environmental problems and their potentially harmful consequences;
2. comprehend how humanity arrived at the fateful condition where
   the long-term sustainability of all living species is in question;
   and, most significantly,

3. recognize and respond effectively to the reality that the only way we may be able to avoid ecological disaster is by transforming our dominant values, social institutions, and manner of living constitutive of modernity (or industrial civilization—what Pirages terms the "Third Revolution in Human Affairs").

In brief, the mission of *Explorations in Environmental Political Theory* is to demonstrate the contribution political theory can make in understanding the environmental crisis, its origins, and a possible resolution. This is done for the purpose of overcoming the crisis by transforming modern industrial civilization into a social order that is ecologically sustainable, socially just, and individually fulfilling to its members. To begin, a statement about the nature of political theory is in order.

Political theory (or political philosophy, or political thought, as it is alternatively called) is the subfield within the discipline of political science that was founded by the thought and works of Plato 2,400 years ago. In contrast to his student, Aristotle, who may be considered the founder of political science with its characteristic (present) emphases upon the (scientific) description, explanation, and prediction of empirically observable phenomena, like revolutions, Plato and his successors in political theory throughout the ages have focused on political values and obligations. Political theorists reflect upon: (1) the historical development of political values and obligations within Western thought and culture; (2) their meaning and applications for both society and individuals; and, perhaps foremost (3) the rational defense of particular political values and obligations. As a result, political theorists prescribe to individuals how they ought to behave, and to societies how they should be organized and how their citizens ought to be treated. Such well-known political concepts and values as justice, equality, freedom, and democracy, form the core of political theoretical discourse. In addition, how these values, once socially understood and agreed to, are to be applied and realized in the concrete, everyday social world is another distinctive component of the field of political theory.

Following the familiar metaphor of the environmental political theory of deep ecology versus shallow ecology (see McLaughlin's essay), we may think of political theory as "deep" politics and environmental political theory as "deep" environmental politics. This terminology is suggested to draw a contrast to the typical scientifically oriented, political study or policy analysis of an environmental issue or government policy, such as air pollution or the Clean Air Act, although I do not wish to stigmatize such scientific or policy studies with a disparaging sense of "shallow." I merely want to point out that such studies do not address the deep issues that include the value-based foundation of the environmental crisis and the resulting need for social transformation, as the contributors to this volume emphasize.

The purpose of this collection of essays, which highlights the convergence of inquiries into the environment and political theory, is to provide examples of the best work done by political theorists on the broad subject of the environment. All of the authors have completed book-length inquiries into the uncharted—until recently—intellectual landscape (hence the term "explorations") where normative (having to do with values) political analyses, environmental limits, and problems intersect. I believe—as this volume's title reflects—that the works of these authors and their colleagues constitute a new and emerging field of study: environmental political theory, where we need to think deeply about what we value as a society, and as individual citizens. It is my hope that the publication of this volume will enable this still developing field to achieve greater levels of public, policy-maker, scholarly, and student awareness, and stimulate more political theorists and environmental researchers to consider its profound subject matter and goals.

I have two objectives in gathering these essays in environmental political theory: (1) to provide a convenient, one-volume source of ideas proposed by a diverse group of environmental political theorists to undergraduate and graduate students within both environmental science and studies programs; and (2) to inform researchers on the environment from all fields about the existence and significance of environmental political theory and how its concentration on political values can improve their work by deepening the overall quality and effectiveness of inquiry into the environmental crisis.

This first collection of political theoretical studies of the environment is intended to serve the student audience in its quest to learn more about the environmental crisis and how we should respond to it across a wide, multidisciplinary curriculum range that encompasses the worldwide academic study of the environment within colleges and universities. In addition, this volume will advance the study of environmental political theory by encouraging college instructors to use these exploratory essays to enrich their teaching and research, regardless of their disciplinary identity, whether in natural, health, or social sciences, or the humanities. Furthermore, it is my aim to put examples of environmental political theoretical discussions before those members of the large and multidisciplinary environmental teaching and research community of scholars who are not currently aware of the systematic study of political values and its role in the study and amelioration of environmental problems. This gap in the perspective of the typical environmental researcher and student needs to be filled if their studies are to be successful. Combined with their environmental expertise, environmental political theory will enable environmental researchers and students to contribute to fundamental changes in our thinking and values. This is necessary—individually, socially, and institutionally—if we are to cope effectively with the environmental threats confronting humanity and all life on our planet.

I have been teaching a political science course on the environment from the approach of environmental political theory for the past twenty years (as distinct from the much more prevalent environmental public policy course). I know firsthand how difficult it is to choose texts for such a course. The subject of the environment is wide ranging and fast changing, and students concerned about the environment and humanity's future are usually unfamiliar with political theory and its focus on the systematic study of values. It is, therefore, understandable how the transmission of the latest scientific hypotheses and data about specific environmental issues, such as global warming, can preoccupy the entire course and readings, resulting in little or no time for raising the essential, political value-laden questions. I have in mind such provocative questions as: What is the nature of the environmental crisis and how did it begin? How do human values relate to natural resource shortages and pollution problems? What social changes are needed to respond to scientific data about environmental problems such as global warming or acid rain? How can we create an ecologically sustainable and socially just world society of 6 billion people? 8 billion? 12 billion?

In response to this normative political gap in the environmental literature, to argue for the recognition of the profound political implications of environmental limits to modernity's key value of ceaseless economic growth, and to prescribe to my colleagues in political theory that we turn our attention to the environmental debates going on at the time, I wrote an article, "The Limits to Economic Growth: Politicizing Advanced Industrial Society,"[1] and a book, *The Death of Industrial Civilization: The Limits to Economic Growth and the Repoliticization of Advanced Industrial Society.*[2] In these publications, I attempted to show the fundamental importance of politics, political values, and political theory to the comprehensive and sound study of the environment, and inform effective individual and social action. Gratifyingly, during the 1990s a substantial literature devoted to environmental political theory (included in the recommended additional reading section) developed. As the new millennium begins, there exists a growing group of environmental political theorists who have authored books to contribute to this volume; it would not have been possible to publish such a collection before the 1990s.

Despite the recent development of environmental political theory, there remain practical problems that obstruct the dissemination of this new field's conclusions. Some instructors who teach courses in environmental studies do not know about this emerging field because academic disciplinary barriers to communication are difficult to overcome. Even those scholar-teachers who are aware of the significance of politics and political values to their subject and would, therefore, be inclined to assign readings in environmental political theory in their courses, do not have the class time to assign one book-length text, let alone several for a diversity of perspectives. Therefore, this anthology is designed to assist both groups. It provides substantial and mostly new essays, not abbreviated excerpts that cannot capture the central elements of each author's argument. I believe that this volume makes available some of the best existing illustrations of environmental political theory by enabling the distinguished contributors to present the main points of their environmental political view in comprehensive essay form.

Multiple discussions brought together in one collection have great classroom potential. The conflict between limited course time and the desire to introduce several political theoretical views of the environmental crisis to students can be resolved by using this anthology; instructors may assign all or some of the essays, thereby integrating several political theoretical views about the environment. This volume provides examples of different positions on issues within environmental political theory, such as the nature of modern values and their role in understanding the environmental crisis, or the relationship of social theory to environmentalism. The recommended reading section contains suggestions for beginning and advanced students of the environment and provides guidance to deepen their understanding of environmental political theory and contemporary environmental problems as defined by the contributors to this volume. For environmental researchers who are new to environmental political theoretical discourse, the works recommended in this section provide an extension of this volume's point of view on the environmental crisis so that they may be used to enhance the researchers' inquiries.

I believe that *Explorations in Environmental Political Theory* offers students and scholars of the environment—vast and profound as this subject is—an important introduction to the ideas of the leading thinkers in a new and vital field. It is my intention that the political theoretical works on the environment contained in this text embody a fundamental tenet within political theory which originates from its creator, Plato: We should discuss goodness every day and we must examine our lives systematically if they are to be worthwhile.[3] Pertaining to the environment, this means that if our investigations into the relationship between humans and our natural environment are to be accurate and effective in achieving our goals of sustainability and justice, we must include within them the examination of both politics and political values. Environmental political theory, exemplified by the essays included here, must become part of our reflections on the humanity/environment relationship and its consequences that are so critical to the future of our planet.

Content

The most important theme of the following exploratory essays on environmental political theory is the emphasis on the political nature of the environmental crisis, particularly the value foundation of the challenges that threaten our earthly home and its inhabitants. The severity of the crisis is acknowledged by every contributor. No detailed descriptions of what the environmental disaster will look like if fundamental changes in our global society are not made—who could formulate such a grim and unthinkable picture? Each author asserts that the challenges to humanity are real, basic, and potentially lethal.

Another unifying element of the volume's essays is the specific set of values and worldview that are claimed to be at the heart of the environmental crisis and thinking politically about this worldview, the worldview of modernity. Although called by different names, there is little divergence over what values and social institutions are being referred to: modernity, neoclassical welfare capitalism, industrialism, market-based society, and global capitalism. All encompass the values and social practices that citizens of advanced industrial societies like the United States, and now with globalization (see Paehlke's essay), virtually the entire human collectivity, consciously hold and pursue: consumerism, competition, individualism, overcoming scarcity, material security, want fulfillment, technology, status, and limitless economic growth. Other values that these political theorists underscore are less obvious to advanced industrial residents and those who aspire to our culture—the denial of limits including environmental and existential limits like death, anthropocentrism, endless consumption as a way to fill the void in our lives, and nature treated as an instrument of human goals (see the Goodin, Kassiola, and Zimmerman essays). Most authors criticize these values and the overall social paradigm associated with modernity. However, Zimmerman reminds us of the positive aspects to modernity and rightfully cautions antimodern, environmental political theorists that the baby must not be thrown out with the bath water; we must preserve modernity's progressivism and its emphasis upon and establishment of freedom in any future, green, postmodern society.

Another important point made both explicitly and implicitly throughout the volume is that since the core of the environmental crisis is based in our value structure, technological improvements alone cannot eliminate environmental conflicts and resulting threats to human (and all other) life (see Milbrath's essay). Only when the environmental unsustainability of modern industrial civilization's values and institutions is socially recognized and the full impact of the environmental crisis is absorbed can transformation of existing social values, institutions, and practices occur. This is analyzed by Dobson as "green utopianism" whose contribution to environmental political theory is to bring realism to typical utopian thought. The catalyst for such a powerful and difficult social learning and change process will be the increased disappointment, dissatisfaction, and tragedy (according to Oscar Wilde's definition) experienced within the futile and flawed modern civilization hooked on endless consumption (Goodin, Kassiola, McLaughlin, and Milbrath essays).

One striking theme of the essays that follow—and of environmental political theory as a whole—is that modernity's success at generating an historically unprecedented productive capacity and quantity of material goods has precipitated both the environmental crisis and industrial citizens' alienation. The former results from the industrial use of natural resources at unsustainable rates, and the pollution of the natural environment at dangerously intolerable levels. The latter is the result of people achieving a never before seen extent of material wealth and who still remain unsatisfied because of the competitive and self-defeating nature of the modern definition of satisfaction. *One basic principle enunciated here is that material wealth alone is not sufficient for human survival and happiness.* As almost all religions propound and as all societies before our relatively recent industrial one were structured, human satisfaction must be found in nonmaterial experiences such as family relationships, relating to nature, or self-fulfilling work (Goodin, Kassiola, McLaughlin, and Milbrath).

Throughout these essays, another important issue is the contribution environmental political theory can make to individual and societal transformation. The mistaken normative and institutional aspects of modernity, and the social and environmental ills that result, must give way to a new, ecologically compatible and limits-recognizing, postmodern social order that is in harmony with our natural environment (see green utopianism discussed by Dobson, and the third major transformation or sociocultural revolution discussed by Pirages). Therefore, the revolutionary consequences of environmental political theory are featured. The authors anthologized here are neither naïve nor utopian (in the standard negative sense of unrealistic flights of fancy); they realize the utmost profundity and difficulty of how such a transformation of modern industrial civilization will occur, and the equally challenging problem of the nature of an alternative, sustainable, and superior society. It is to these paramount issues that environmental political theory may be able to make its greatest contribution (as discussed by Dobson, Kassiola, Milbrath, Paehlke, and Pirages).

Some contributors discuss the need for a worldwide green, or environmental, social movement for change to achieve this revolutionary goal (McLaughlin and Milbrath), whereas others are concerned about the possible effects such a social movement may have on our other values (Paehlke and Zimmerman). Before any prescription for a global green revolution can be persuasive, the critical thinker must concede the daunting social fact that no advanced industrial society has ever undergone such an enormous cultural transformation to a postmodern society with new values and institutions and absorbed the dramatic developments associated with globalization, the current hegemony of ever-expanding transnational corporations and mass media in the newly created global marketplace and consumerist world order (Paehlke). To create a fundamentally different worldview and ecologically sustainable society based on environmental political theory's call for revolutionary conceptual and normative change from the modernist perspective, the mass publics within our materially rich industrial societies must understand and appreciate the value bases of the environmental crisis. Several theorists (Kassiola, McLaughlin, Milbrath, and Zimmerman) emphasize the dissatisfaction of modern life and its preoccupation with endless consumption and limitless economic growth and the ecological impossibility of pursuing these modern values and practices by the nonindustrialized world (Pirages), and consider these social facts to be a necessary catalyst for the industrial masses to begin the arduous process of seeking, defining, and implementing alternative values and social institutions. Milbrath terms this "the social learning process."

Some postmodern values that provide alternatives to the dominant contemporary ideals are discussed by all of the authors, but Goodin focuses exclusively on green values. This author makes explicit what is usually taken for granted and suppressed in modern industrial society—anthropocentrism, or the presumed superiority of humans to other elements of nature. This important value within modern ideology is addressed within the larger general concept of the theme of the relationship between humanity and nature (Goodin; see also Dobson, and McLaughlin on the deep ecology platform). The human value of nature, according to this green theory of value, is its capacity to allow us to experience our lives in a larger natural context (Goodin).

All the essays reinforce the crucial point that in order to understand the environmental crisis we must first understand the misconceived and undesirable character of modern values and the culture derived from them on a much deeper level than is usually presented in school or the media. One modern and antispiritual (or antinonmaterialist) value that is highlighted is the civilization-wide political and economic role of consumerism in contemporary industrial society (Goodin, Kassiola, McLaughlin, and Zimmerman). *I would say that along with the political value basis of the environmental crisis, the essential trait of ceaseless material consumption within modernity and its ultimate and necessary failure to produce human satisfaction is a pervasive theme throughout this volume and the environmental political theoretical literature as a whole.* A vital part of the environmental education of the public must include more than the latest ecological information; for our survival, environmental education must include a thorough normative analysis of modernity, market-based society, globalized capitalism, and the defining futile characteristic of our social order—endless material consumption as the only means to fulfill ourselves. Therefore, environmental education, currently widely defined only within the scientific realm, must be expanded to incorporate environmental political theory and its quintessential foci as illustrated in this volume—modern political values, consumption-based society, anthropocentrism, limits and the human condition, limitless economic growth, nature/humanity relationship, postmodern social change, the nonmaterial composition of goodness, sustainability, and, finally, social justice.

The profound perception of some of the environmental political theorists whose essays are included herein may come as a shock to readers who were educated during the cold war, absorbing its invectives against communism and assuming a clash between capitalist and communist ideologies. Great similarities exist within both capitalism and communism (or socialism) (Paehlke and Zimmerman)! One does not need to be a specialist in political theory to see the realities of this view demonstrated as virtually the entire world's nations now seek material wealth, economic growth, and to live like rich capitalist industrial societies (most striking in the former Soviet Union societies and China). The significant lesson drawn here by environmental political theorists is that the usual framework of conventional political rhetoric—even sophisticated scholarly discourse—of left/right (communism/socialism-capitalism) dichotomies that still continues despite the collapse of the Soviet Union is not deep or profound enough to be useful in understanding the environmental crisis. When the deeper level of the ultimate or fundamental values of society are examined, both ideologies are seen to be modern or industrial in nature (McLaughlin and Paehlke). Environmental political theorists stress the crucial point that these common industrial social values, their conceptual presuppositions, and institutionalization within modern civilization, are inconsistent with ecological limits and are producing an unsustainable, unsatisfying, and undesirable society.

It is my hope that this collection of explorations in environmental political theory will help the reader comprehend Paehlke's statement used as an epigraph to this introduction and illuminate the nature of sound and practically effective thinking about the environment. We are confronting a unique set of fatal environmental threats to our global existence, and environmental political theory in response to these threats must be bold and profound. The ambitious goal of this volume is to introduce the reader to the gravity and the normative basis of the environmental crisis. We must examine all that we value in modernity if we are not to succumb to the deadly excess of our modern ways. Time is short, so I urge you to give the ideas contained in the following essays and related recommended works your most serious attention, and, furthermore, integrate their insights into your thoughts and actions. It is not hyperbole to say that your own happiness and the fate of the planet may lie in the balance.

1

The "Tragedy" of Modernity

How Environmental Limits and the Environmental Crisis Produce the Need for Postmodern Values and Institutions

Joel Jay Kassiola

> In this world there are only two tragedies. One is not getting what one wants, and the other is getting it. The last is much the worst, the last is a real tragedy!
>
> —Oscar Wilde, *Lady Windermere's Fan*

I would like to begin by examining Oscar Wilde's paradoxical conception of human tragedy and relating it to the self-defeatist nature of modernity, the normative basis of the environmental crisis, and the obligation for transforming our society into a postmodern social order. What did Wilde mean by "getting what one wants"?[1] Conceding that Wilde enjoyed being a nonconformist who satirized the social values of his time and place, late nineteenth century British society, his statement of the *worst* tragedy in life being *getting* what one wants seems quite puzzling, if not perverse, to the contemporary reader at the beginning of the twenty-first century. In our current world, human wants appear limitless both in number and diversity and ceaseless in their creation. Getting what one wants is our social definition of individual happiness; for the society as a whole, having its citizenry get what it wants is the prime indicator of national priority and success—certainly not tragedy! Indeed, the satisfaction of human want seems to be the very opposite of tragedy, especially not the *worst* tragedy, making Wilde's passage quite perplexing and requiring elucidation.[2]

I propose that what Wilde communicates about the nature of human tragedy, and why it appears so enigmatic to the contemporary reader within an advanced industrial society, such as the United States, will illuminate the environmental crisis and its consequences for modern society's transformation to postmodernity, and furthermore, why such transformation is both necessary and desirable.

Wilde's observation provides an excellent entrée to the theme of this volume: the introduction to the emerging, wide-ranging, and important field of environmental political theory, or the convergence of environmental studies and political theory. Too many scientific studies of the natural environment ignore the political realm completely (which is understandable, given the specialized scientific training and experience of the environmental scientists conducting this research), and moreover, until recently political scientists themselves, particularly political theorists, left the urgent field of environmental studies and the problems raised by the environmental crisis to their colleagues in natural science (except for students of public policy since 1970 who studied the environment among other issues involved in the public policy-making process). The new field of environmental political theory, whose leading contributors are contained in this book, is specifically designed to correct this serious omission by providing its readers with discussions of the normative political nature and consequences of environmental problems. Special emphasis will be placed on the value foundation of the current global environmental crisis. It is my hope that the publication of this volume will make these studies in environmental political theory more accessible to both scholars and students, so they will be inspired to pursue further their inquiry into this vital field of study.

Human Wants, Modern Futility, and Dissatisfaction

"In this world," as Wilde begins, could refer either to the human condition per se, for all time, or merely the state of humanity in Wilde's own British society, which was the first, and most advanced, modern industrial society in its day. Given Wilde's inclination to comment on humanity as a whole,[3] the former meaning is probably the more accurate reading. Nonetheless, the latter interpretation emphasizing the particular cultural traits of modern Great Britain also suits my understanding of the view of human tragedy contained in the passage and its profound lessons especially well, as I hope will become clear as this discussion advances.

Wilde's first human tragedy is the omnipresent fact experienced by nearly all humans many times throughout their lives: not getting what one wants. Prior to the industrial revolution, virtually all humans were preoccupied with attempting to avoid this negative outcome with regard to the basic biophysical requirements for human existence. This life and death struggle remains true today for our planet's poor industrial and nonindustrialized citizens who constitute a large majority of the human population.

This fundamental characteristic of human life, the failure to satisfy one's wants, asserted by Wilde as one form of human tragedy, is so commonplace that little more need be said about it except to note that critical reflection upon such aspects of prosaic reality can be valuable in making explicit what is usually left implicit or ignored. Such is the case, I believe, when considering the human condition and the inevitable reality of our wants remaining unfulfilled.

The concept and phenomena associated with limits usually are taken for granted, and therefore left unanalyzed; existential limits to human knowledge and life reflect humanity's fallibility and mortality. Significantly, for this discussion, environmental limits must be added; they create the unavoidable scarcity of natural resources for human use as well as inescapable restrictions upon the safe absorption of waste products from human existence and activities. All limits contribute to the first of Wilde's two forms of human tragedy—want unfulfillment. (We shall return to this crucial point of essential limits and their consequences for human life shortly.)

What needs explanation is Wilde's second tragedy—getting what one wants—and particularly, his additional claim that success at satisfying our wants is "much the worst" tragedy compared to the usual experience of human failure at this endeavor. I suggest a very unlikely source for explicating Wilde's paradoxical second notion of "tragedy" is Henry Kissinger, a former American secretary of state and political scientist. A comment from his nationally-televised analysis of American society during the tumultuous period of the Vietnam War bears an uncanny resemblance to Wilde's passage:

> To Americans usually tragedy is wanting something very badly and not getting it. Many people have had to learn in their private lives, and nations have had to learn in their historical experience, that perhaps the worst form of tragedy is wanting something very badly, getting it, and

finding it empty. And to get this sense of historical humility and of limitation, which is the experience through which we are now going as a people, is extremely painful.[4]

Whether Kissinger consciously quoted Wilde's play is not relevant to this essay's purpose. What is significant, I contend, is his point about the worst form of human tragedy consisting of wanting something, getting it, and then "finding it empty." Achieving success at getting what one wants and then finding this success unsatisfying or "empty," as Kissinger put it, forces us to reconsider our taken for granted values and goals in a manner that *not* getting our wants does not. When we fail to achieve our objectives, our values and goals remain intact and unquestioned as we persevere in our struggle for success at getting our wants. In a discussion on the meaning of human disappointment in social life, the economist and social theorist Albert O. Hirschman emphasizes how far people will go to reconstruct or misperceive reality in order to deny disappointment or to admit error as its cause:

> The denial of reality that is practiced testifies to the *power* and *vitality* of the disappointment experience. We engage in all kinds of ingenious ruses and delaying actions before admitting to ourselves that we *are* disappointed, in part surely because we know that disappointment may compel us to a painful reassessment of our preferences and priorities.[5]

Wilde may have considered getting what one wants as the worst form of tragedy because of the pain involved in judging such achievements empty and producing "a sense of humility and limitation," as Kissinger noted, or disappointment with the accompanying pain of the "reassessment of our preferences and priorities," as Hirschman astutely observes.

It should be noted here as a possible objection to Hirschman's point that not getting a particular want, like not making an Olympic team or becoming president of one's company, might also lead one to reconsider her or his values and goals ("preferences and priorities") when it becomes evident that the want will not be accomplished. This deflating and humiliating process could be what is at the heart of the often described "mid-life crisis" wherein people recognize that their longstanding, even lifelong and self-defining, objectives will not be realized. This necessitates a reexamination and reconstitution of one's value system and set of life goals; one's worldview is shaken at its foundations. This returns to Wilde's first and lesser form of human tragedy: not getting what one wants. Thus, such a "reassessment of our preferences and priorities" occurs not only when we get what we want and find it disappointing because unsatisfying, but also when we do not reach our goal, and therefore, Hirschman's point about the distinguishing consequence of disappointment is nullified.

However, it may be observed that when humans fail to attain our wants, we are constantly advised (in modern Western culture, at least) to overcome adversity and continue to dream. The pursuit of unfulfilled wants figures prominently in high school and college commencement speeches. Much thought about the strategy and tactics to achieve success in realizing this goal is encouraged, but usually one is not reflective about *why* the unattained objective remains a value. Rarely do we question whether the desired goal does, or should, constitute a want of ours, including why we desire what we do. We seldom conduct an inquiry into the nature of our values underlying the quest for our objective to be reached. The social ethos in such a situation is simple: Put one's "shoulder to the wheel" and commit ourselves to work harder and smarter to get our want. The contemporary cultural emphasis when failure to achieve our wants is experienced (Wilde's lesser form of human tragedy) is to redouble our efforts to attain success and not to be a quitter!

Contrast the negative human experience of failing to realize our goals to Wilde's second and much the worst form of human tragedy: success at obtaining our wants, wherein we get what we want but find it dissatisfying or empty. In this event, the emotional reaction is much deeper, demanding more of us than perseverance in our quest by working harder and smarter. We must substitute some other goal now that the attained one has been a disappointment! (Why such a substitution of another want seems absolutely necessary to most people acculturated with modern values will be discussed subsequently.) Reconsideration of one's values and goals is more likely to be stimulated by the unsatisfying experience, or Wilde's "real tragedy," after a want has been "gotten" or fulfilled. The point is that it is easier and quite natural to maintain our preexisting values and goals when we do not achieve them and experience Wilde's lesser degree of tragedy—where putting more effort or using a different strategy for success are deemed appropriate responses—than when we *do* achieve our objectives but find them unsatisfactory and, according to modern society, must create other wants or objectives to strive for.

Wilde's concept of human tragedy implies that getting our wants necessitates reflection about our values, goals, and view of the world, thereby raising the specter of value change. The less tragic experience of not accomplishing our goals, according to my reading of Wilde, requires considerably less analysis or soul searching. Thus, human dissatisfaction precipitates reconsideration and reconstitution of our values in a manner not demanded by the failure at meeting our desires.

A philosopher has described what he terms the "value erosion" or "realization erosion" process in his discussion of fundamental value change, which, I think, can shed some additional light here.

> The status of a value can be eroded away when, in the wake of its substantial realization in a society, the value "loses its savor" and comes to be downgraded by disenchantment and disillusionment. Some examples would be: "*efficiency*" in the era of automation, "*progress*" in the age of anxiety, "*economic security*" in a welfare state, "*national independence*" for an "emerging" nation in socioeconomic chaos.[6]

When these ideas concerning the prime motivation for people to change their values—achieving them and then discovering that they have "lost their savor"—are applied to the social level, they help us to understand the devastating impact of the value "realization erosion" process upon modern industrial civilization. Achieving our wants and then becoming disenchanted with them because of their emptiness, or according to Wilde, getting what one wants, and experiencing real and much the worst tragedy leads us to examine critically these wants and their value bases and to become more receptive to their change for superior alternatives. When human wants and their associated values lie at the foundation of society and are so eroded through unsatisfying realization, the transformation of the dominant social paradigm, and its corresponding social structure, is made increasingly possible by the phenomenon of value realization erosion or Wildean tragedy. "In contrast to other crises in history, which have been caused by visibly negative factors such as plague and draught—the 'cause' of the current crisis—material growth—is generally considered good."[7]

The current environmental crisis may be explained along these lines of the *success* of the modern social order in generating unprecedented material wealth—and waste products—and experiencing the value realization erosion process that results from the conflict between the existence of environmental limits and the supreme industrial value of unlimited economic growth. The more we accomplish of the modern value of unlimited material growth, the more this value is eroded because it is recognized as insatiable, even threatening to our survival because of external environmental limits. Furthermore, this value is also found to be empty or inherently dissatisfying because of its self-defeatist and futile nature. *We may, therefore, conclude here that the environmental crisis is basically value driven and attacks the very heart of modernity—unlimited economic growth and its implied modern denial of limits.*

Human Satisfaction and a Possible Criticism

A critic of this normative analysis of modern tragedy and its revolutionary consequence could object that my interpretation of Wilde's passage on tragedy is faulty because I have based it on the dissatisfaction with realized values or gotten wants, using the insights of Kissinger and Rescher. This critic might go on to pose the following question: "What if we *are* satisfied with our gotten wants and do not judge them to be *empty* or eroding of our lives because these values have not 'lost their savor,' and therefore, do, indeed, produce the satisfaction we seek?" Does this unexamined and happy possibility not occur, and if so, does not the existence of such pleasing occurrences undermine the proffered analysis? Moreover, does not this possibility also contradict Wilde's claim that the outcome of getting our wants will produce tragedy, let alone much the worst tragedy, as compared to not realizing our goals?

In thinking about these hypothetical questions, I suggest we consider two possible conclusions regarding human wants: not getting what we want and getting it (leaving aside, as Wilde himself did, the very real complication of the partial realization of our objectives which would thereby presumably result in partially tragic consequences, according to Wilde's account). Focusing in on the allegedly *real* tragedy of getting what one wants, there are two possible results (highlighted by the critic's challenge ignoring partial results): getting what one wants and finding it dissatisfying, exemplified by Kissinger's explanation of the worst form of tragedy and Rescher's value realization erosion process, or getting what one wants and judging it satisfying, as the hypothetical critic points out. Although the critic may agree with the analysis pertaining to the first and disappointing result when we achieve our objectives but find them empty or lacking in savor, this critic might ask, "Does not the happy alternative for humanity, wherein we get what we want and find

Figure 1   **Human Wants and (Dis) Satisfaction**

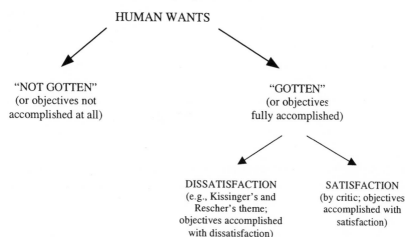

it satisfying, negate Wilde's view of both tragedy and the human condition which must include this real and clearly nontragic possibility?"

By attempting to answer these penetrating questions, and by exploring the product of human action whereby human wants are satisfied with no regrets and full gratification, we may obtain a deeper understanding of modern society's worldview and its fundamental flaw. First, I wish to grant the point that, happily, not all human desires are realized in an unsatisfying manner—humans *do* achieve satisfaction when getting their wants or achieving their desires. However, the key question for this discussion remains: Might Wilde's observation about the human condition where, counterintuitively, getting what we want is much the worst tragedy, still hold true when human wants are satisfied with no negative reaction? Can the human experience of satisfaction still be thought of as tragic, or even much the worst tragedy? I offer the schema above to assist the reader in comprehending the possibilities of human action considered here.

The problem raised by the need to explain Wilde's position on tragedy in the circumstances where human wants are happily realized underscores, I believe, the profound nature of these questions raised by Wilde's view for citizens of modern industrial society, and the remaining nonindustrialized population which now seeks the modern way of life. Political theory can play a role in this effort to understand the human condition and the environmental crisis with all of its social ramifications. Exploring the fundamental nature of humanity is a time-honored tradition within the history of political theory since its founding by Plato nearly two and a half millennia ago. All canonical political theories have either an explicit or implicit theory of humanity that grounds the theorist's positions on political issues, large and small.

The Birth of Modern Political Theory: Hobbes's Unlimited Desirer Conception of Humanity, Its Significance and Undesirability

One of the most important reflections on the human condition within the entire grand tradition of political theory, and certainly the most significant for comprehending modernity—and its fundamental deficiencies—is the view proposed by the seventeenth-century British philosopher, Thomas Hobbes, who is generally considered by political theorists as the founder (or cofounder with Machiavelli) of modern political thought. Without going into a long discussion of Hobbes's entire and widely influential political theory which is clearly beyond the scope and purpose of this essay, I would like to nominate the following paragraph of his as the most important single paragraph in modern political theory; this paragraph provides, I suggest, rich insight into the nature of modern life and values. It will assist us in clarifying Oscar Wilde's passage on tragedy and the modern human condition.

> The felicity of this life consists not in the repose of a mind satisfied. For there is no such *finis ultimus*, utmost aim, nor *summum bonum*, greatest good, as is spoken of in the books of the old moral philosophers. Nor can a man any more live whose desires are at an end than he whose senses and imaginations are at a stand. Felicity is a continual progress of the desire from one object to another, the attaining of the former being still but the way to the latter . . . I put for a general inclination of all mankind a perpetual and restless desire of power after power that ceases only in death. And the cause of this is not always that a man hopes for a more intensive delight than he has already attained to, or that he cannot be content with a moderate power, but because he cannot assume the power and means to live well which he has present without the acquisition of more.[8]

There is so much to comment on in this one pivotal paragraph, which is why I consider it so noteworthy and deserving of a unique place in modern thought that it is almost overwhelming:

1. Hobbes's—and modernity's—denial that human happiness consists "in the repose of a mind satisfied";
2. Hobbes's—and modernity's—discarding of the 2,000–year-old
   grand, moral and political tradition concerning our "utmost
   [moral and political] aims";
3. Hobbes's—and modernity's—identifying human life with ceaseless desires ("continual progress of the desire from one object
   to another"), so that the ending of desires means death with the
   implication that the satisfaction of human desires is merely temporary and thereby requires the need for additional desires to
   take their place in order to avoid the dreaded state of "senses
   and imaginations at a stand" which is equivalent to death for
   Hobbes;
4. the attainment of human felicity is simply the means to the "continual progress of desire from one object to another" that "ceases
   only in death"; and
5. that humans perpetually desire power that "ceases only in death"
   not for more delight than they already have attained nor for lacking "contentment with moderate power," but for the *security* of
   their power and means to live well *already attained*!

According to Hobbes, all of these purported human characteristics
and actions exist not for the achievement of human happiness or some
other supreme value, as moral and political theories were logically structured within the long history of Western moral and political thought
prior to Hobbes. Rather, human desire functions solely and merely to
retain or make secure our current "means to live well" by seeking more
power, desires, and acquisitions endlessly. Hobbes's paramount concern with the bedrock of the insecurity of life and the resulting competition with other humans is considered by commentators the hallmark of
Hobbes's entire political thought. Even more important, because of the
insight into modern life provided by Hobbes's political theory, it is the
hallmark of modern society.[9]

How does this paragraph by Hobbes and his view of insatiable human nature relate to Wilde's remarks about human tragedy? Hobbes's
position, reflected in the modern social order as a whole, conveys the
point that since human life is the pursuit of one desire after another
ceaselessly until death, then when want satisfaction is achieved, we must
create and seek new, unmet wants in order to stay alive! We are com-

pelled to spend our entire lives seeking wants satisfaction or pursuing our desires continuously until death. Thus, even when we do experience satisfaction of our desires, we still cannot rest happily, according to Hobbes. In modern society's worldview, so influenced by Hobbes, "repose of a mind satisfied" does not constitute human felicity.

In the eighteenth century, the French political theorist, Jean-Jacques Rousseau, criticized both Hobbes's theory and actual modernity. Rousseau captured the horrors of Hobbesian society as follows, "Civilized [modern] man, on the other hand, is always moving, sweating, toiling, and racking his brains to find still more laborious occupations; he goes on in drudgery to this last moment."[10] Could Wilde be referring to this kind of Hobbesian, and quintessentially modern, experience of the satisfaction of one want merely producing the necessity of creating and pursuing others endlessly until death? Is this the *real* and much the worst tragedy than not getting what one wants that Wilde had in mind?

Putting aside textual analysis for the moment, how can achieving satisfaction of human wants—especially when fully gratified and not disappointing in the results—be less attractive than not achieving satisfaction? What kind of theory of humanity and worldview would lead to this unhappy vision of social life? While radical environmental critics of modernity have often been accused of gloom and doom regarding their apocalyptic reflections about our planet's future, I would respectfully propose that the defenders of modernity, the current social arrangements and the modern values at the foundation of such a social order, perpetuate the doom and gloom of the Hobbesian view of human nature: no rest, no satisfaction, constant insecurity, and the quest for additional desires and power until death! (Does this view explain the gravestone epitaph: "Rest in Peace," where the only restful peace humans can experience is upon death?) Rousseau's words above seem quite apt; we experience modern life in the Hobbesian manner. Would we be better off if our wants remained *ungotten* or unfulfilled as Wilde implies? Does Wilde's position on the nature of tragedy seem more relevant and persuasive now, even if it is based on an undesirable worldview? I firmly believe that Hobbes's path-breaking, even revolutionary if gloomy, conception of the human prepolitical condition, the infamous Hobbesian view of the "life of man[as] solitary, poor, nasty, brutish, and short,"[11] and its implications for social life are seriously mistaken. (I refer to Rousseau's more positive alternative, but much less influential, view on modernity.) Yet, Hobbes's influence within modern industrial ideology, alas, cannot be denied as I tried to show in my volume, *The Death of Industrial Civilization*. If the Hobbesian concept of insatiable human nature with unlimited desires is correct, it leads to the conclusion that people are unable to reach long-term or meaningful satisfaction *even when their objectives are accomplished*, because they must constantly create and seek the next desire, *endlessly*.

How short lived is satisfaction in our society? For insight into this revealing characteristic of modernity, let us examine professional sports teams who win championships. This illustration, I believe, will illuminate the Hobbesian view of humanity and Wilde's view of human tragedy. Do not consider the "losers" who fail to get what they want—winning the Super Bowl, World Series, Stanley Cup, or the National Basketball Association (NBA) championship—but look at the ones who succeed in winning these much desired symbols of professional athletic accomplishment. Victorious teams and their fans have precious few moments at the end of a very long, arduous and anxiety-filled season to enjoy a world championship before the coaches and members of the team are asked by the media about their *next* season in the very locker room where the celebration of the final victory of the current season is occurring. Expressing sentiments that remarkably echo Wilde's, a writer on the harmful nature of competition within modern society cites a commentator on the Dallas Cowboys football team after winning the Super Bowl:

> Despite their excitement, however, winning fails to satisfy us in any significant way and thus cannot begin to compensate for the pain in losing. . . . *Winning offers no genuine comfort because there is no competitive activity for which victory is permanent* . . . Subjectively, the status of being envied and targeted by others may be superficially gratifying, but it is also deeply unsettling. Objectively, the reality is that it is only a matter of time until one becomes a loser again. [George Leonard] "The problem is this: even after you've just won the Super Bowl—*especially* after you've just won the Super Bowl—*there's always next year.* If 'Winning isn't everything, it's the only thing,' then 'the only thing' is nothing—emptiness, the nightmare of life without ultimate meaning."[12]

Professional sports teams in advanced modern society are, I think, illuminating instances of the Hobbesian worldview and the worst Wildean tragic experience. Their members (and fans to a lesser but significant degree) live from season to season, most of the time losing the championship—not getting what they want (consider baseball's Chicago Cubs not winning the World Series since 1908!). Then, the *real* or much the worst tragedy occurs when they get what they want and experience "But what about next year?" immediately after the championship victory has been won, indeed, during its very celebration. The televised image of the great basketball player, Michael Jordan, pleading with the Chicago Bulls owner to keep the 1997 championship team together for the next season during the postgame celebration *minutes* after winning the team's fifth NBA championship is vivid evidence of this phenomenon. This scene was incredibly repeated after the Bulls sixth NBA championship in 1998!—and now we know it was not honored because the Bulls were in fact broken up and disbanded with its stars traded and Jordan (temporarily) retired (and then left the team for another), producing the feared "loser" status for the Chicago Bulls that remains until today.

Therefore, even when human values have not gone sour or lost their savor or found to be empty after accomplishing our objectives (the second possible reaction to the successful attainment of our goals discussed earlier), the Hobbesian view of fulfillment of human desires is short lived and merely an intermediate point to the next desire ("the former [felicity] being still but the way to the latter [additional desires from one object to another]")—a process that continues endlessly until death. *As a result, even gratified desire is ultimately unsatisfying.* This way station or "unlimited, continuous desirer" view of the human lifetime as a struggle for means with no ends, or with no ultimate values or satisfied goals, terminated only by death, renders the accomplishment of objectives almost meaningless and human satisfaction fleeting. Presumably, the same is true of life itself—a truly grim and alienating perspective that I believe we experience profoundly in the advanced stages of modernity.

In Wildean terms, "getting what one wants," like winning a championship, paradoxically is "much the worst" tragedy because of the extremely brief nature of such an accomplishment and its resulting momentary satisfaction producing the need to continue on to the next want or desire even with the rare and auspicious outcome of realized goals not found to be initially disappointing. According to Wilde's statement and, I contend, the Hobbesian conception of life, no matter how one's wants are gotten, humans end up dissatisfied, clarifying how desired results can nonetheless produce real and much the worst tragedy. Either our accomplishments are unsatisfying because they are found to be empty or eroded when realized, or even when the results are satisfactory, they only gratify us for a short period of time before we resume the never ending human process of seeking our desires. *Both* the possible results of the attainment of sought-after goals, whether they produced disappointment or satisfied us temporarily, necessitate the creation of the next want ad infinitum, ad nauseum, according to the Hobbesian and Wildean positions.

The Crisis of Modernity and the Concept of Limits

The contrast between the quintessential modern views of Hobbes and Wilde and the view of the ancient Greeks is stark. This is indicated by Hobbes's explicit denial of the supreme goods of the "old moral philosophers" in the paragraph cited earlier, exemplifying the moderns' typical disdain for the old and eagerness to discard it. They prefer the new, viewing ancient and traditional morality with skepticism, if not outright rejection. The ancients, represented for the moment by Aristotle, recognized and appreciated the phenomenon of *pleonexia*, or the insatiable and unlimited human desire to have more. Pleonexia was considered to be a moral and political fault; therefore, society needed to have this inclination combated by the social order through its social institutions, especially in its economy.[13] This and any view of life that contradicted Hobbes by claiming that human happiness consisted of meaningful satisfaction based on the acceptance of ultimate values and ends would be both anti-Hobbesian and antimodern.

Wilde's statement that the worst human tragedy is the realization of our desires (or getting what we want); Hobbes's view of humanity and society based on the constant want seeking, made necessary by human insecurity and ceasing only in death; and the Aristotelian, premodern recognition that unlimited desires have undesirable consequences that can and must be thwarted by the right social institutions, all raise the crucial issues of limits and limitations to human desires. Given this discussion of the conceptions of human desires as unlimited and socially unchecked or guided, genuine and meaningful human satisfaction will not be possible, and therefore, as Wilde formulated it, humanity would either experience the (lesser) tragedy of not getting what we want, or the (greater) tragedy of getting it!

This desperate conclusion reminds me of the dark comedy of the modern writer and filmmaker, Woody Allen:

> More than any time in history, mankind faces a crossroads. One path
> leads to despair and utter hopelessness, the other to total extinction. Let
> us pray that we have the wisdom to choose correctly.[14]

To avoid such paralyzing despair described by the contemporary novelist Kurt Vonnegut Jr. as "utterly terminal pessimism appalled by all
that an insane humanity might yet survive to do,"[15] we need to examine
the central idea of limits pertaining to human desires and its role within
modernity more thoroughly. *The problem of the nature of human wants
and their limitations is essential to social life and our understanding of
it.* Human tragedy and disappointment—as well as triumph and fulfillment—depend upon our wants, which in turn depend upon our values.
This point has fundamental importance for our individual and social
lives and provides the stimulus for thought and action that will lead us
to desirable social transformation. I believe that human tragedy (as formulated by Wilde and Kissinger), the erosion of human values caused
by their realization (as analyzed by Rescher), and the Hobbesian worldview of the ceaseless and unlimited nature of human wants all reflect a
fatal flaw within modern thought and society.

This flaw of modernity is highlighted by the environmental crisis,
including various challenges to human health and the modern way of
life caused by the environmental crisis, fomented by ecological limits.[16]
The environmental crisis could be utilized for the purpose of transforming modern society into a superior postmodern civilization founded upon
alternative values and institutions. Our modern Hobbesian social order is
being threatened by its own success, getting what it wanted. The materially
richest society in human history is characterized by an endless flow of material products *and* wants. Contrary to Karl Marx's belief that modern capitalist society would destroy itself because of its economic failures, we seem
to be self-destructing through our very success at getting what we want!

An important point to remember is that the apparent origin and driving force for the current crisis of modernity was environmental in nature.
The contemporary crisis of modernity with its ideology of limitlessness
is considered to have begun in the 1960s and 1970s as a result of dramatic ecological events: the harmful effects of DDT, an oil spill off the
California coast, breakup of huge oil tankers, the effects of our oil dependency and the resulting energy crises, water and air pollution, global warming, stratospheric ozone depletion, acid rain, deforestation,
soil erosion, global population growth, toxic and nontoxic waste

disposal, world hunger and starvation, depletion of resources, environmental diseases, and the endangerment of plant and animal species. All of these occurrences have had the accumulated effect of forcing citizens and policy makers to question our post–World War II optimism about the future and the basic premise of modern society, which is unlimited economic growth and ceaseless economic progress. Erich Fromm, a psychologist and social theorist, captures this modern concept of unlimited progress succinctly when he asserts:

> The Great Promise of Unlimited Progress [was] the promise of domination of nature, of material abundance, of the greatest happiness for the greatest number, and of unimpeded personal freedom. . . . With industrial progress, from the substitution of mechanical and then nuclear energy for animal and human energy to the substitution of the computer for the human mind, we could feel that we were on our way to unlimited production and, hence, unlimited consumption . . . [and] the trinity of unlimited production, absolute freedom, and unrestricted happiness formed the nucleus of a new religion, Progress. . . .[17]

The path-breaking and shocking volume, *The Limits to Growth*,[18] first published in 1972, articulated the environmental crisis with the rigor of scientific data and computer analyses. This work challenged the modern notion of unlimited progress, including its supposedly limitless components of material production, consumption, economic growth, natural resources, freedom, and happiness. Although more citizens of our society have acquired more material possessions and desired more material wants than in any previous social order, affluent modern citizens increasingly find such goods and wants unsatisfying, manifesting Wildean tragedy, value realization erosion, and Hobbesian *angst* or anxiety. Modern industrial capitalism has been able to modify itself to avoid the lethal economic contradictions and self-destruction predicted by Marx; yet it has not been able to overcome the potentially fatal contradiction between modernity's promise of unlimited progress with its unlimited dimensions and the inescapable existential and environmental limits made undeniably clear by the environmental crisis since the 1960s. The latter, in combination with the resulting global, radical, environmental social movements, have provided the impetus to confront the deficiencies of modernity, increasing the mandate for a new postmodern society. *The single most important aspect of the environmental crisis may be its normative basis and unique demonstration of the unsustainability and undesirability of modernity, in a manner that no previous challenge to this seemingly invincible social order has faced in its history.* In addition, the corresponding need to transform our hegemonic modern industrial civilization has become evident.

By focusing on the concept of "limits," I think we can avoid what Rousseau perceptively realized was Hobbes's fundamental methodological mistake: The error of considering modern human behavior and values as natural or part of human nature in reality instead of recognizing that alternative behavior and values were not only possible but superior. Rousseau, the most penetrating early critic of modernity, understood that the insatiable behavior and values described by Hobbes as humanity's essential nature, illustrated by Wilde's conception of human tragedy or by my example of professional sports teams, are really social constructions by misguided modern society. Unlike Hobbes, and like the ancient Greeks, Rousseau astutely perceived the unacceptable normative costs of founding a social order on insatiable and limitless desires. This achievement constitutes one of Rousseau's great contributions to modern thought. In his famous work, *A Discourse on the Origin of Inequality,* Rousseau criticizes his predecessors in political theory, most notably Hobbes, when he asserts:

> The philosophers, who have inquired into the foundations of society, have all felt the necessity of going back to a state of nature; but not one of them has got there. . . . Every one of them, in short, constantly dwelling on wants, avidity, oppression, desires, and pride, has transferred to the state of nature ideas which were acquired in society; so that, in speaking of the savage, they describe the social man.[19]

Beginning with Hobbes, I contend, the foundational idea of modernity, its values, worldview, and social institutions has been to deny the possibility—or even desirability—of the satiation of human wants and the limits to the human condition such satiation would imply. Let us recall Hobbes's statement that "the felicity of this life consists *not* in the repose of a man satisfied," and Wilde's "much the worst" tragedy of "getting what one wants."

Adam Smith and Modern Materialism

Rousseau agreed that Hobbes's view of human nature was descriptively accurate but not normatively acceptable. When we examine the thought of Adam Smith, the eighteenth-century British moral and social theorist and important contributor to the development of modern thought and society, Hobbes's modernist view of human nature takes a decidedly materialist turn, forming the foundation of modernity: the ceaseless preoccupation with material wants and possessions, making the economy, economic values, and economic goals the most important aspects of modern society dominating the life of the modern citizen. Smith expresses this crucial point for understanding modernity in his essential work, *The Wealth of Nations:*

> The principle, which prompts to save, is the desire of bettering our condition, a desire which thought generally calm and dispassionate comes with us from the womb, and never leaves us till we go into the grave. In the whole interval which separates these two moments, there is scarce perhaps a single instant in which any man is so perfectly and completely satisfied with his situation, as to be without any wish of alteration or improvement of any kind. An augmentation of fortune is the means by which the greater part of men propose and wish to better their condition.[20]

Note the significant similarity of Smith's view to Hobbes's: the central modern idea of the insatiability or limitlessness of humanity's desires ceasing only with death, and the impossibility of humans achieving meaningful satisfaction. Once these limitless desires are tied to material objects, Smith argued, the ubiquitous and endless human desire to "better our condition" occurs, awakening the propensity in human nature to "truck, barter, and exchange one thing for another."[21] Hence, the birth of modern materialism, influencing the thought and lives of humanity across the planet ever since.

Smith's philosophy accomplished the transfer of the Hobbesian infinite desirer concept of human nature and the vision of social life derived from this concept to material objects and economic activity, now supported by the production prowess of the modernist capitalist economy. For the most advanced stage of this social order (exemplified by the United States with its multitrillion dollar economy, the other advanced industrial societies, and the contemporary phenomenon of globalization), virtually all of the Earth's inhabitants now fit the Hobbesian-Smithian model, pursuing materialist goals endlessly. VCRs, DVDs, large projection, high definition televisions, expensive basketball shoes, digital cameras, luxury cars, and so on are grist for the marketing mill as their manufacturers strive to create a global market for luxury goods by drawing on the lack of satiation, the absence of the "repose of a mind satisfied," and the limitless desire to "better our [material] condition till we go into the grave."

One of the leading limits to growth theorists, economist Hermann E. Daly, turns to the Bible to demonstrate the attack by modernity and its denial of limits upon the wisdom of the ages ("the books of the old moral philosophers," as Hobbes put it) which emphasized the existence of limits. After noting Jesus' reply to Satan that man does not live by bread alone, Daly eloquently writes:

> Man, craving for the infinite, has been corrupted by the temptation to satisfy an insatiable hunger in the material realm. . . . The proper object of economic activity is to have *enough* bread, not infinite bread, not a world turned into bread, not even vast storehouses full of bread. The infinite hunger of man, his moral and spiritual hunger, is not to be satisfied, is indeed exacerbated, by the current demonic madness of producing more and more things for more and more people. Afflicted with an infinite itch, modern man is scratching the wrong place, and his frenetic clawing is drawing blood from the life-sustaining circulatory system of his space-ship, the biosphere.[22]

As this powerful passage suggests, a major precept of the limits to growth, environmental critique of modernity is that for all of its tremendous power, the industrial juggernaut has not accomplished the impossible: to overcome the existential limits of the human condition which provided the bases for the limits-emphasizing tradition as old as Western civilization.[23] "Modernity has accomplished many far-reaching transformations, but it has not fundamentally changed the finitude, fragility, and mortality of the human condition."[24]

While grade school students learn about the industrial revolution in terms of scientific advances, innovations in machinery and fuels, little is taught about the revolution in values and social institutions that changed society. An economic theorist describes this transformation, providing an excellent summary to this section's discussion:

> In distinction from previous societies where the pursuit of wealth and hard work were considered as inferior activities and as a curse, left to slaves, women, and inferior social groups, industrial society made the acquisition of wealth morally acceptable and considered it as a moral obligation. [Smithian] Economic thought justified this attitude by assum-

ing this acquisitiveness and the propensity to truck, barter, and exchange in order to increase one's wealth is a basic human propensity. Here a unique historical phenomenon, the acquisitive attitude, was interpreted as a universal human inclination.[25]

The basic premise of modern materialism that the ceaseless and limitless net increase in material goods will produce a corresponding ceaseless and limitless increase in human happiness is essential to the modernist's denial of the satiation of human wants, and the resulting claim of their endless nature. It is this belief that makes economic growth the most adhered to value on Earth. Yet, this materialist conviction is false and constitutes an erroneous foundation for our entire modern value and social structure. The whole modern political theoretical tradition, starting with Hobbes and Rousseau and leading up to political economists and social theorists Thorstein Veblen[26] and Fred Hirsch,[27] attests to the futility of realizing the self-contradictory and foundational modern value of ceaseless, unlimited, unfulfilled wants where the only escape from their tragic pursuit is death!

Conclusion: The Modern Denial of Limits, the Environmental Crisis, and Postmodernity

How does this political theoretical analysis of the tragedy of modernity relate to the environment, the current environmental crisis, and the worldwide environmental movement for social change? The answer, in brief, is that the most recent form of the environmental social movement began in the 1960s and 1970s with the publication of Rachel Carson's *Silent Spring* in 1962, the first American Earth Day in 1970, the publication of the *Limits to Growth* volume in 1972, and the United Nations first conference on the environment in 1972. Spectacular ecological disasters like the Santa Barbara oil spill, the Three Mile Island nuclear accident, the Prince William Sound oil spill, the Chernobyl nuclear disaster, and various floods and famines have dramatically increased the industrial public's consciousness of the existence of environmental limits and their consequences for our supreme modern value of unlimited economic growth. Environmentalists have researched, publicized, and attacked the many sources of pollution and the hazards of nuclear power and have recognized and sought to protect the limited quantities of nonrenewable and renewable energy resources, minerals, animals, and plants.

In these ways the environmental movement has addressed, and continues to address, the unlimited economic growth as a dangerous foundation of modern society that threatens the survival of the planet and all of its living inhabitants.

The environmental crisis facing modern society today is essentially a *normative* crisis at its root, as I have attempted to demonstrate in this essay with its focus on the tragedy of modernity derived from our faulty values, worldview, and social institutions; it demands a transformation to alternative, postmodern values, worldview, and institutions. This conclusion, if correct, should have profound meaning for the modern citizens, researchers, and especially for the elite, who view the environmental crisis in a reformist manner as merely a set of technological problems with no negative implications for our modern values.

The paramount modern value of unlimited economic growth for modern individuals and society is based, as we have seen, on an Hobbesian view of the world and its emphasis on unlimited human desires. This, in turn, produces the Wildean tragedy. Let us consider here the relevance of the twentieth-century French social theorist and novelist, Albert Camus, and his *philosophie des limites* (philosophy of limits). Camus insightfully proclaimed that "man is the only creature who refuses to be what he is," a limited being confronting a limited world.[28] A central theme in Camus's fictional and nonfictional writings[29] is modern humanity's refusal to recognize the limits that confront us and the fundamental negative consequences of our state of denial, characterizing modernity at its most basic level. Camus prescribes full recognition of these limits as an inescapable part of the human condition and recommends that we live according to them without engaging in denial.

Camus emphasizes the human limits of mortality (the limit to life) and fallibility (the limit to knowledge). I argue that it is also crucial to underscore the limits to our satisfaction through material acquisition and, by extension, the limits to economic growth and the quintessential modern value of materialism. Once we cease the modern "escape," which Camus termed humankind's refusal to be what we are, recognize and accept our existential limits,[30] we may then construct a social order consistent with these unavoidable limits. Camus echoes the goal of the ancient Greek poet Pindar who is quoted in the epigraph to *The Myth of Sisyphus* as follows, "O my soul, do not aspire to immortal life, but exhaust the limits of the possible."[31] We must heed Pindar's admonition, endorsed by Camus, and "exhaust the limits of the possible." Only then, I maintain, will contemporary humanity end the damaging process of modernity's refusal to be what we are: limited beings in an ecologically limited world. We would, thereby, comprehend the basic error of modernity and all of its pernicious ramifications: the modern denial of limits, especially pertaining to human wants, resulting in the denial of human satisfaction and destruction of our environment.

Two distinguished social theorists, Daniel Bell and Lewis Mumford, have commented on this defining characteristic of modernity. Their formulations are so important that they deserve the most serious consideration by the reader (note also their similarity to Camus's view). First, Bell:

> The deepest nature of man, the secret of his soul as revealed by the modern metaphysic, is that he seeks to reach out beyond himself; knowing that negativity—death—is finite, he refuses to accept it. Behind the chiliasm of modern man is the megalomania of self-infinitization. In consequence, the modern hubris is refusal to accept limits.[32]

Mumford, the renowned student of modernity, explains the idea of limitlessness that has characterized the modern worldview from its earliest stages:

> The desire for life without limits was part of the general lifting of limits which the first great assemblage of power by means of the megamachine brought about. Human weaknesses, above the weaknesses of mortality, were both contested and defied. . . . From the standpoint of human life, indeed of all organic existence, this assertion of absolute power was a confession of psychological immaturity—a radical failure to understand the natural processes of birth and growth, of maturation and death.[33]

This modern denial of limits and the megalomania of modernity takes several forms: the political violence resulting from political absolutism of the twentieth century that Camus focuses on; the fascination with absolute power, mechanization, speed, and militarism that Mumford describes; and the value supremacy of unlimited economic growth and materialism as means to unlimited progress based on the unlimited desirer conception that I have argued in this essay. It is my belief that the current environmental crisis can stimulate an awakening to the undesirable nature and consequences of this basic modern conception once it is recognized that most of the participants in the environmental crisis literature have been natural scientists who have overlooked its political and philosophical implications. Environmental political theory can make its most urgently needed contribution by correcting this omission.

Our modern misconceptions of the human condition, human wants and satisfaction, as well as the associated value of unlimited economic growth, have produced the numerous excesses now challenging the various ecological limits in advanced modern society. It is here that the environmental movement, informed by environmental political theory, can make its greatest impact by elucidating the errors of modernity on the deepest normative levels, and thereby inspiring us to create alternative postmodern values and institutions. This should reflect humanity's real condition: a fundamentally limited nature with more than materialist needs (see Zimmerman's discussion in this volume on our nonmaterial needs and modernity's exclusive preoccupation with material scarcity). We must not aspire to the impossible, unlimited materialist life, but exhaust the limits of the possible, limited as it may be;[34] that is, we must begin to recognize human and environmental limits that modernity, since its advent, has refused to do.

Not all human wants are infinite and limitless, nor are they capable of satisfaction by economic growth alone. Contrary to the modern worldview, once this fundamental view of the human condition is fully understood and appreciated, we can attempt to address the daunting challenge that it implies: the creation and acceptance of postmodern values and institutions. I invite the reader to engage in this essential task, beginning with her or his own life, followed by the hard work of implementing this alternative postmodern view for society as a whole. Before we can begin, let alone conclude, the process of transforming modernity and reversing its disastrous effects for human life and satisfaction, our planet, and all other forms of life, we must recognize and correct modernity's tragic illusion of limitless economic growth.

2

Envisioning a Sustainable Society
Lester W. Milbrath

In my judgment, the most important reality in today's world is that modern industrial civilization cannot be sustained. Even though many world leaders do not recognize this fact, it is nevertheless true.

I spent three months in Southern California, teaching at the University of California at Irvine. I shocked my students when I made the point that North America has the two most unsustainable societies on the planet (Canada and the United States) and that Southern California is the most unsustainable part of North America. The Southern Californians have erected a huge metropolitan area with nearly 20 million inhabitants on a terrain of mountains and valleys that is essentially a desert and is highly susceptible to earthquakes. The city must import all its water, energy, and food. Its transportation system depends overwhelmingly on heavy, fast automobiles that travel on multilane freeways that crisscross the area. If Southern Californians had intentionally set out to design an unsustainable society, they could hardly have exceeded the reality of today's Los Angeles area.

On January 17, 1994, a moderate earthquake struck the northern part of the metro area and reminded its inhabitants how vulnerable they are to the disruption of their imported services. Two hundred years ago that earthquake would barely have been noticed in the area. Today, water, energy, and transportation links were broken in addition to the loss of life and buildings. One might have thought that people would see the folly of their situation and abandon the area but almost none did. The possibility of not rebuilding the freeways never came up for public discussion; there was no public awareness of the unsustainability of the city. The people in the area took for normal what is entirely unnatural, and hastily set about rebuilding what had failed them.

The most important problem faced by mankind is: *How do we trans-*

form an unsustainable society into one that is sustainable? That question raises a series of additional questions: How did we get into this predicament? Why is modern society unsustainable? What happens if we do not change? What must be changed if human society is to survive? What can we do to bring about the requisite changes? I will discuss all of those questions, but I cannot promise to have all the needed solutions.

How Did We Get into This Predicament?

We did so by becoming too successful. It did not occur to people in the Los Angeles area to abandon the city because it is, for them, successful. They assume it will continue to be successful indefinitely. Our vision is blinded by tragic success of the human species. Homo sapiens have lived for only a tiny fraction of the time our planet has existed. If the time of the earth's existence (4.6 billion years) were compressed into one calendar year, human existence would extend for only eleven minutes; civilization would have lasted only one minute; modern industrial society would have lasted only two seconds. Nearly all of the changes that threaten the existence of our civilization transpired in the last two seconds. We are now so powerful that by using science and technology we can move mountains, slash down forests, fly to the moon, and destroy all life—even our own.

Nowadays we often hear that we face an environmental crisis. But do we properly understand our predicament? Is this an environmental crisis? Try this thought experiment: Imagine that suddenly, poof, all the humans disappear but leave behind the buildings, roads, shopping malls, stadiums, factories, skyscrapers, automobiles, ships, planes, and so forth. Now, imagine that three or four centuries pass. What will have happened? Nature will have swiftly taken over; buildings will have crumbled; vehicles will have rusted and fallen apart; plants will have grown into and broken up roads and parking lots; much of the land will have been recolonized by forests. Water, air, and soil will gradually have been cleansed by nature; most endangered species will once more flourish. Nature, you see, would thrive splendidly without us.

That experiment makes it clear that we do not have an environmental crisis; we have a crisis of the human species. More accurately, we have a crisis of human civilization. It was not until humans became civilized and took more and more of the biosphere to serve our exclusive needs that we began to reproduce at epidemic rates. Just in the twentieth century, human numbers doubled twice, from 1.5 billion to 3 billion, to 6 billion. Population will double again within the next fifty years, bringing us to 11 or 12 billion. Still another doubling would carry us beyond 20 billion. Allowing that to happen would be total folly. If reproductive success is the sign of a successful species, we have become tragically successful. (Compare to Kassiola's discussion of the tragedy of modernity in the previous chapter.)

Why Is Modern Society Unsustainable?

Our use of resources and discharge of wastes more than doubles with each doubling of the human population. Those growth rates cannot help but force a great transformation. Growth simply cannot continue for two reasons: More than half the resources in the earth's crust have been consumed and scattered, and there simply will not be sufficient resources for all those new humans, even at present consumption rates.

Even more important, the emission of greenhouse gases (carbon dioxide, methane, nitrous oxides, and chlorofluorocarbons) is beginning to change the way the biosphere works. Scientists estimate that the earth will warm three to five degrees Celsius in the next seven decades, perhaps sooner (with even more heating up predicted in the most recent research findings in 2001). That will be sufficient to change climate patterns. We cannot be sure that the climate will change gradually and then settle down into a new pattern; it is likely to oscillate unpredictably and bring unexpected catastrophe. You have probably read predictions of good farmland turning to desert, devastating floods, rising sea levels, killer hurricanes. Climate change and loss of the ozone layer will injure ecosystems all over the planet and reduce their productivity at the very time all those new humans will be looking for sustenance.

Equally devastating, climatic instability would destroy the confidence people need in order to invest. People will not be sure that they could ever live in the house they would like to build. Entrepreneurs would have little confidence that their business could get supplies or that their goods would have a market. Investors would fear that their stocks, bonds, and loans would become worthless. Young people would not know how to plan for a career. If the climate oscillates unpredictably, we will become victims of our own success. Be forewarned: Chaos in climate patterns means economic catastrophe.

By just doing what we have been doing every day, we are unintentionally conducting a giant planetary experiment to see how far we can perturb biospheric systems before they change their patterns and drastically change everything about our lives. By being single-mindedly successful at doing what society expects of us, we have created a civilization that is headed for breakdown. We are facing a massive transformation of modern society that we cannot avoid. We should change the direction of our society now before we find out the answer to that unintended experiment. In Earth time we have less than one second to make the necessary changes. Either we learn to control our growth in population and in economic activity or nature will control it for us. Remember, nature's solution is death.

What Happens If We Do Not Change?

If we persist on our current trajectory, we can expect, as already mentioned, that we will double human population within fifty years. We will triple or quadruple world economic output. That will lead to swift depletion of the world's resources and to the emission of such a torrent of pollutants that the planet's ecosystems cannot assimilate them. Most seriously, we are likely to change the pattern of the planet's biogeochemical systems with all of the terrible consequences that I already have mentioned. We are likely to seek technological solutions to those problems, but it is my considered opinion that trying to solve societal problems with more and better technology will fail. We will belatedly and painfully learn that most socioeconomic problems are not amenable to a technological fix, and, moreover, that the environmental crisis is not a technological problem but is based on our values (see introduction to this volume).

Not only has modern industrial society created this crisis, but in my judgment, it is not capable of producing a solution. It is blinded to the existence of the crisis and disabled in trying to avoid it by the values it pursues. Think of the values upheld as good in contemporary political discourse: economic growth, consumption, efficiency, productivity, jobs, competitiveness, taking risks, power, winning. Societies pursuing those goals cannot avoid depleting their resources, cannot avoid degrading nature, cannot avoid poisoning life with wastes, and cannot avoid upsetting biospheric systems. Will we thoughtfully transform our society to a sustainable mode, or will we stubbornly refuse to change and have change forced upon us by the collapse of society's fundamental underpinnings? *Resisting change will make us victims of change. I repeat for emphasis, resisting change will make us victims of change.*

What Must Be Changed If Human Society Is to Survive?

How do we transform our present unstable society to a new sustainable society? We all know that both societies and people resist change. Achieving change is not as easy as giving an order; even the most powerful dictators must persuade the people that they will be better off if they change. My answer—I believe it is the only answer—is that we must *learn* our way to a new society. The key aspect of our relearning is to transform the way we think. *It is absolutely essential to change the way we think.* All other attempts at change will fail if we do not transform our thinking. If we can make the right changes in our thinking, the necessary changes in society will follow.

Can we learn in time? We all know that social learning usually is slow and painful, but not always; sometimes we cross a threshold and learning comes about astonishingly swiftly. Who among us would have predicted the sweeping changes that occurred in Eastern Europe in the fall of 1989? How many foresaw that the Soviet Union would disintegrate with hardly a shot fired? When people changed their thinking the old order simply disappeared. When a society has no other choice than to change, we get little guidance from the past; we cannot predict the future from the past in those circumstances.

Can we manage to look ahead and make careful plans to bring about the changes that we know must come, or will we resist change and have it painfully forced upon us? Either way, our only option is to relearn; nature, and the imperatives of its laws, will be our most powerful teacher as we learn our way to a new society.

I characterize the new society that we must create as sustainable; but what do I mean by "sustainable"? A sustainable society does something more than keep people alive; living is more than merely not dying. In a sustainable society, people conduct their lives so that nature can cleanse itself and living creatures can flourish. People living sustainably husband nature and resources so that future generations of people, and other creatures, can enjoy a life of decent quality.

The values appropriate to a sustainable society are displayed in Figure 2.1.

Figure 2.1 **A proposed value structure for a sustainable society**

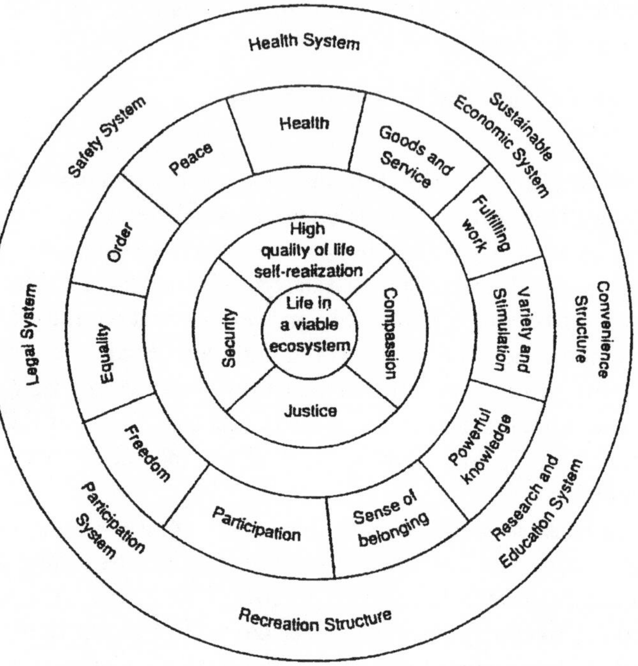

Contrasting Values and Goals Between Sustainable and Modern Societies

Life in a viable ecosystem must be the core value of a sustainable society. Viable ecosystems nurture all life, not just human life. Ecosystems function splendidly without humans but human society would die out without a viable ecosystem. Individuals seeking quality of life require a well-functioning society that must be supported by a well-functioning ecosystem. If we follow the logic of those statements, we must give top priority to the good functioning of our ecosystem, second priority to the good functioning of our society; only when the viability of both systems is assured is it permissible to seek quality of life in any way we choose.

But do we live according to the priority of those values? Obviously not! Leaders in modern society equate material consumption with quality of life. They urge us to swiftly exploit resources to maximize economic output without careful forethought about future consequences. By placing top priority on economic values, they sacrifice the good functioning of vital life systems, making it unlikely that those systems can support the huge increase in human population that is coming. At the very time when all the capabilities of life systems will be needed, our lack of foresight will have greatly weakened them.

A sustainable society affirms *love* as a core value. It extends love and compassion not only to those near and dear but to people in other lands, future generations, and other species. It recognizes the intricate web of relationships that bind all living creatures into a common destiny. Life is not mainly conflict and competition between creatures; rather, a sustainable society emphasizes partnership not domination; cooperation more than competition; love more than power.

A sustainable society affirms justice and security as other core values. Those are core values in every society but the way they are realized differs from society to society. A modern industrial society that emphasizes wealth, power, competition, and domination generates great differences in status that seem inherently unjust to those of lower status. Individuals often resort to crime and violence to improve their situation. The values of justice and security are continually under assault in such a society. A sustainable society that emphasizes love, partnership, compassion, and cooperation can more easily provide justice and security.

A sustainable society would encourage self-realization as the key to a fulfilling life. A sustainable society would help persons become all they are capable of being whether they possess a talent that is highly valued in the labor marketplace or not. Work should be redefined to become a means to self-realization and not merely a block of time to be traded in the labor market. Modern competitive industrial society encourages firms to replace workers with machines and wastes the creative talents of hundreds of millions of unemployed people. The problem will explode into a permanent crisis as the world's population doubles in the next fifty years.

A first step to extricate ourselves from this problem will be to change our thinking to distinguish work from employment. We presently reward only the employed and look down upon the unemployed as less than fully human. Our faulty thinking fails to recognize that nearly everyone works even if they do not have a job. Persons doing their own work, or nonpaid contributors to family and society, should be valued as much as those highly paid. Self-esteem should not be linked to employment but should derive more from skill, artistry, effort, and integrity.

Reconsideration of Modern Society's Focus on Economics

Economic growth is a means and not an end; it cannot be our top priority—a viable ecosystem must be society's top priority. Current rates of economic growth are impossible to sustain. Modern political leaders constantly proclaim economic growth as their top priority even though societies that do so are bound to fail. Our current misplaced emphasis on growth must give way to a recognition that there are limits to human population growth and to economic growth; otherwise, society will lose more highly treasured values, such as the continued good functioning of global biogeochemical systems, the vitality of ecosystems, the continued availability of vital resources, and the health of all creatures.

We must forthrightly recognize that there are limits to Earth's resources and to the ability of life systems to absorb pollutants; those limits will necessarily restrict population growth and economic activity. A sustainable society would recognize that basic fact and would emphasize making quality products to be loved and conserved for many years. Products would be designed to be safely and easily recycled to other uses when their original use is finished. People would learn to love beauty and simplicity. Packaging would be kept to a minimum and would be designed to be reused or recycled.

A sustainable society would support simple lifestyles by diminishing the role of advertising in communication and entertainment. Modern society fails to recognize that advertising that urges everyone to buy, consume, and throw away will so injure ecosystems that it will lead to that society's painful demise.

A sustainable society would utilize both planning and markets as basic information systems that supplement each other. Both are needed to guide economic activity and public policy. Modern society fails to recognize the fundamental inability of markets to anticipate the long-term future and to adequately assign social value to public goods, such as clean air and parks. Modern society puts too much faith in markets; it even abdicates responsible moral choice to markets by allowing them to demand closing or moving factories, to make harmful and wasteful goods, to freely release pollutants, to insist on public subsidies, and to insist on favorable laws and regulations.

A sustainable society would recognize that public goods (those that are available to everyone, such as schools, highways, parks, national defense, environmental protection, etc.) are just as important for quality of life as private goods. It also would recognize that markets by themselves are incapable of providing public goods; therefore, it would expect government and other public agencies to provide public goods and to justly assess taxes to pay for them.

In contrast, many leaders in modern society mistakenly assert that only personal goods can bring quality in living, and neglect public goods in order to reduce taxes. My country, the United States, vigorously promotes businesses, and a market economy oriented to the production of personal goods, to the point that Americans now live in a society in which privileged people have personal affluence while all experience public squalor. Many millions of Americans cannot succeed in that system and are unable to earn enough income for a decent life. Their anger and frustration lead to unprecedented levels of violent brutality. We cannot find quality in living in that way.

Science and Technology in the Service of Society

Science and technology are not value free; they make values, they change values, they are guided by values, and they profoundly influence everything about modern life. Yet, leaders in science, business, and government continually proclaim that science and technology are value free and should be promoted as positive steps toward progress and the good life. The public is told that it is not proper for society to control science and technology. This abdication of public responsibility gives the ability to direct those forces, and to collect their benefits, over to those who can pay for specialized talents and equipment (especially business and government); therefore, science and technology primarily serve the values of the established order. Those who control science and technology can use them to dominate all other creatures—they can literally destroy any or all life.

A sustainable society would encourage further development of science and technology for the good they can do, but it would anticipate their potential for evil and would learn to develop social controls of those powerful forces. In contrast, modern society eagerly promotes their development without foresight as to consequences or recognition of the need for controls.

Powerful new technologies can induce sweeping changes in economic patterns of lifestyles, governance, and social values. They are even more powerful than legislation for inducing permanent change; we can repeal legislation but we do not know how to repeal a powerful new technology. Therefore, a sustainable society would not allow deployment of new technologies without careful forethought regarding the long-term impact of a proposed technology. It would learn how to design and enforce social controls of the deployment and use of technologies.

Social Learning as the Dynamic of Social Change

Social learning is different from the learning of individuals. When a society learns, the individuals within it also learn, but individuals often learn without the society learning. Even though a society cannot be said to have a mind, societies, as social entities, can be said to know or believe something. Social learning is embodied in societal memory, conventional terms of discourse, social norms, laws, institutional patterns, institutional memories, shared perceptions, and so forth.

Societies always have learned despite their inherent tendency to preserve the status quo; but we can make swift social learning a conscious societal policy. A society desiring to be sustainable would do this not only to deal with pressing problems, but also to help that society to realize its vision of a good society. No single individual, not even a government, has the power to order a society to change. Meaningful and permanent social change occurs when nearly everyone learns the necessity and wisdom of accepting the change. Therefore, a society hoping to survive and thrive would emphasize swift social learning as its best strategy for evolving sustainable modes of behavior that also lead to quality in living.

In contrast, modern industrial society, driven by the desire for power and wealth, uses the market to guide its destiny. Markets cannot look ahead to deal with problems until they become powerful immediate threats. A society that hopes to become sustainable must use enhanced foresighted learning to anticipate problems and avoid crisis policy making.

We cannot make a society sustainable without changing the way we think. A sustainable society must cultivate ecological thinking which is different from the thoughtways in modern society. Amazingly, most people in modern society do not know the fundamental laws of nature such as the First and Second Laws of Thermodynamics. For example, environmentalists derive four key maxims from the First Law of Thermodynamics which says that matter and energy can neither be created nor destroyed, they can only be transformed: (1) everything must go somewhere; (2) everything is connected to everything else; (3) we can never do merely one thing; and (4) we must continually ask, "and then what?" These maxims are routinely violated in contemporary thinking and discourse. Every school child should learn them; yet almost none are given this instruction. A sustainable society would reaffirm the belief, once held in primitive societies, that a knowledge of nature's workings is basic to being educated. It would act on that belief by requiring environmental education of all students as it now requires every student to study history.

Ecological thinking recognizes that the geosphere and biosphere are systems and that proper understanding of the way the world works requires people to learn how to think systemically, holistically, integratively, and in a futures mode. Everything is connected to everything else; we must learn to anticipate second-, third-, and fourth-order consequences for any contemplated societal action.

Modern society, in contrast, emphasizes simple cause and effect "mechanistic thinking," which fails to alert people that most actions have unanticipated consequences. It encourages narrow expertise and short-term planning, while simultaneously discouraging holistic, systemic, and futures thinking. A sustainable society would correct that distortion and accord esteem to those who practice foresighted ecological thinking.

A society desiring to be sustainable would redesign government to maximize its ability to learn. It would use the governmental learning process to promote social learning. In chapter 14 of *Envisioning a Sustainable Society,*[1] I describe a learning system for government that would encourage inputs from citizens to enhance its learning ability. This learning system would add a new branch to the government designed to give it a much needed foresight capability that I call a "Council for Long Range Societal Guidance." This learning system not only would help government to learn by enlisting the learning of the entire society but the government learning process would also help the society to learn.

In contrast, modern society takes a short-range perspective and mistakenly assumes that the future will be like the past. It insists that planners and decision makers must be immediately practical, which generally means that economic needs take precedence over all other values. It ridicules people who peer into the future and make plans to forestall future problems; it calls them "impractical dreamers." Yet, as we well know, modern society is constantly scrambling to deal with crisis after crisis that it did not anticipate.

The era when governors needed only to command and citizens meekly obeyed has passed. A learning sustainable society would affirm the inherent value of persons by requiring that governors listen to citizens. A sustainable society not only would keep itself open for public participation but also would cultivate mutual learning between officials and citizens as the central task of governance. The most successful governance occurs when citizens and officials mutually understand their problems and acknowledge the appropriate solutions.

A sustainable society would recognize that we are part of global biogeochemical systems; and that our destiny is tied to the continued good functioning of those systems. Our health and welfare are vitally affected by how people, firms, and governments in other lands behave. Therefore, it would strive diligently to build an effective planetary politics. It would encourage its citizens to join transnational social movements (like the anti-World Trade Organization social movement made up of nongovernmental organizations worldwide), and political parties because they can make effective common cause with movements and parties in other countries and work together to preserve the visibility of global biogeochemical systems. It would nurture social learning all around the planet, because the cooperation of all is needed to preserve the good functioning of planetary life systems. This necessity to work together may one day lead to the formation of a world society with a world government.

Learning Our Way to a Sustainable Society

Learning our way to a new society not only is the preferred way; it is the only way—in my judgment; there is no shortcut. No individual has the power and the trust of the people to order new ways of thinking, new ways of perceiving, new architecture for institutions, new laws, new norms, new ways of making and doing things. We get those new ways of thinking and doing only by learning—it must be the learning of the entire society.

Fundamental relearning cannot occur, however, until people become aware of the need for change. So long as contemporary society is working reasonably well and its leaders keep reaffirming that society is on the right track, the mass of people will not listen to a message urging change. For that reason, life systems on our planet probably must get worse before they can get better. Nature will turn out to be our most powerful teacher. We probably will not be able to listen until biospheric systems no longer work the way they used to and people are shocked into realizing how much their lives depended on the continued good functioning of those systems.

After a severe shock to wake us up, in times of great systemic turbulence, social learning can be extraordinarily swift. Regretfully, injuries to life systems already may be very great by that time. Life probably will not cease, but many will die and others will be gravely injured. Why can't we learn at less cost?

Even if I know they will be difficult to achieve, here are some specific recommendations about next steps to be taken to bring about a sustainable society. If we could wave a magic wand to obtain the cooperation of people and their governments, the following actions would be effective:

- Change the way we think as swiftly as possible. We need to clarify our values and adopt new priorities. In the process we should define our responsibilities so that people see what their part of the overall task is and the necessity to do their share. All of us must learn to think systemically, holistically, integratively, and in a futures mode. Renewed reflection on the true meaning of quality of living should be part of this relearning effort.
- Control and gradually eliminate weapons of mass destruction.
- Stop population growth as quickly as possible. With heroic efforts, population rise might be leveled off at 8 or 9 billion.
- Reduce material consumption in the more developed countries and use that reserve capacity to help the less developed countries meet their subsistence needs.
- Cut back as much as possible on use of fossil energy; develop and adopt more energy efficient technology; cut out energy waste wherever found; stop using fossil energy simply for thrills, fun, ease, or comfort; convert to use of solar energy.
- Aggressively reduce economic throughput so as to preserve more resources for future generations and to reduce discharge of wastes into the biosphere. Failure to do so will seriously reduce the carrying capacity (or how much life the ecosystem can biologically support) of life systems.
- Find ways to share employment so we do not need to make unneeded goods just to provide jobs for people. Work should be redefined to become a means of self-realization, not merely a pawn in economic competition.

- Emphasize making quality products that can last lifetimes—beautiful things to be cherished and preserved. Products should be designed to be easily repaired and for safe eventual disposal. They should be marketed with as little packaging as possible.
- Diligently reuse, restore, and recycle materials that we now throw away. Carefully dispose of the remainder of the wastes.
- Eliminate use of chlorofluorocarbons (CFCs) to allow the stratospheric ozone layer to restore itself (agreed to in a United Nations treaty but must be implemented fully). Recapture CFCs from current uses and destroy them (break them down into original constituents).
- Stop the release of toxic environmental chemicals into the environment.
- Protect and enhance biodiversity; revitalize ecosystems that have been injured by human actions; husband nature and resources so that future generations and other creatures can enjoy a life of decent quality.
- Plant billions more trees.
- Phase out energy and chemical intensive agriculture so as to develop methods of tillage that are sustainable.
- Restore degraded ecosystems to flourishing health wherever possible.
- Develop an ethic that constantly alerts people that their actions should impact Earth systems as lightly as possible.
- Affirm love (caring for others) as a primary value; it should be extended not only to those near and dear, but to future generations, other species, and people in other lands.
- Diminish rewards for power, competitiveness, and domination over others. A sustainable society emphasizes partnership rather than domination, cooperation more than competition, justice more than power.
- Develop a procedure for careful review and forethought regarding the long-term impact of a proposed technology. Bad consequences of new technology are easier to avoid or manage if they can be anticipated from the start.
- Redesign government to maximize its ability to learn; then use the government learning process to promote social learning. Develop a new government institution to better anticipate future consequences of proposed policies, laws, and technologies.

- Societal learning of environmental thinking should become a national project. Require that every child receive environmental education (it is just as basic as history); institute environmental education programs for adults; make a special effort to educate media employees about environmental concepts and thinking.
- Do not merely work for a living but work for something that is truly important.
- Keep a sense of humor; sing, dance, affirm, love, be joyous in your oneness with the earth.

Our common journey promises to be challenging and exciting, even though difficult. It will be much easier, and more likely to be successful, if we face it optimistically with a deep understanding of the pace and character of social transformation. We humans are special. Not because of our reason—other species can reason—rather it is our ability to recall the past and foresee the future. We are the only creatures that can imagine our extinction. That special gift of understanding places a unique moral responsibility on humans. Once we have contemplated the future, every decision that could affect that future becomes a moral decision. Even the decision not to act, or to decide not to decide, becomes a moral judgment. We humans, given the ability to anticipate the consequences of our actions, will become the conscious mind of the biocommunity, a global mind that will guide and hasten social transformation. Those who understand what is happening to our world are not free to shrink from this responsibility.

3

Building Sustainable Societies
The Third Revolution in Human Affairs

Dennis Pirages

The early twenty-first century is at once a fascinating and troubled time for an international system that is rapidly becoming a global one. It is characterized by substantial population growth and rapidly increasing demands for natural resources for the bulk of the human race in the less industrialized areas of the world. But those countries that have reached mature industrialization are undergoing a transition to some sort of postindustrial condition. Populations are no longer growing, service industries are expanding, and demand for natural resources seems to be stabilizing. At the same time, technology induced change is causing considerable social, economic and political strains in relations among countries. The next few decades will mark a fundamental turning point in the worldwide expansion of the industrial revolution as the human race grapples with long-term sustainability problems: how to deal with environmental limits to growth on a global scale and how to develop and manage new technologies that will ease environmental pressures.

Theories that can shed light on the twenty-first century sustainability issues are best anchored in basic ecological principles that govern the relationships of all species with nature. The forces shaping human societies and behavior are often quite the same as those shaping possibilities for other species. These forces include demographic change, shifts in climate, and availability of natural resources. Although Homo sapiens is beginning to gain some control over these factors, throughout most of history they have been substantially beyond human domination.

Homo sapiens has coevolved with millions of other species and is in many ways similar to them. Human beings live in biological populations, require similar resources for survival, are subject to the laws of nature, and is physically adapted to the environment through natural selection processes. But Homo sapiens has emerged as the dominant species, at least temporarily, not because of sharper claws, more strength, or greater speed, but because of the parallel evolution of a complex culture. Both of these evolutionary processes provide information that is critical to the survival of the species. The human genetic endowment, honed by millions of years of interaction with nature, represents a storehouse of survival wisdom that is passed biologically from one generation to the next. But human beings also learn from experience and profit from a parallel process called sociocultural evolution. Thus, Homo sapiens is a unique species because its members adapt to the surrounding world in two ways: through the harsh process of biological natural selection that is common to all species, and through the unique process of observing, learning, and passing verbal and written survival information from one generation to the next.

Human beings are also unique in exploiting technology to enhance well-being. Two bursts of technological innovations have been responsible for major transformations in the nature of the information passed from one generation to the next. The first, the agricultural revolution, began about ten thousand years ago in the Middle East and has now spread to encompass the entire world. It has been supplanted in many places by an industrial transformation that is still spreading to the more remote areas of the planet. Yet growing evidence shows that this second revolution cannot be sustained, and that we are entering a third revolutionary period. This nascent revolution is characterized by concern for the long-term sustainability of the human race. It is anchored in the understanding that this type of industrial development cannot be transferred to the bulk of the human race. A more affluent world population that might reach 10 billion can be sustained only by a major transformation in the relationship between Homo sapiens and the natural systems that are essential to collective well-being.

Defining Sustainability

On one hand, thinking about the nature of a sustainable society is easy. Living sustainably means that human populations would prosper within the constraints of nature and have no long-term negative impacts on the environment or opportunities for future generations. But on the other hand, building sustainable societies for the next century is a complex and difficult task because all industrial societies are, to at least some extent, living beyond the long-term carrying capacity of the territory that they occupy. The industrial modernization that originated in Europe nearly 400 years ago and still is spreading to the more remote parts of the world has culminated in value systems, consumption patterns, institutions, and habits that only can be sustained within environments of resource abundance and unlimited opportunity. But they are much less appropriate for the future, particularly for the dense and growing populations in many of the presently less industrialized areas of the world.

Building more sustainable societies in the contemporary world means finding ways to maximize human satisfaction while minimizing human impact on environmental services. Thus, perfectly sustainable societies would be those in which economic activity takes place using only renewable or recycled resources, placing zero long-term burden on the environment. The policy emphasis in such societies would be on meeting human needs rather than stimulating human wants and on the quality rather than the quantity of consumption. Progress toward more sustainable societies would be indexed by new definitions of efficiency stressing the effectiveness with which resources are used and the durability of resulting products.[1]

There are two paths leading to more sustainable future societies. Following the first path involves continuing to muddle toward sustainability by making sporadic and clumsy adjustments to the tightening constraints of nature. Following the second path requires more human initiative and creativity and involves the use of anticipatory thinking to develop policies that can mitigate some of the harshest aspects of muddling through to a possibly less benevolent, yet somewhat sustainable, world. (See social learning emphasized by Milbrath.) There are currently powerful demographic, technological, and environmental forces of change grinding away slowly to transform consumer societies and associated materialistic values and behavior patterns into greener, postindustrial, postmaterialist ones. But creating more sustainable societies rapidly and less painfully is a policy-relevant activity that can be informed by scientific research.

The Passing of Industrial Societies

Human societies and value systems have been transformed previously by at least two readily identifiable revolutionary currents of change.

The first of these pulses, the agricultural revolution, began gathering momentum around the year 8,000 B.C. in the Middle East and slowly spread to encompass almost the entire world. This revolution was driven largely by technological innovations in agriculture, including the domestication of plants and animals that greatly enhanced the available food supply. The sociocultural impact of this revolution was considerable. Hunting and gathering bands were transformed into sedentary populations, a much more refined division of labor developed, human populations began to grow, civilization as we know it emerged, and a major change in the relationship between human beings and nature took place. Almost all societies have now experienced the agricultural revolution. There are very few remaining hunting and gathering societies.

The more recent and relevant transforming pulse, the industrial revolution, began gathering momentum in fifteenth- and sixteenth-century Europe and helped to forge an international system composed of sovereign states. Initially enhancing human productivity by harnessing energy found in fossil fuels to do the work of human beings and draft animals, industrial era technologies also have been instrumental in fundamentally changing the nature of the impacted societies. Agrarian cultures have now been transformed into more secular and materialistic ones, villages have given way to cities, farmers have become factory laborers, nature has become something to be dominated in the name of economic progress, and human psychological and physical mobility have been greatly enhanced. Most important, this revolution has created a secular, materialistic, rational, pragmatic, utilitarian belief system that has been deepened by decades of seemingly increasing material abundance.

The evolutionary products forged by these two great transformations are shared social paradigms: collections of perceptions, beliefs, norms, values, institutions, and survival rules that provide a common frame of reference and make social life possible.[2] Cultural clashes that have accompanied the more recent industrial modernization process are fundamental conflicts between agrarian and industrial paradigms, very different ways of perceiving reality, treating nature, and defining a good life. Over a 400–year period, the industrial revolution has spread material abundance as it has penetrated more remote areas of the planet, but it also has created psychological dilemmas, economic disparities, and social discontinuities. Continued increases in population and consumption now threaten the future course of industrial progress and the sustainability of the human race.

The industrial transformation, which is customarily called "development," has been a very destabilizing period in human history. Its spread has been characterized by massive social upheavals and destruction of existing social orders. Industrial development and modernization also have been associated with severe environmental deterioration, the onset of world wars, political revolutions, and other episodes of large-scale bloodshed. During this period of turmoil, however, some countries managed to increase material consumption enormously, often through large-scale importation of commodities from less industrialized countries. Other countries, however, became the victims of imperialism and are still mired in economic stagnation. But during this period of intense industrialization, there was little assessment of the likely environmental or social impacts of technological innovation and diffusion, and thus human beings could do little to mitigate the harsher effects of wholesale transformation.

But to this point, modernization has been a positive experience, and only a few people would opt to return to truly agrarian circumstances. This productive epoch has yielded unprecedented material abundance, rising living standards for a large part of the world's population, a revolution in human rights, and much increased human social mobility. There is mounting evidence, however, that industrial civilization in its present form may no longer be sustainable or exportable to the large numbers of people in the less industrialized world, and a third major revolution in thinking may well be under way.[3] But compared to the last revolution, there is now greater understanding of the dynamics involved, and it should be possible to follow the second path by making intelligent policy choices to smooth the harshest effects of another protracted period of sociocultural transformation.

The Origins of Sustainability

Numerous societies at different times and in different places have encountered local sustainability crises as demands on nature have exceeded regenerative capabilities. But academic and policy concerns over global sustainability have been apparent only for about three decades. The origins of these concerns lie in the combined global population explosion, industrial expansion, and rapid increase in demand for raw materials of the 1960s and early 1970s. The reasons for this rapid expansion of demand for natural resources and environmental services were many, but the result was an awareness that growth in raw material consumption and environmental exploitation could not long continue without serious consequences for the quality of life in a more densely populated world. Increasing numbers of human beings and higher levels of per capita consumption set off alarm bells over the earth's ability to respond to the demands of future generations.[4]

Growing demographic and environmental concerns catalyzed the publication of *Limits to Growth* and subsequent debates over the future of the human condition in the 1970s.[5] One of several studies commissioned by the Club of Rome, the "limits" computer simulation led to the conclusion that without significant reduction in rates of population growth and new resource efficiencies in industrial production, some sort of major ecological collapse would be inevitable. Publication of this book, the first oil crisis, and the 1972 Stockholm Conference on the Human Environment raised public awareness of environmental issues and sparked an extended debate over potential future limits to growth in resource consumption. The response to these growing ecological concerns was a search for a development model that would permit social progress without environmental deterioration. Thus, the idea of a "steady-state" or "sustainable" society emerged as a possible solution to the perceived limits to industrial growth.[6] While more sustainable societies would have to be somewhat more frugal, there would be possibilities for new efficiencies and satisfactions within steady-state economies aimed at maximizing human satisfactions while minimizing the throughput of raw materials.[7]

Many of these ideas finally received an official seal of approval by the World Commission on Environment and Development in 1987. This so-called Bruntland Commission, concerned with the many dilemmas and issues associated with the future development of less-affluent countries, defined sustainable development as "development that meets the needs of the present without compromising the ability of future generations to meet their own needs."[8] This statement was a marked departure from previous development thinking in two ways. First, it focused on meeting human needs rather than wants. Second, it officially abandoned the assumption, championed historically by liberal economists, that successive generations would naturally be better off than their predecessors. The commissioners concluded that changes in access to resources and in the distribution of production costs and benefits necessitated a new concern for social equity between and within generations.

Concern over future sustainability grew significantly and gathered political momentum in the 1990s. The 1992 United Nations Conference on Environment and Development in Brazil produced Agenda 21, a forty-chapter action plan dealing with many aspects of sustainable development. National, regional, and local commissions on sustainability have been appointed in dozens of countries. Scholars and activists also have tried to create measures of sustainability. In reviewing these attempts, Walter Corson has identified more than a hundred suggested indicators of sustainability.[9] What was once an uncomplicated response to perceived limits to industrial progress has blossomed into a significant social phenomenon.

Sustainability as Process

Creating a more sustainable world is best envisioned as a dynamic process associated with moving from materialist and environmentally destructive industrial to postindustrial and postmaterialistic societies.[10] This process not only involves changing how resources are used and allocated, but also involves reshaping values and institutions that have been molded by generations of increasing material influence. There are thus two aspects of the evolving sustainability problematique. The first concerns relationships between human beings and nature, addressing the requisites for maintaining a balance between environmental capabilities and material demands. The second focuses on assessing and preserving, where possible, many of the ideals and institutions that have evolved during this era of material prosperity. The task of maintaining or restoring more livable environments cannot and should not be accomplished at the expense of new social standards that are to be taken to be the determinants of social progress.

The sustainability problematique is therefore a cluster of environmental, economic, social, and political paradoxes associated with resolving issues resulting from the waning of an industrial way of life while simultaneously creating more sustainable societies that preserve nature, retain some socially acceptable vision of affluence, and preserve many of the hard-won freedoms of industrial modernization. But during times of economic affluence there is often little concern about the future and thus there is inaction on these critical issues. During times of economic turmoil, however, these future issues are frequently discussed, but there are few resources available to devote to systemic transformation.

Thus, the recent weakening of the global economy complicates the transition to a more sustainable world. The slower growth and periodic recessions that have the benevolent side effect of reducing global pollution also increase the poverty, unemployment, and discontent that lend themselves to reactionary retrenchment as easily as to any paradigm shift. It is difficult to explain to an army of the unemployed and downwardly mobile that their predicament is making a contribution to long-term ecological well-being.

Building more sustainable societies is also best seen as an ongoing diverse process rather than a specific condition to be reached because relevant constraints and possibilities differ over time and space. What is sustainable under one set of circumstances may well not be under others. For example, steps to create a more sustainable future for oil-rich Saudi Arabia would be quite different from those required for resource-poor Japan. Future sustainability will be influenced by patterns of population growth and decline, changing environmental constraints, and technological innovations. Thus, following the second path and moving in an organized way toward a more sustainable world requires that diverse alternatives be explored with an emphasis on preserving the greatest possible flexibility in social organization.

Creating more sustainable societies is therefore a continuing process of economically and ecologically positive change, moving away from environmentally destructive definitions of progress toward postindustrial visions using different prescriptions in different situations. But building more sustainable societies need not require performing acts of ecological penance such as forced vegetarianism or basing fashion industries on sackcloth. Rather, real intellectual excitement and a renewed sense of political purpose can be generated by devising new ways to enhance human satisfaction without substantially increasing the burden on nature.

Muddling Toward a More Sustainable World

The process of becoming more sustainable by design requires levels of international cooperation that may be difficult to maintain. Thus, it is very likely that considerably more muddling through in fits and starts will be required. There are presently three sets of factors that are operating to both destabilize and transform the existing environmentally destructive global economy. The first of these drivers of change is a widespread and growing perception of new types of environmental limits to traditional forms of industrial growth. The second is demographic shifts, both population explosions and implosions that threaten to limit growth in consumption on a global scale. Finally, the advent of post-industrial technologies in areas such as telecommunications and bio-technology is leading to a structural transformation of industrial economies.

Perceptions of various kinds of global growth limits are not new, but recently more refined climatological observations have been added to them. Scientific speculation about the future integrity of the earth's protective ozone layer was followed by observations that thinning was taking place. A general consensus on the severity of the problem led to international agreements to reduce and eventually eliminate produc-tion of chlorofluorocarbons and related chemicals. More recently, how-ever, abundant evidence of global warming due to carbon dioxide buildup has given credence to earlier environmental fears and led to a flurry of diplomatic activity, including the Kyoto Protocol on halting greenhouse warming, to restrict carbon dioxide emissions. Curbing carbon dioxide emissions has become a priority item in international negotiations and potentially a significant limit on traditional forms of transportation and industrial production.

Demographic changes are also reshaping global consumption pat-terns and creating a somewhat unexpected force for greater sustain-ability. Rapid population growth in Africa, the Middle East, and parts of Asia and Latin America is outstripping capital formation and dim-ming prospects for future industrial growth. During the period from 1980 to 1993, for example, the bulk of the less industrialized countries experienced a decline in measured per capita income. Of the 121 coun-tries for which World Bank data are available, 53 experienced an annual decline in per capita gross national product (GNP) for this thirteen-year period.[11] Assuming that a 1 percent per capita growth rate is nec-essary just to build and maintain infrastructure to cope with growing population density and related complexity—constructing highways, building schools, installing traffic signals, dealing with pollution—another 18 countries failed to make any significant real per capita progress over this period. And more recently, many of the Asian NICs (Newly Industrialized Countries), considered to be the economic suc-cess stories of the last two decades have plummeted into deep reces-sions. In addition, official development assistance from wealthier countries is stagnant and future decreases are likely. Thus, the capital formation required for the spread of industrial consumption patterns is not occurring in nearly half of the less industrialized countries.

But on the other side of the demographic coin, a population implosion is also serving to dampen potential demand for big-ticket items such as environmentally unfriendly automobiles. Many European countries have reached or dipped below zero population growth. Taken as a whole, the population of Europe is now declining at .1 percent annually. And people in industrial countries are living much longer. The net result is that almost one in five Europeans is now over the age of 65 and that percentage will grow rapidly over the next two decades.[12]

The net result of these two kinds of demographic shifts is that demand for many kinds of consumer goods will likely increase much more slowly than historic norms. In much of the less industrialized world, lack of purchasing power means very slow development of new markets, whereas in many of the more industrial countries aging populations scraping by on pensions will hardly have the purchasing power to boost sales of industrial products. Thus, world demand for raw materials is presently growing much more slowly than originally forecast in the 1970s and likely will slow even further over the next two decades.

Finally, in line with the projections made by Daniel Bell nearly thirty years ago, present patterns of technological innovation and entrepreneurial activity indicate continuing momentum toward postindustrial conditions and greater sustainability.[13] Growth in non–resource-intensive industries, for example, is creating a shift from blue collar to white collar employment. While this type of structural transformation is taking place unevenly, just as fossil fuel–intensive technological innovations drove the industrial revolution and became a growing burden on the environment, a broad range of biomedical and telecommunication technologies are slowly moving economic activity in more sustainable directions.

Pains of Transition

The transition to a more sustainable world, whether by design or muddling through, will generate issues and conflicts between vested interests that wish to cling to traditional sunset types of growth and those who advocate sunrise types of progress. While social conflicts during a period of erratic growth and socioeconomic transition are not likely to be as violent as those that accompanied the shift from agrarian to industrial societies, a paradigm change from laissez-faire quantity growth to more targeted quality growth is bound to continue to raise political controversies.

One of the most fundamental political and economic questions of the impending transformation is how to keep score; how to define and measure progress. Gross domestic product (GDP) has long been the commonly accepted measure of well-being. But GDP is nothing more than an undifferentiated indicator of material throughput, a throwback to a bygone era in which growth of any type of consumption was considered to be positive. Prison construction and school construction are considered to be of equal merit. Mining coal and clear-cutting forests are as laudable as building windmills.

This unsophisticated approach to defining progress is finally yielding to increased scrutiny. While even many economists have long criticized GDP as an indicator, the ongoing transformation has finally created the momentum to replace it with more reasonable and information-rich indicators. One example of such an attempt is the genuine progress indicator (GPI) recently developed in the United States in order to foster debate over the quality of growth.[14] Composed of twenty-six components, the GPI for the United States peaked in the early 1970s and declined rapidly thereafter. Similar indicators have been created for more than a dozen other countries.

The slowing of traditional types of progress also raises important ethical issues concerning intergenerational welfare and mobility, both within and among countries. The old model of progress assumed that technological innovation would make each generation materially better off than its predecessors. But this can no longer be assumed. Slowed growth has fostered unemployment and underemployment in many parts of the world. As opportunities have shrunk, the potential for intergenerational conflict has increased. In the industrial countries, both new entrants to the labor force and those near retirement age often have been the victims of structural transformation and increasingly cutthroat global competition.

Data that, for understandable reasons, are not politically popular or well publicized clearly reveal a generation in industrial countries that is not as well off as the previous one in many ways. Unfunded and underfunded entitlement programs are already fostering tensions between those who are collecting benefits and those who do not expect to collect in the future. Existing generous public and private pension plans in industrial countries simply will not be viable when a much smaller work force will be supporting a much larger retired population. For example, in the year 2030 in the United States, there will be only three workers potentially in the labor force for every person in retirement. In the same year there will be only about two workers in the Swiss labor force for every retired person.[15]

Intergenerational sustainability issues are also found on the international level. Latecomers to industrialization, such as China and India, assume little responsibility for the existing cumulative pollution that they claim has been caused by generations of previous industrial development. Global warming issues only can intensify the debate between the global rich and poor and may well become a surrogate for many other issues of international wealth redistribution.

China and India contain more than 40 percent of the world's population and, for ecological reasons, simply cannot be raised to current European or American levels of resource consumption. Thus, some sort of new planetary bargain is needed if the demands of this generation of global poor are to be taken seriously. Even if there were to be an unprecedented transfer of capital to the less industrialized world, it still would be impossible for the bulk of humanity to live near levels of consumption reached by the early industrializers. Suppose that China were miraculously raised to U.S. consumption levels. An ecological disaster would surely result. Energy consumption in this hypothetical China would be roughly fourteen times the current level and 25 percent higher than the total world consumption.[16] In spite of world automobile manufacturers' present attempt to penetrate the Chinese market, a China dominated by freeways, suburban shopping malls, and homes with two-car garages could not be sustained for any extended period of time by the resources potentially available on this planet.

Finally, building more sustainable societies runs contrary to long-term, worldwide trade liberalization. There already is significant controversy between domestic environmental policies and the General Agreement on Tariffs and Trade and now, the World Trade Organization (WTO), principles of free trade. Several high-profile cases pitting environmentalists against free-trade advocates have already surfaced, and the World Trade Organization, staffed largely by lawyers and economists, will increasingly encounter cases where national environmental policies clash with free-trade principles. The process of becoming more sustainable will sharpen these kinds of conflicts, and it will be difficult to reconcile many sustainability initiatives with the industrial growth orientation of the WTO institutions.[17]

Toward Sustainable Transportation

The internal combustion engine and the privately owned vehicle are at the center of the industrial paradigm and the sustainability debate. While governments of industrial countries emphasize the need for worldwide sustainable development, at the same time they encourage their automotive industries to penetrate the Chinese and Indian markets. But it is the automobile and its close relatives that account for the bulk of contemporary petroleum consumption and a substantial portion of worldwide atmospheric pollution. The automotive approach to mobility also has had a tremendous impact on the spatial distribution of human settlements, the nature of urban areas, and the relationship of human beings to natural systems. But just as many societies were originally transformed by automotive technologies, the nascent postindustrial revolution has given birth to new mobility concepts.

Worldwide diffusion of existing approaches to transportation, with their emphasis on fossil fuel–dependent, privately owned vehicles, cannot long continue in a more sustainable world. This approach to mobility is a reflection of the American environment and culture in which the automotive industry initially prospered. This kind of transportation system made sense in a large and lightly populated country blessed with an abundance of petroleum. But these systems have been emulated in Europe, Japan, and Korea, regions that are much more densely populated and petroleum deficient, at a very high environmental price. Traditional European cities have been Americanized as core areas served by mass transit have given way to urban sprawl, freeways, and suburban shopping centers. Seoul, Bangkok, and other Asian cities have become virtually impassable during rush hours as the transportation infrastructure has sagged under the growing onslaught of privately owned vehicles. While Japan's automobile industry has been an international economic success, domestically it has been an environmental failure. The air in Tokyo and other large Japanese cities is now extremely polluted. And heavy dependence on petroleum imports from the Middle East now limits Japan's foreign policy options.

The impending era of sustainability means that the automotive industry no longer may be a transformer of environments, but is likely to be transformed itself by sustainability requisites. Future transportation systems increasingly will be shaped by environmental and cultural factors. Thus, the Chinese market, far from being penetrated by Tokyo, Stuttgart, or Detroit, may well redefine mobility systems. It is difficult to conceive of Shanghai being leveled by freeway and parking lot construction or Chinese from inland areas driving privately owned vehicles to the beach for summer vacations. In fact, the Chinese National Academy of Sciences recently issued a report concluding that the privately owned automobile has little future in China.

An era devoted to developing a more sustainable world will thus open up creative mobility options. Technological innovations will lead to new kinds of mobility while demographic and environmental limits will close down others. Large and densely populated countries like China and India likely will never experience the kind of industrialization and associated pollution experienced by the early industrializers. The unfolding telecommunications revolution and associated psychological mobility may well serve as a substitute for an automotive revolution in these areas.

Conclusion

Homo sapiens is now poised on the threshold of a third major transformation in sociocultural evolution. An industrial era is waning as various limits to growth and challenges to the industrial way of thinking are becoming apparent.[18] The two previous transformations were far from smooth since the people caught up in clashes between paradigms had little understanding of the processes that were underway. But this revolution may be different because it is now possible to use anticipatory thinking, itself a product of sociocultural evolution, to develop a process for making the transition to a more sustainable world with minimum violence and social dislocation.[19]

4

Janus-Faced Utopianism

The Politics of Ecology

Andrew Dobson

It almost seemed, during the 1980s, as if both the left and the right had conspired to drive utopianism from the political stage. On the right, neoliberalism, with its hard-headed and largely successful appeal to instincts of self-aggrandizement and self-preservation, made capitalism seem the untranscendable horizon within which any political project would have to be written. On the left, the 1980s represented the steady demise of actually existing socialist societies that, even though discredited within many socialist circles anyway, still comprised the practical repository of socialists' utopian dreams. The dream ended definitely in 1989 with the collapse of the Berlin Wall, as if the wall had determined to provide us with concrete (!) evidence of the apotheosis of liberal democracy's victory in the war of ideologies, first prefigured in Francis Fukuyama's article, "The End of History?" in the *National Interest* in the summer of that same year.

But as capitalism rose and socialism fell, another player emerged on the political scene—capable, it seemed, of kick-starting history and breathing life back into utopian political projects. This new player has come to be called "ecologism." Many people flocked to this novel political banner, and from all walks of political life. The confusion this eclectic support has sown will be evident in what follows, since ecologism's relationship with utopianism is not a simple one, but it seems clear that—prima facie at least—ecologism promised some succor to those who despaired at the apparently terminal one dimensionality of political life in the 1980s and early 1990s.

In what follows, I shall be spending more time on social theory than on literature (insofar as the distinction holds). Those who reflect on utopia as a genre standardly point to the division between literature and social theory, and some claim that utopian texts must be written in the literary idiom for them to be part of the genre at all. Krishan Kumar comes close to this when he claims that "Utopia . . . is first and foremost a work of imaginative fiction," but then he makes the useful distinction between utopia and utopian social theory.[1] So while Rousseau (for example) might never have written a utopia in the sense of a "story of the ideal society,"[2] the proposed harmony between individual wills and the General Will is a piece of utopian social theory. Utopian social theory is what I primarily shall be concerned with.

I shall be working toward the ideal that ecological politics is in ambiguous relationship to utopianism, and this ambiguity can be regarded as either a benefit or a burden from a political point of view. I shall claim that ecological politics can be viewed in utopian terms, but that its utopianism is Janus-faced, looking both forwards and backwards. The benefit of this is that such eclecticism brings with it the possibility of transcending political boundaries, thereby casting the net of potential political support as wide as possible. The burden, though, lies in the potential for confusion due to the inability of supporters of the radical environmentalist project to identify just where they stand on the utopian frontier. I shall weigh up these benefits and burdens near the end of the chapter before concluding with an assessment of the role of the latest challenge to green utopianism as I conceive it—the challenge of ecological modernization.

Green Utopianism

The central motif of green utopianism, I believe, is a presaged harmony of human beings with the nonnatural world. Most utopias are characterized by the absence of conflict between human beings, and this theme is given a specific turn in the case of green utopias with the pacification of relationships not only among human beings, but between human beings and their natural environment. The intellectual basis of this pacification can take two forms, only one of which—I believe—can properly be characterized as a green utopianism. The first (and nonutopian) argument for the reconciliation of human beings with the nonhuman natural world is that it is in the interests of human beings to protect the natural environment, and this is because human survival depends on the so-called life-support systems that the natural world provides. This argument looks particularly strong when future generations of human beings are taken into account. Given that we cannot be certain what the effects of present actions on the environment will be in the future, and assuming that we want to pass on the conditions for existence to future generations, we should be precautionary rather than Promethean (the argument runs) in our treatment of the nonhuman world. In this way, a pacified relationship between human beings and their natural environment is arrived at by arguing that the interests of both generally coincide.

Note that this version of harmony between the human and the natural demands no transformation of human beings. The argument is for a coincidence of the interests of human beings *as they are* and the environment. While this might be right (and the case is powerfully argued by Bryan Norton in his *Toward Unity Among Environmentalists*),[3] it is not, to my mind, an argument from utopia. The utopian sensibility, in general, is underpinned by a belief in our "more or less indefinite malleability," as Krishan Kumar puts it.[4] Utopias are not written in the language of the here and now, but of the yet to be. Marx may have berated the utopian socialists for their political naivete and for their failure to embrace historical materialism, but his refusal to write recipes for the cookshops of the future is an implicitly utopian recognition that the nature of communist society was inexpressible in contemporary language. Human beings under capitalism and under communism would be different and, similarly, green utopias arrive at a harmony between human beings and nature through the transformation of human beings. In the green utopia, human beings have abandoned their acquisitive, instrumental, and use-related relationship with their natural environment, and it is this transformation, and the harmony that issues from it, that lies at the heart of green utopianism.

Green Antiutopianism

Such a view, though, is immediately open to the objection that many green political tracts are written in the language of limits, with the obvious antiutopian connotations that this conveys. The utopian sensibility, on the face of it, is most accurately mirrored in the idea of an expanding universe, inventing itself as it occupies space that does not exist until time and matter create it. The green political project, on the other hand, seems better expressed by the idea of the steady-state universe with its limits fixed and its boundaries more or less static.

There is plenty of evidence for this latter view, not least in the text which did more, perhaps, to get the contemporary environmental movement off the ground than any other—the *Limits to Growth* report of 1972. In the revised and updated 1992 sequel to the report, Donella Meadows and her colleagues reiterate their fundamental point that:

> The earth is finite. Growth of anything physical, including the human population and its cars, buildings and smokestacks, cannot continue forever. . . . The limits to growth are limits to the ability of the planetary *sources* to provide those streams of materials and energy, and limits to the ability of the planetary *sinks*, to absorb the pollution and waste.[5]

So it seems that to the degree that limits to production and consumption are fixed by the earth's finitude, the human condition—as far as political ecologists are concerned—is also fixed. Most presentations of political ecology do indeed begin with an inventory of the environmental resources at our disposal and go on to outline how they are being used up at unsustainable rates, before pointing out—as Meadows and her colleagues do above—the dire consequences of continuing to do so. Dystopia, then, for political ecology, is written into the dynamics of present social, political, and economic practices.

But dystopia is not fully with us, and most political ecologists believe that the unvirtuous, unsustainable spiral can be broken. Meadows and her colleagues themselves, indeed, follow their dystopian warning by saying that, "[T]his decline is possible," and that, "A sustainable society is still technically and economically possible."[6] This squares with Lyman Tower Sargent's belief that "a defining characteristic of the dystopian genre must be a warning to the reader that something must, and by implication, can be done in the present to avoid the future."[7]

The difficulty presented by this, though, is that if political ecologists believe that the human condition is unalterable, as the limits thesis seems to suggest, then how can political ecology have anything to do with utopia if a precondition for utopian thinking is a belief in our "more or less indefinite malleability" as Kumar thinks it is?[8] There seems to be tension, at least, between an imagined future in which human beings are utterly different from the way they are today, and the belief in a fixed human condition. On this reading, the apparently antiutopian themes in political ecology seem to block the utopian impulse. The antiutopian temperament presents itself as the sum of ripe old human wisdom, a storehouse of cautionary but essential truths about human nature and human strivings distilled from the collective experience of mankind.[9]

This reminds us of Edmund Burke, of course, but it also has echoes in political ecology: In modern farming the farm worker is increasingly isolated from the soil he is tilling; he sits encased in his tractor cab, either with ear muffs to shut out the noise or with radio blaring, and what goes on behind the tractor has more to do with the wonders of technology than with the *wisdom of countless generations of his predecessors.*[10]

Burke's point is that what he calls an "entailed inheritance" provides "a sure principle of conservation and a sure principle of improvement. It leaves acquisition free; but it secures what it acquires."[11] Burke prefers wisdom to reason because the former conserves the latter designs, and in designing wisdom, reason may lose benefits acquired over many generations. In these respects, Burkean conservatism and political ecology (as I have been describing it) are as one, and both are opposed to the carelessness expressed in utopian talk of indefinite malleability. The antiutopian's principle target, says Kumar, is *hubris,*[12] and so is the political ecologist's. If utopians uncompromisingly believe that "[T]here are no fundamental barriers or obstacles to man's early perfection [and that] scarcity can be overcome,"[13] then the gap between utopians and political ecologists is as wide as it can be; scarcity is the most basic and unalterable feature of the human condition as far as political ecologists are concerned. So, utopianism demands malleability and political ecology's interpretation of the human condition denies its possibility. Does this imply the impossibility of green utopianism?

The crucial and relevant distinction here is between malleability of the human condition and malleability of human nature. It is perfectly possible to believe that the human condition is fixed, while human nature is not, and this is indeed what political ecologists believe. Political ecologists do not possess the "pessimistic and determinist view of human nature" that is common to antiutopians,[14] nor do they believe in "original sin"[15] if by this we mean unredeemable sin. They do believe that there are (more or less) fixed limits to production, consumption, and waste, but they have a utopian sense of what is possible within those limits. Kumar himself recognizes this, and in his assessment of different types of utopia, he refers to "ecotopia" as a "gesture towards realism" that "abated nothing of its utopian character."[16] It might seem curious to speak of realism and utopianism in the same breath, but this accurately summarizes the contribution that political ecology has made to the utopian tradition: "Far from being beyond necessity, freedom might consist in a new recognition and understanding of it, and the reorganization of its sphere along ecological lines."[17] The green utopia is one that operates with nonnegotiable ecological constraints and one in which dystopia is always actually or potentially present. Green utopias, in other words, demonstrate (to their own satisfaction at least) that "hard-head realism"[18] can be as much a part of the utopian, as of the antiutopian, sensibility.

Green Conservatism and Utopianism

The relationship between the politics of ecology and the utopian tradition is further complicated by the immense variety of ideological positions available to political ecologists. An examination of green texts reveals that the nature of the social, political, and economic relations that underlie the pacification of human/nature relations is heavily contested, and this means that the extent of the relationship between ecologism and utopianism will be contested, too. Another reason why it might be argued that ecologism harbors ineliminable antiutopian impulses is the apparently enduring conservatism in green thinking. John Gray, for example, from a principled conservative position, has tried to appropriate ecological themes for the conservative tradition. Gray argues that:

> Many of the central conceptions of traditional conservatism have a natural congruence with Green concerns: the Burkean idea of the social contract, not as an agreement among anonymous ephemeral individuals, but as a compact between the generations of the living, the dead and those yet unborn; Tory skepticism about progress, and awareness of ironies and illusions; conservative resistance to untried novelty and large-scale social experiments; and perhaps most especially, the traditional conservative tenet that individual flourishing can only occur in the context of forms of common life.[19]

Even though Gray's prospectus willfully ignores all the progressive and leftist elements in green thinking, few would deny that what he says makes good sense as far as it goes. Now, we do not normally speak of utopian and conservative politics in the same breath, and, indeed, Krishan Kumar has pointed out that conservative themes seem to amount to antiutopianism:

> The utopian denies original sin, and believes that men can perfect them-
> selves by creating the right environment. The anti-utopian . . . sees weak
> human creatures constantly succumbing to the sins of pride, avarice and
> ambition. . . . His pessimistic and deterministic view of human nature
> leads him to the conviction that all attempts to create the good society on
> earth are bound to be futile.[20]

So, if indeed the politics of ecology can sensibly be thought of as inhabiting conservative space, as Gray thinks it can, and if conservative sentiment is fundamentally antiutopian, as Kumar thinks it is, then attempts to link green and utopian thought seem doomed to failure.

But even if we accept that ecologism is either partly or wholly bound up with the conservative political tradition, there seems no reason to deny the possibility of a green conservative utopia, and I shall illustrate one below. Second, even texts usually regarded as inhabiting the conservative wing of the politics of ecology betray obvious utopian impulses. I shall take just one example: William Ophuls's *Ecology and the Politics of Scarcity.*[21] When Ophuls sets about describing the characteristics of the steady-state society, it is true that he enlists the support of conservative sounding ideas and thinkers. He writes that "we shall necessarily move from liberty toward authority" (p. 226) and "away from egalitarian democracy toward political competence and status" (p. 227). Likewise, Edmund Burke makes several loudly applauded appearances in the book (as he does in Gray's chapter, to which I referred above), because "steady state values bear a particularly uncanny resemblance to his ideas" (p. 233)—ideas such as stewardship, a scepticism towards progress, the acceptance of limits, and the need for a balanced, harmonious, and organic social order. Ophuls concludes that "in our search for a set of social and political ideas that correspond to an ecological world view, Burke will surely have to teach us" (p. 234).

But although Ophuls is regarded as something of an ogre by those determined to regard political ecology in a leftist light, his riffle through the card index of political thought for ideas that might undergird the "steady-state society" actually turns up a much more eclectic set of notions than that suggested by the bare resume of the previous paragraph. For one thing, Burke's political prescriptions are explicitly rejected by Ophuls: "It by no means follows that we must adopt Burke's political doctrines," he writes: "Rule by a landed aristocracy is now anachronistic at best and reactionary at worst" (p. 234). Second, the move from liberty to authority mentioned above in the context of the likely contours of the sustainable society is not as dramatic as might appear—Ophuls means no more than constitutionally limited authority, and checks on the use of property in "ecologically destructive ways" (p. 226). These prescriptions are hardly likely to offend any but the most committed libertarian. Third, Ophuls's other principles, such as communalism, stewardship, modesty, diversity, holism, and a sense of spiritual morality (pp. 226–32) are notoriously double edged as far as the political prescriptions that can be derived from them are concerned. Ophuls's own pessimism of the intellect obliges him to recognize the possibility of a "monolithic and totalitarian" (p. 236) solution to the conundrum of living with the politics of scarcity, but his optimism of the will leads him to prefer the route of "ecological self-restraint" (p. 236). His book, indeed, concludes on a recognizably utopian note when he writes joyously of "a life of self-restraint and simple sufficiency in natural harmony with the earth" (p. 244). So even apparently conservative sources of political ecological prescription are prone to utopian dreaming.

The tension between conservative and progressive utopianism in green thinking can be further illustrated through an examination of work on green communities—an archetypal utopian political form in itself, of course. Green utopians tap into a long line of utopian writing that revolves around the self-reliant community. In such communities, it is said,[22] personal autonomy can be reconciled with collective responsibility, personal fulfillment is found through creative work rather than industrial(ized) labor, and Aristotle's dictum that "man is [potentially] a political animal" is made real through face to face, rather than faceless, relationships. What utopian political ecologists add to this is that the self-reliant community is an environmentally responsible community of low resource use, living necessarily within the energy and resource budget provided by the locale.

They also believe that living in small self-reliant communities engenders a strong sense of ecological and political place. It is well known that political ecologists argue that human beings are as much a part of a nonhuman biotic community as of a political human community. Membership of the biotic community, they suggest, brings with it specific duties and constraints that should inform the nature of the political community. Political ecologists further believe that large-scale industrialized societies are, in their nature, partly to blame for our losing touch with the biotic community of which we are part. This has both ethical and practical implications: ethical in that we "lose sight" of those nonhuman entities toward which we have (they say) moral obligations, and practical in that we have no immediate sense of the physical limits imposed upon production and consumption by our natural condition.[23]

Small communities also occupy an important place in green strategies for social change. Perhaps the best-known exponent of this monastic approach to green change is the German social theorist, Rudolf Bahro. Bahro has argued for a "new Benedictine order"[24] of a small-communal life in the belief that:

> The single community can strive to live self-reliantly, so that it can picture to itself the possibility that the whole species could be organized in analogous cells, responsible for *Gaia*—having an appropriate contact with the world of animals, plants and minerals, and with the original elements of earth, water, air and fire.[25]

But the green experience is also awash with examples of communities of a less spiritual kind, ranging from city farms to the sophisticated but nevertheless communal Centre for Alternative Technology in Wales. Each of these communities tries to live the sustainable future for which it argues—small experiments designed to change the world through force of example.[26] Krishan Kumar has noted Martin Buber's suggestion in this connection that "the value of utopian communities . . . lies . . . in indicating the social substance, the germ cells, of the new society,"[27] and says himself—correctly, as far as the experience of political ecology goes—that "something of the same project of cellular reconstruction has been clear in the many counter-cultural and ecotopian communities that sprang up in the West in the 1960s and 1970s" (p. 79).

The Janus Face of Green Utopianism

But while the self-reliant community is a common thread in green utopianism as I present it here, there is no agreement as to the location of this community in chronological time, and it is this that further complicates the relationship between ecologism and utopianism, yet enables us to make some political sense of it. There are three possibilities: first, the recovery of a perfect past moment; second, the grafting of parts of the past onto parts of the present; and third, the imagining of a wholly new future. Edward Goldsmith, cofounder of *The Ecologist* and a coauthor of the text that did much to get British political ecology off the ground,[28] is an archetypal representative of the first strand of green utopianism. He imagines a world of "largely self-sufficient communities, carrying out their economic activities at the level of the family, the small artisanal enterprise and the community itself, largely to satisfy local needs via local markets" (p. 331). In terms of a possible typology of utopias, Krishan Kumar defines one type as the "golden age" utopia, which he describes in the following way:

> Virtually all societies have some myth or memory of a Golden Age, a time of beginnings in which humanity lived in a state of perfect happiness and fulfillment. Most frequently this myth takes on a primitivist form. The "original" time or condition was one of simplicity and sufficiency. There was an instinctive harmony between man and nature. Men's needs were few and their desires limited. Both were easily satisfied by the abundance of nature.[29]

Seen from this perspective, Goldsmith's sustainable society has a distinctly Golden Age utopian air about it. This utopia insists on the recovery of an imagined ideal historical movement—with all the unreconstructed political and social problems this brings in its train for those of a politically progressive persuasion. Goldsmith has become marginal to leftist British political ecologists through his insistence that social problems are largely due to the breakdown of families, his patriarchalism, and his exclusivist sense of personal and political identity: "Mixed marriages between natural exogamous social groups . . . threaten the critical order of society and thereby that of the cosmos of which it is a part."[30]

Goldsmith's plump for the past is undoubtedly a part of the overall green picture, and it amounts to the green conservative utopia to which I referred earlier. It is, however, modulated somewhat in the second instance of green utopianism, in which putatively ideal features of the past and present are combined. William Ophuls, for instance, writes that, "the picture of the frugal society . . . represents something like the city-state form of civilization, but on a much higher and more sophisticated technological base."[31] This vision combines the past (city-state form of civilization) with the present (modern technology) with the intention of overcoming some of the limitations of golden age utopianism.

André Gorz speaks for the third type of green utopianism. Gorz talks of "decentralizing and scaling down production units in such a way that each community [is] able to meet at least half its needs,"[32] and echoing Marx, he writes of a society where the chimera of environmental responsibility under capitalism has given way to:

> a society . . . without bureaucracy, where the market withers away, where there is enough for everyone, where people are collectively and individually free to shape their own lives, where people produce according to their fantasies, not only according to their needs; in short, a society where "the free development of each is the condition for the free development of all."[33]

This society does not exist and has never existed, except in an imagined future, and in this respect it differs markedly from the other types of green utopianism. The great mistake, though, would be to try to reduce green utopianism to any one of these possibilities. The principal and most interesting point is that all three can legitimately lay claim to articulating something important about the green utopian sensibility—and while this might show confusion it also may harbor positive political potential, as I shall try to show shortly.

But first we can make a little more analytical progress by putting these different views on green utopia in the context of disagreements over the objectives associated with the Enlightenment tradition. Each of the chronological possibilities referred to above relates to a possible position in respect to the Enlightenment. First, and as Tim Hayward has pointed out in an excellent study,[34] radical ecologists often style themselves anti-Enlightenment, calling into question the Enlightenment project and laying the blame for environmental and social dislocation at its door.[35] Goldsmith is one such radical ecologist. Ophuls, second, argues for the grafting of Enlightenment successes (the development of technology) on to putatively attractive features of the past (the direct democracy associated with the ancient Greek city-state). Gorz, finally, will suggest that virtually none of the promises of the Enlightenment have been redeemed, and that the way forward is not through re-enchanting the natural world, as Goldsmith would wish, but by bringing it under the sway of an ecological rationality.

This third position—that of locating the green utopia wholly in an imagined, and as yet unrealized, future, is interestingly represented in ecologically-oriented readings of Jurgen Habermas. Kumar has pointed out that "Habermas . . . has offered something approaching a utopian model of social relations in his account of the 'ideal speech situation',"[36] and John Dryzek, in particular, has made fruitful use of this by developing what we might call an ecological utopia of process rather than of product. Dryzek suggests that "intersubjective discourse presupposes some ecological—and not just linguistic—standards."[37] His belief is that under the (utopian) conditions of communicative rationality—that is, where "social interaction is free from domination . . . strategizing by the actors involved, and (self-) deception"[38]—people would recognize that they had a generalizable interest in ensuring the "continuing integrity of the ecological systems upon which human life depends." (p. 55) What this means is that there would be a happy coincidence between the utopia of uncoerced discourse and the utopia of an ecologically sustainable society, or in other words, the procedural utopia of discursive democracy produces one of the objectives of ecological politics: a sustainable society. Dryzek is clearly a redeemer of the Enlightenment promise rather than an abandoner of it, and to the extent that his is a green utopia it is quite opposed in form to that of, say, Goldsmith.

For the sake of a tentative conclusion to this part of the chapter, and before moving on to consider a potent challenge to green utopianism in the form of ecological modernization, we can reduce our three types of utopia to just two, which I shall call "golden age" and "imagined future" utopias. It should be clear by now that both these types of utopia are present in green thinking, and while I have chosen to represent them through the work of Edward Goldsmith and André Gorz, respectively, their places could be filled by any number of theorists and activists from a wide range of political cultures. I want to reiterate that it would be a mistake to try to reduce these takes on green utopianism any further. They both express aspects of the green political sensibility, and while they are self-evidently in tension with one another, this tension might be regarded as potentially productive from a political point of view.

At the level of political persuasion, intellectual detail is of relatively little importance: What is important is to get people behind large ideas. The British political culture, for example, was changed beyond all recognition by Margaret Thatcher's hitching together of the two most long-standing and deep-rooted themes in British political life: individualist liberalism and traditional Burkean conservatism. This mixing and matching was brilliantly captured in her oft-quoted idea that "there is no such thing as society; there are only individuals and their families." The latter half of this phrase (which is rarely quoted) brings liberalism and conservatism into contact in a way that makes sense of their juxtaposition yet obscures their contradictions. My broad point is that while these contradictions might be exposed by a little intellectual spade work, the deeper ebb and flow of political culture can always be enlisted to hide them away again.

In the context of green utopianism, the imagined future and golden age types both speak to large political constituencies, and there may be some mileage for greens in embracing them both rather than in trying to shoehorn the green political project into either one or the other or— perhaps worse—trying to construct some spurious and deeper connection between them. If there is a deeper connection, it is simply that they are both forms of utopianism in the sense I outlined near the beginning of the chapter; that is, that they both operate on the basis of transformed human beings, human beings who have "abandoned their acquisitive, instrumental and use-related relationship with the natural environment" as I put it earlier. There is some sense in saying that this transformation points both back to the past and toward an imagined and fundamentally different future, and that therefore the Janus face of green utopianism should be regarded as a political strength rather than an intellectual weakness.

The Present: Ecological Modernization

But none of this will matter very much if green utopianism is fundamentally irrelevant to contemporary environmental politics, as some are currently suggesting. Since the (re)birth of the contemporary environmental movement in the late 1960s and early 1970s there have been two waves of radicalism and two waves of reaction. The first radical wave coincided with the *Limits to Growth* report of 1972, which led to suggestions that a return to steady-state low-throughput societies was the only way of guaranteeing a sustainable human life into the future. This was met by the reaction that the 1972 report was too pessimistic about resource availability and that human ingenuity would overcome any apparently fixed biospherical limits.[39]

The second radical wave came with the birth and growing success of what the late Petra Kelly called "anti-party" green parties, particularly in Europe, and more particularly in (West) Germany. These parties took much of the limits-to-growth critique on board, but placed it in the context of a wide-ranging critique of contemporary economic and political practices. They also added an ethical dimension to the debate by arguing that environmental degradation was due, at least in part, to an exploitative attitude of humans toward the nonhuman natural world.

The reaction to this second wave has come in a variety of forms, but for the purposes of this chapter, I want to refer to the one that goes by the name of "ecological modernization." Albert Weale, in his book on *The New Politics of Pollution*,[40] describes how in the 1980s ecological modernizers began to challenge the green fundamentalist view that there was "a zero-sum trade-off between economic prosperity and environmental concern" (p. 31). The view that economic prosperity (or at least economic growth) was dysfunctional for the environment was (and is) an article of faith for those who argue(d) for some variant of the steady-state economy. Moreover, the steady-state economy is present in one form or another in the green utopias to which I have been referring. So the thesis of ecological modernization presents a principled challenge to the need for this kind of green utopianism.

Ecological modernizers present three arguments: First, "[I]f the 'costs' of environmental protection are avoided the effect is frequently to save money for present generations at the price of an increased burden for future generations";[41] second, "[I]nstead of seeing environmental protection as a burden upon the economy the ecological modernist sees it as a potential source for future growth . . . a spur to industrial innovation" (pp. 76, 78); and third, "[W]ith the advent of global markets, the standards of product acceptability will be determined by the country with the most stringent pollution control standards. Hence, the future development of a post-industrialist economy will depend upon its ability to produce high value, high quality products with stringent environmental standards enforced" (p. 77).

Each of these arguments can be confronted with some degree of success by radical political ecologists, but I do not propose to outline their defense in any detail here.[42] The important thing in the present context is to say that this decoupling of economic growth and environmental degradation has the apparent effect of drawing (at least one of) the principal sting(s) at the disposal of radical ecologists. In strategic terms, why bother with radical ecological ideas if we can, as it were, have our cake and eat it? The attraction of Weale's ecological modernizers is that they offer us a both/and solution rather than an either/or one: *both* economic growth *and* environmental protection, *both* productivity *and* ecosystem preservation.

It will not have escaped notice either that dystopia plays no part whatever in the ecological modernizer's story. Global markets will not, they say, lead to ever more intensive and irresponsible use of resources, but to the global tightening of pollution control standards. The goal of productivity will not override that of environmental protection, but will enhance it through the opportunities for industrial policy. Ecological modernizers will therefore claim that utopia is unnecessary and dystopia is unlikely. There is some evidence that European policy makers (even British ones) are increasingly subscribing to the ecological modernizers's thesis. As the thesis gets an increasingly firm hold on the policy-making community, and as environmentally concerned publics became aware of the thesis and its strengths, it is possible that the tenuous grasp of green utopianism on the public's imagination will weaken still further. Yet, green utopianism—like any utopianism—has the capacity to disrupt the developing consensus.

Of all the many commentaries on ecological modernization that have appeared recently, one of the most suggestive from my point of view is Peter Christoff's. Christoff argues that there are now fundamentally two types of ecological modernization on offer, which he refers to as "weak" and "strong" types. The weak type is that to which I have been referring above: Its characteristics, according to Christoff, are that it is "economistic, technological, instrumental and technocratic."[43] The strong type, on the other hand, is "ecological, systemic, communicative and deliberatively democratic" (p. 490). This is not the place for a detailed analysis of these terms; the important point is that Christoff's strong ecological modernization contains recognizable echoes of a radical green program—a radical green utopianism, even. Green utopianism is a disrupting influence, and this is likely to be its role in environmental politics in the twenty-first century. When brought into contact with what seems to be a settled and ever more hegemonic notion such as ecological modernization, it acts like a corrosive acid, eating away at apparently secure foundations and demanding an opening up of the terms of reference, rather than their closure. This, then, is green utopianism's eternal (and most effective) role: calling the reformists to order when they stray too far off line during their march through the institutions.

5

Environmentalism and Progressive Politics

An Update

Robert C. Paehlke

The 1990s were an ideologically volatile decade. A decade ago, when I began writing *Environmentalism and the Future of Progressive Politics*,[1] the cold war was yet at the core of global politics. Neoconservatism was entrenched in power in most of the rich English-speaking democracies—entrenched, but yet to reach the heights of ideological dominance it achieved about 1992. At the same time, in the late 1980s, environmental concern was near the peak of its second wave, easily as strongly and widely felt as it had been in the early 1970s.[2]

As state socialism crumbled, it seemed at the time I wrote that book that the ideological future might well be marked by an ongoing struggle between neoconservatives and greens—a struggle which would be quite central to the everyday politics of many richer nations. This may yet prove to be the case, though other possibilities now seem as likely. The most frightening but not utterly implausible future is one where globalization and corporate media dominance are in combination so thoroughgoing as to set boundaries on the very existence of meaningful politics and effective government. More optimistically, from the hindsight of the early twenty-first century, we can see that environmental advances have and will likely continue to come in periodic surges. The surges almost inevitably wane as nonenvironmental concerns (e.g., unemployment, governmental deficits, or other forms of economic instability) return to the fore, as they did in the early 1990s and in the new millennium, but return as the urgency of economic and social issues recede.

On what is from a progressive green perspective another optimistic note: In a world where the very word "socialism" now seems passe, neoconservatism seems also to be less ascendant. Pragmatic political moderates were leading several wealthy nations toward the balanced public budgets and attendant prosperity that neoconservatives championed endlessly until the worldwide recession from the beginning of the new millennium to the present, but rarely delivered when in power. It is possible, then, that neoconservatism's day of ideological hegemony has also passed. One possible reason for the waning of neoconservative hegemony, ironically, is the likelihood that without a godless socialist enemy at the gates, a politics of paranoia wears a little thin with time. Welfare moms and the United Nations bureaucracy just cannot threaten prosperous and powerful nations over the long haul quite as thoroughly as the KGB and nuclear weapons pointed in our direction. Without either an ongoing external enemy, runaway governmental deficits, or economic instability, the mobilization of the potential forces of the extreme right is far harder to achieve. Indeed, one might hypothesize, positive waves of environmental opinion (as in the late 1960s/early 1970s and the late 1980s) will be coincident with the relative absence of economic instability unless and until environmental issues are effectively resolved.

Environmental politics remained a force in the late 1990s and early in the new century, but has not yet achieved again the public policy centrality that seemed possible within the crest of the second wave of environmental concern (1985–1992), during which time *Environmentalism and the Future of Progressive Politics* was written and published. One important reason for this semi-failure of environmentalism is the ongoing and accelerating transformation of the world economy by a force that has come to be called "globalization," and an increasing media dominance by global corporations and individuals, often with an extreme right outlook. Globalization threatens to do nothing less than to render politics itself, at least politics within nation-states, all but obsolete—little wonder that environmental politics now captures public attention only intermittently (although globalization itself could be used to engender revival of the environmental social movement such as with the anti-World Trade Organization (WTO) protest movement). Globalization creates a climate wherein governments—all governments at all levels—are unable to act independently and decisively as regards the environment or social equity for fear that corporations will redirect the location of production or opt against employment or investment expansion, or (especially in smaller economies) the nation's currency will fall from favor with international banks and money traders. Ideologies of all varieties, from moderate to right to progressive and/or green seem unable to challenge the current economic transformations which proceed as if they were mere technical exercises devoid of political and ideological content (which is precisely what the nongovernmental organization–based, anti-WTO movement is trying to combat by calling attention to the political nature of these transactions).

At the same time, environmental politics has evolved and adapted since 1989. Biodiversity, old growth forests, habitat losses, endocrine disruptors, hazardous waste exports, ozone depletion, climate warming, fishery collapses, and the Association of Southeast Asian Nations haze have all risen to the fore of international attention within that short timeframe. Green concerns have become an important part of the global political agenda despite the limited political successes thus far of stand-alone green political parties. Despite this new reality, national governments, when out of the public eye, can and will defend domestic (polluting) industries within trade proceedings. Moreover, decisive steps regarding fundamental challenges such as climate warming and the protection of tropical rain forests have not yet been taken in many political jurisdictions. Promises have been made under the pressure of the global spotlight, but thus far have rarely resulted in effective action. Overall, without ideological engagement, broad publics have simply not addressed the central question about the sustainability and desirability of the postindustrial, globalized world in the making; hence the importance of the recent anti-WTO protests.

This chapter, then, will address some of the implications of these sweeping political changes for both environmentalism and progressive politics. The consideration will begin with a brief updated summary of the themes and arguments of *Environmentalism and the Future of Progressive Politics*. The next section will provide some reflections on the ideological and political importance of the end of the cold war and the seeming demise of the far left in contemporary political life. Next is a section on globalization and what seems now a near impossibility of avoiding a return to the worst ravages of nineteenth-century capitalism. Will we really see a return to sweatshops and child labor, to catastrophic pollution and resource destruction, replayed in poorer nations of the world a century and half after the first round of unrestrained capitalism? A fourth section will consider some of the implications of globalization for politics in the richer nations, including the increasingly closed nature of contemporary global decision making and the politics of deregulation. The final section will focus on the evolution of environmental politics in the 1990s with an emphasis on the potential for new approaches and postregulatory environmental policy tools.

Environmentalism and Progressive Politics: A Summary

Environmentalism and the Future of Progressive Politics was first and foremost an assertion that environmental concerns were political concerns and that the best way to understand environmentalism was as a complex set of political ideas—a central theme of this volume. I asserted that environmentalism was not a passing issue or series of issues but rather the first new and truly distinctive political ideology since socialism, and as important as liberalism, conservatism, and socialism in their time. Moreover, the book asserted that it was important that environmentalism was different from any of the other ideologies in several important ways. The book looked at the deep and rich history of environmental concerns including pollution and health, conservation and wilderness, and resources and sustainability from some centuries ago to the present day. It showed the ways in which environmentalism has been rooted in a particular set of values and is quite unique in the extent to which it is the only ideology truly based (in part) in the natural sciences (early Marxist claims to this effect notwithstanding). Environmentalism as an ideology, it was argued, is deeply immersed in some sciences (ecology, toxicology, epidemiology), yet is frequently at odds with some of the practitioners (and some of the products) of other sciences, especially applied sciences.

Environmentalism as an ideology, I argued in some detail, was neither left, nor right. This assertion was not original with me, but I did make the case in several new ways and at several levels. The works of leading and varied eighteenth- and nineteenth-century classical political theorists—such as Karl Marx, John S. Mill, Edmund Burke, and Benjamin Disraeli—were shown to have expressed ideas that were quite prescient as regards contemporary environmental concerns. If political theorists of this range of diversity could take such views, clearly it could be said that there might be something different about this nascent set of ideas. Second, contemporary environmental thinkers from Barry Commoner to Amory Lovins to Paul Ehrlich to Garnett Hardin and others were examined in terms of their political leanings, and it was found that environmentalists, while they perhaps are most commonly inclined to the moderate center-left, do indeed cover the whole of the left-right political spectrum. Third, it was noted that existing governmental regimes in practice—both those of the left and of the right—had to that point handled environmental concerns rather badly. As regards the now collapsed regimes of the far left, we now know even better how badly.[3]

What I did not fully appreciate at the time is that there is an additional way to demonstrate that environmental politics is different from the traditional politics of left, right, and center. I did not discuss in *Environmentalism and the Future of Progressive Politics* what would now be called environmental policy tools. Doing so would have allowed me to demonstrate that environmental objectives can be advanced using the tools with which many on the political right could (and can) in principle be comfortable (e.g., the selective removal of economic subsidies or the use of user fees to alter environmentally doubtful behaviors as in the case of per unit charges for municipal solid waste). Other environmental objectives, or for that matter the same environmental objectives, can also be achieved through the use of tools which would have greater appeal to those on the political left (e.g., public supports for keeping the cost of public transportation low, or tough regulations and enforcement to decisively halt environmentally dangerous actions including pollution and poor land use practices).

What I was clear about at the time of writing the book was that, while environmentalism itself was inherently neither left nor right, choices regarding left/right social and political implications of environmental policy decisions must nonetheless be made. As environmentalists, we all still stick our heads in the sand sometimes with regard to all of the social and economic equity concerns associated with environmental protection initiatives. Mercifully, this is now far harder to do given the rise, perhaps at opposite ends of the environmental spectrum of ideas, of environmental justice and wise use organizations and voices. It remains the case, though, that different environmentalists can make different choices as regards the equity impacts of environmental protection initiatives, but it is very hard to avoid having to make such choices one way or the other within the process of policy advocacy and decision making.

This consideration, the multiple ways in which one can resolve or mitigate environmental problems, is one of the problems that face all stand-alone Green parties. In *Environmentalism and the Future of Progressive Politics* I expressed doubts about an emphasis on green parties unless there existed a system of proportional representation and a multiparty system. My fear was (and still is) that green party political efforts are likely to prove futile, or nearly so, and that even when successful will find the green party torn about in the face of inherent left-right (and other) internal divisions. That is, when a full array of political and administrative decisions must be made, greens cannot, as a group, easily resolve their differences, and on many important political questions tend to have no position at all. Environmentalism, I asserted, was a truncated ideology. Environmentalists often need to know better where they stand on core issues of left and right politics. Moreover, environmentalists need political allies, and I asserted then, and I still feel, that the best fit is with the moderate left with some openness to some—not all—of the tools and concerns of the moderate political right (e.g., community, opposition to corporate welfare, and even fiscal conservatism in the sense of balanced public budgets, though not in the sense of deep tax cuts).

In *Environmentalism and the Future of Progressive Politics* I tried to show that many policies advocated by the traditional moderate left had unseen, generally positive, environmental implications and thus were simultaneously important, for different reasons, to both moderate progressives and environmentalists. In effect, I argued that environmentalism, understood as antipollution and prowilderness, is too narrowly conceived. For example, public spending on education, health, social services, and the arts are socially useful, employment intensive, *and* very low in terms of energy use or environmental damage per dollar of the gross domestic product, or per job. Thus, decent levels of public spending are likely to be better environmentally than are the corresponding alternative tax reductions. Galbraith is also right about private wealth and public squalor for reasons other than those he asserted so eloquently. So, while environmentalism of the left, right, or center makes sense, so does common cause on some policies which tend to advance environmental quality only indirectly.

What I did not see fully at the time of writing the book were how many environmental problems in rich countries and poor were to some extent rooted in economic and social inequality generally. I was mindful of some, but *Our Common Future*[4] (which only shortly preceded my book) identified many more and the environmental justice movement (which largely came afterwards) made very clear that so long as the siting of environmentally undesirability facilities was comparatively (politically) easy (owing both to racism and social inequality), real solutions to environmental problems could and would be systematically avoided. Social justice, or at least environmental justice, must, therefore, precede effective environmental protection in many cases. Were I rewriting the book today, I would give the environmental justice movement a prominent place in the argument.

Environmentalism and the Future of Progressive Politics asserted that environmentalism should be more urban oriented and that environmentalists should more often recognize that relatively compact urban forms and settlement patterns (and more extensive use of public transportation) are crucial to air quality and to other concerns such as habitat preservation and energy use. Automobiles, and the urban forms with which they exist in symbiosis, eat up space and energy in amounts quite unlike any other single human device. More than that, urban environments are an everyday concern of more people and as such are crucial to the political success of the environmental movement. Indeed, only after the concerns of the conservation movement were eclipsed by, or amalgamated with, (primarily urban-oriented) pollution issues in the 1960s and 1970s, did the environmental movement gain significant political ground. Interestingly, my discussion of urban form and environmentalism was but one part of one chapter, but received as much attention in reviews and elsewhere as did some points over which I labored longer and spent many more words. I was invited into further studies on this particular subject and learned better after the book came out just how important this issue is to both environmentalism as a movement and to the quality of everyday life.

Specifically, after 1990 I undertook additional studies on the environmental implications of urban form and urban planning, and later studies of the environmental impacts associated with the extraction and production of building materials (forests, aggregates, iron and steel, cement) and related matters. This work strongly reinforced my view that the solution to many environmental problems, including many contemporary wilderness protection problems, are rooted in the social problems of North American cities and the technical problems of urban and transportation policy and planning. Environmental justice advocates and deep ecologists are often seen as polar opposites within the environmental movement and are sometimes seemingly antagonists, but looking through the window of urban form, urban design, and building materials decisions they are two sides of the same coin. William Rees's concept of "ecological footprints"[5] and the exciting recent work of Fischer-Kowalski and Haberl[6] reinforce this view. Human settlement patterns, energy and materials use, and transportation mode choices that are inherent in those settlement patterns animate many of the concerns of both deep ecology and the environmental justice movement.

Environmentalism and the Future of Progressive Politics was, in the end, about the many intersections of social policy, economic policy, and environmental policy and politics. The debates over sustainable development and sustainability in the late 1980s and 1990s also have been very much in this same territory. So are the even more contemporary public debates about globalization. I remain convinced that environmental values are and should be at the core of a coherent critical assessment of neoclassical economics and neoconservative (now more often called neoliberal) politics, and of unrestrained global free trade itself. I did not fully see it in 1989, but I would assert more forcefully and directly now that such an alternative vision is important to the effective functioning of democracy in a global era. At the same time, I still would say now, as I did then, that environmentalism does not simply stand in opposition to a right-wing view of economic policy. For example, long-term governmental budgetary deficits (with or without the Keynesian rationale) make no more sense from the environmentalist perspective, than from a conservative perspective. In this Reagan, Thatcher, and others were correct in principle (though for the wrong reasons), but wrong in practice in that they, especially Reagan, did not actually reduce public deficits in timely fashion.

Environmentalism and the End of the Cold War

Marxism and capitalism may yet be dancing their century-plus long macabre dance despite the little lamented demise of one dance partner. Marx himself was an apt critic of the faults of capitalism as a form of sociopolitical organization—it was and is yet a system prone to overproduction and to highly cyclical and inequitable successes. However, the sociopolitico-economic system built in Marx's name was, unfortunately, worse than the one whose excesses he assessed and found so wanting. Communism was worse in any number of ways, including— irony of ironies—social equity.

As a science, Marxism also failed because it did not allow for the possibility that those who managed the capitalist system would read and understand the assessments of Marxists and sometimes, when pressed by political circumstances, compromise in ways that undermined the political appeal of Marxism itself. Humans make poor objects of science —we are far too literate. Now, wonderously, just when Marxism-in-practice has been exposed for the social, environmental, and economic fraud that it was, capitalists in most locales suddenly imagine themselves now free, finally, to be what Marx assumed that they and their system long since, and inevitably, would become.

Was the end of the cold war the end of history? Not for long, one might argue, when capitalists finally feel free to be the selves that Marx assumed that they absolutely had to be. The new digitalized, globalized, and automated economy may have whipped the bondholder scourge of inflation, but has not, as William Greider has noted, found any way to counter its tendency to surplus productive capacity.[7] The recent financial crises in Asia may serve to compound that tendency and the errors and imprudence of North American bankers and Asian conglomerates will be borne by everyday Asian citizens and possibly non-Asian societies, and the economic woes will spread as the new century develops. They will consume less and work harder and in so doing impose downward pressure on industrial wages elsewhere on the world. It sounds hauntingly familiar.

Marx's analysis was born—and had wide and widening appeal— amidst long hours, repression of trade unions, child labor, minimal state intervention of any kind, and generally deteriorating work conditions of Europe and North America a century ago. Global corporations, headquartered in nations where such conditions have not recently existed for the majority, are now selling goods produced under working conditions very near to the nineteenth-century British nightmare that Marx, and especially Engels, documented in detail. These same firms have also, throughout the 1990s and continuing into the new millennium, simultaneously jettisoned millions of lifelong employees in their home countries, leaving some to live on mediocre early pensions and many of their children to the not-much-better-than-Indonesia-or-Mexico opportunities of the North American retail economy, fondly known as "McJobs."

The point here is that history is suddenly not over precisely when it seemed to be. The dance band may play again in other venues. Hopefully, the band will play a different tune the next time around. The tune will be different for the same reason Marx's scientific certainties were merely possibilities the first time around. If the potential dancers turn off their TVs and read history, we will hopefully this time see that both communism and those forms of capitalism which are unrestrained by democracy can be false gods. Can we learn that only an activist state providing social programs and permitting or even promoting a viable trade union movement can prevent massive excesses in productive capacity? If that were not enough to hope for, can we also simultaneously learn that there are ecological limits to the kinds and the quantity of industrial production that is desirable in net terms?

It is a problem and in a sense also a blessing that capitalist corporations only can expand capacity so far before they run out of customers with money in their pockets. There are, in the end, only so many buyers when average wage levels are steady or falling, and there only is so much restorative power and resilience in nature. These are not, unfortunately, offsetting contradictions—it is for the most part the already poor whose wages fall, and environmental problems are rooted far less in product selection and production technologies than in growth in the gross domestic product. Raw corporate power must therefore be doubly restrained and guided, but few restraints remain in the first decade of the new millennium when at present not even false, alternative visions have either ideological force or political power. More checks on power yet exist, of course, than existed within the old Communist regimes. However, fewer exist than existed when capitalist economies were more mixed and less global, or when international economic competition was between nations with roughly comparable wage levels and rules of the game, including comparable environmental regulations. And far fewer exist than are necessary and/or desirable.

What is lacking, then, is any alternative vision to unchecked, technologized, global capitalism—clearly a role for environmental political theory and books like this one. One need not, however, be utterly pessimistic. The end of the cold war opens new possibilities. The human imagination can now see beyond the often sterile notions of left and right. The world is truly more complicated than that. Markets do work, but they can be tools of, rather than substitutes for, other human and natural values. The entrepreneurial spirit would survive, and perhaps could even thrive, in a fairer and more ecologically sensitive world order, despite the protestations of profiteers to the contrary. Capitalism can adapt, even to a world where other institutions and values thrive as well. Governments could tax energy and raw materials more and low incomes less. The technological possibility of extremes of automated production could result—without the mythological revolution—in more leisure, rather than the constant threat of high unemployment. Several

European nations are already moving in this direction, as we did in North America early in this century, and could again.

The end of the cold war also has resulted in many quite direct benefits, both in terms of improved environmental protection, especially in some Eastern European locations, and in terms of the spread of at least nominal democracy. For example, both total pollution and climate warming emissions have been reduced in the new united Germany and elsewhere in Eastern Europe. Moreover, almost all of the nations of the world can now meet with civility and good intentions regarding many issues, from land mines to climate warming to debt management. (And terrorism might be added here post–September 11). While the outcomes are not always ideal by any means, the cold war posturing is gone and some steps forward can be achieved and quite broadly accepted. As well, until the recent economic difficulties in Asia (and now spread throughout the world), economic well-being in some poor nations has advanced more rapidly than it had previously, and human population growth rates have, correspondingly, if unevenly, declined.

Whereas the excessive expansion of productive capacity within former state socialist regimes, such as China (coupled with rapid growth elsewhere) carries risks both economically and environmentally, it may yet help to open significant net positive outcomes both socially and politically. Finally, the demise of the often antigreen socialist left in both Europe and North America may open a window of opportunity for the eventual development of new, distinctive, and popular critical perspectives which integrate many things from social justice to vigorous environmental protection to alternative entrepreneurialism. The ideological future need not be the ideological past even if (social and environmental) industrial productions in many poor nations bear an uncanny resemblance to those of a hundred years ago in nations that are now both rich and suddenly moving backwards in terms of social equality.

Globalization and the Environment

In the wake of the cold war, global trade expansion and global trade regimes have rushed to fill the vacuum and to make the entire world safe for global corporations. In the 1980s such firms were, of course, important, but today they are utterly dominant. Such firms can bring enormous pressures to bear on governments regarding the nonenforcement or virtual disestablishment of environmental regulatory regimes by threatening to withhold or transfer investment. They always could do this, of course, but such threats are now more credible when capital movement, reengineering, downsizing, and plant closures are utterly normal. We already forget that only ten years ago it was not assumed that everyday business decisions were made without regard to decades-long community presence, or that lifetimes of devoted service from employees counted for nothing.

This all bears on the important question of the centralization or decentralization of environmental protection initiatives. The smaller the unit of government, the less economically diverse the political jurisdiction, and the higher the local unemployment rate, the greater the relative power of large mobile corporations. This is why, even more today than in 1989, decentralization of environmental decision making is (as I argued then and still believe) generally a dangerous thing. What I did not anticipate at all in *Environmentalism and the Future of Progressive Politics* was that even the national politics of the environment was soon to be overwhelmed by the international politics of economics and trade. *Globalization is thus, in my view, a change larger even than the end of communism and the cold war.*

A distinction needs to be drawn here between, on one hand, the fact of extensive global trade and the easy global relocation of multinational firms and, on the other, the negotiated trade regimes, such as the North American Free Trade Agreement (NAFTA). When a firm can pay quite skilled manufacturing workers a dollar or two a day in Indonesia, China, or Mexico, it can easily afford to pay quite high tariffs to sell into the United States, Japan, Canada, or Europe. This is especially true if at the same time firms escape utterly from any system of legal protection for those wishing to form independent unions, from workplace health and safety regimes, and from enforced environmental regulations. The treaties do not cause these problems; they just help to speed and codify the process. But trade treaties also may provide an opportunity to harmonize (average) upward rather than downward on labor and environmental standards—to gain more in less advanced regimes, perhaps more than is lost within more advanced regimes. As with the NAFTA Side Agreement on Labor and the Environment, which could have been part of the original stronger treaty, there is no technical (as distinct from political) reason why trade treaties could not contain all manner of progressive social and environmental provisions.

Only politics and power prevent, for example, NAFTA from pegging the Mexican minimum wage as a minimum percentage of the average North American minimum wage, or as a slowly rising percentage of the average U.S./Canadian industrial wage. Such a measure would slow and socially alter the pace of industrial transformation, but it would not stop it. As I will note below, there are some reasons why globalization as a whole is not necessarily in and of itself a bad thing, but rather that it is especially the pace (and present design) of change that is socially and environmentally problematic. There also is nothing that prevents international enforcement of common environmental and workplace safety regulations as is virtually now the norm within the European Union. Nothing prevents these things now except the unavowed intent by industry and, often, by our own governments to undermine such regulations at home and indeed everywhere, or at the very least to assure that such rules can easily be avoided elsewhere, whenever necessary.

The pace of socioeconomic and political change in the past ten years has been spectacular. Downsizing, downshifting, reengineering (and reinventing government) are new to our vocabulary in the past decade, but they already have significantly changed family and community life and political attitudes throughout North America. There is, further, little reason to think that the pace of change will slow in the future—automation has just begun and globalization has a very long way to proceed. Rifkin and others have documented how some of these changes have affected employment security and income levels.[8] Again, the changes are not all bad by any means. Inflation has been controlled by insecurity and downward pressure on wages (though deflation may not be). Fewer people anywhere imagine now that they will have a career with only one firm or even necessarily in one city or one country. That can be socially and politically dangerous when unemployment rates are high, but could be stimulating when other and equal options are plentiful.

These new realities have enormous implications for environmental policy. Even in the richest nations, and in local government circles and among employees everywhere, there is now a thoroughgoing political timidity. Every government now fears losing employment investment and tax revenues. Almost any social behavior—including child labor—is somewhere justified in terms of global competitiveness, and employees and firms everywhere must compete with that new standard. No level of profit, or level of executive or product-endorsement compensation, is seen any longer as distasteful or greedy. Also quite normal is the environmentally intolerable, even outrageous, behavior in faraway places like Nigeria, Indonesia, and Guyana, combined with good corporate citizenship on the environmental front in the Netherlands, Canada, and/or the United States.[9]

We seemingly have gone back to the nineteenth century in so many ways. We are not far from the extremes of wealth and poverty that supported the old mansions of Fifth Avenue and Newport, Rhode Island. The low-wage gap has been automated or globalized or both. The digital/communications billionaires of today do not need so vast a legion of employees, just a few by comparison to the coal, steel, and railroad barons of yore. The running-shoe barons micromanage their production operations from the other side of the planet and focus their principal attention on product image. As well, the nineteenth-century rich went to Newport with hundreds of servants; the Bill Gates's Pacific Northwest mansion is served more by electronic devices than by human employees. Maybe the latter is a positive social change, but there was some sense of personal obligation to one's servants unfelt at fast food enterprises, and the net effect of all the changes is a McWorld.[10]

Interestingly, some of today's billionaires, not a reborn International Workers of the World leadership, are often the very people openly raising questions about the ways to balance corporate power in the age of globalization. George Soros argued, "Laissez-faire capitalism holds that the common good is best served by the uninhibited pursuit of self-interest. Unless it is tempered by the recognition of a common interest that ought to take precedence over particular interests, our present system is liable to break down."[11] James Goldsmith, perhaps the most eccentric British billionaire resident in France is more direct:

> Forty-seven Vietnamese or forty-seven Fillipinos can be employed for the cost of one person in a developed country, such as France. Until recently. . .4 billion people were separated from our economy by their political systems, primarily communist or socialist, and because of a lack of technology and of capital. Today, all that has changed. Their political systems have been transformed, technology can be transferred instantaneously anywhere in the world on a microchip, and capital is free to be invested anywhere the anticipated yields are highest.[12]

Goldsmith comes to unexpected conclusions from this kind of assertion—for example, he holds to something of a finger in the dike politics which opposes European integration. I would come to the opposite conclusion.

An economically integrated globe needs more political integration, not less. Goods produced with few employees in automated plants or at one forty-seventh of the average wage of the buyers of those goods do pose spectacular social, political, and economic problems at both ends of the transaction, and even more so pose problems for the environment we all share. I have always had a fear about the automation of industries wherein there were severe health hazards for employees. Not that one would not celebrate the escape of fellow humans from conditions whereby they "traded their lives for a living." Indeed, *Environmentalism and the Future of Progressive Politics* discusses sympathetically the important links between occupational health and environmental health. But, without someone at the work site and within the firm to fight to control the use of harmful chemicals and to make it more expensive to use them, those hazards might more often be released into communities and into nature. Similarly, if goods can be produced for almost nothing at the other end of the earth, why bother to repair them, and why not have three of them when you need only one. The rate of energy and material throughput made possible by the combination of automation and super-low wage levels may come to overwhelm nature even with a functioning system of environmental regulations.

If Southeast Asian forest workers earned even half the wages of those in the Pacific Northwest, the rate of destruction of tropical rain forests would slow considerably.[13] If Caribbean bauxite miners were paid half what a miner would earn in Germany or Japan, there likely would be less aluminum foil that was not recycled (though I'm aware that in this case those wages are far less a factor than the price of electricity at the site of the smelter). The broad point is that the social and the environmental are tied together in numerous ways, in ways that just were not visible to me in 1989. Employment insecurity undermines environmental concern in both poor countries and rich. The rapid change and geographic mobility associated with globalization and continuous and constant reengineering undermines the ability and desire to protect any particular environment setting. It does nothing good for the stability of family life either: twice as many family units, twice as many refrigerators and pots and pans, and less time available for community and for politics, environmental or otherwise.[14]

This is not to say that there is no good—environmentally or socially— that has, will, or could result from the digital/global age. There has been a significant increase in private investment and industrial and other employment in many very poor nations. Industrial wages in India, China, and elsewhere are brutally low, but many Asian, Latin American, and African nations, including some very poor ones, have made relative and absolute economic gains in recent years. As well, and more important environmentally, there is potential for significant reductions in energy and material throughputs associated with digital and communications technologies, especially in terms of such throughputs per dollar of the gross domestic product. As *Environmentalism and the Future of Progressive Politics* emphasized, this variable is a key to achieving increments of environmental impact reductions across the board. Another indirect (and highly unpopular) source of environmental gain is the fact that globalization exerts downward pressure on wages in rich countries. If one were to assume that the planet is a zero sum game, or that even present industrial output levels are unsustainable, the only way to level up the poor nations is to level down the rich. This ignores, however, the fact that the leveling down in the rich nations has been borne almost entirely by poor individuals within those rich countries.

The possibility that adequate environmental protection might ultimately limit economic growth was an issue that troubled me in 1989, and I felt that I did not resolve it satisfactorily in my book. My views are now only modestly clearer on this point. It is probable, in my view, that there is no environmentally suitable way to lift the whole world to North American living standards, especially if one assumes that human population will at least double again, one more time. Ecological footprint analysis suggests that it would take three Earths(!) to achieve this feat of leveling to present North American living standards.[15] This analysis, however, assumes that the gains in the poor nations will be in terms of all the materials we use with roughly the same levels of energy and materials intensity, and that the rich nations will not improve in this regard. That need not be true in either case. It is easy to envision a gross domestic product/energy and materials ratio twice or even three times as good as we achieve at present, but this still leaves us several planets short if human populations indeed double as now seems all but inevitable.

In the end, if one prefers a world that is both more equitable and environmentally sustainable, it is hard not to be open to the idea that the rich nations are rich enough, at least in terms of energy and material consumption. It would seem, though, the poor in rich nations could hardly use less of anything than they presently do—unless they can find ways to gain in quality of life terms while holding their ground in energy and materials use terms. This is, of course, possible. One can hypothesize (and advocate) the introduction of high quality, low cost public transportation, permitting the scrapping of broken down, fuel-inefficient automobiles. One can also imagine a restoration or expansion of demand-side management initiatives by public and regulated private electrical utilities (giving away efficient refrigerators, lighting fixtures, and air conditioners to poor customers). Clearly, there is a great deal that could be done; some of the policy tools that might help to advance on that policy front are discussed in the concluding section of this chapter. But it remains the case that the rich in the rich countries cannot be sustainably supported even at present consumption levels if the poor everywhere are to gain any significant ground.

One way to begin to resolve these interconnected problems, as touched on above, is to develop social, human rights, and environmental agreements that parallel the WTO to incorporate such initiatives within such treaties themselves. At present, this is a formidable task politically, to say the least. North Americans and Europeans must come to understand that wages, working conditions, social safety nets, and even human rights will tend toward, but not ever get fully to, a common level to the extent that global trade advances. The world truly is interconnected as never before, for richer and for poorer. All these factors will tend to level consumption upwards in some of the poorer nations and downwards in at least some of the richer nations—the question is how quickly will the leveling proceed and how far will the bottom rise and the top fall.

Why would one even imagine that the rich in the rich countries would ever accept such outcomes? For one reason, environmental damage exported is environmental damage that will frequently find its way back home—on imported food, in climate warming, and in the worldwide movement of air, water, and wildlife. As well, extinct species are lost not just for all time, but to all humanity and all nature. People understand this increasingly. There is also a trade-off for the rich were they (we) to accept steady or even a modest decline in consumption over time. The trade-off commodity is time—shorter work weeks, earlier retirements, less consumption dominated, more leisure oriented lives. The environmental movement must come to be as global as the most global of corporations—to convey the price we all pay for ecological damage in distant locations—and it must come to advocate more explicitly a modest time for money trade-off as, simply, a better way to live.

Domestic Politics and the Closed Nature of Global
Decision Making

One of the issues that I came to understand more fully shortly after
Environmentalism and the Future of Progressive Politics was published,
is the relationship between environmentalism and democracy.[16] One of
the defining characteristics of the emerging environmental movement
in the United States in the 1960s and 1970s, as distinct from the earlier
conservation movement, was that environmentalists had serious doubts
about the existence of a public interest in resource policy that could and
would be determined by technical elites within public bureaucracies.
Environmentalists reacted to all closed door determination of an objective public interest and to any purely scientific determination of
that same elusive notion. Environmentalists were more often of the
view that both science and values were a necessary part of the public interest within environmental realms and that no one, no experts
of any kind, had a special and overriding advantage in determining
what was best environmentally.

It has been widely argued by environmentalists that environmental
decision making should be conducted in the open and with a maximum
of public participation. Sometimes mistakes may be made in open processes, but policies will be improved if they are not in the hands of
closed bureaucracies where bargaining with special interests is the norm.
Too often, it was observed, the individuals involved in closed decision
making processes moved from public to private bureaucracies seamlessly
shared a common outlook. Even public interest watchdog groups are
prone to such cooptation. Iron triangles (consisting of mutually influencing groups of congressional committees, executive agencies, and private corporations) can emerge in policy circles with no one serving nature
vigilantly and no one serving disadvantaged people effectively. Thus, in
1969, the National Environmental Policy Act included protections to
keep environmental assessment processes open and visible. In the 1970s,
virtually all of the major pieces of domestic environmental legislation
in the United States included public participation provisions and open
public decision processes.[17]

At the international level the world of decision-making is, however,
less open, visible, and participatory. The protection of the national interest is typically in the hands of appointed figures who say very little in
public (like the international World Trade Organization). There was a

frank exchange of views, it is reported, until such time as a decision is reached. The toasts at the banquet are on global television; the discussions behind closed doors are not available. No unofficial citizens of any nation have any significant input whatever into most international proceedings of substance. Suddenly, by the start of the 1990s, much environmental policy had been thrust increasingly into this insulated world, behind the closed doors of international trade dispute panels peopled by lawyers and anonymous, unelected, international bureaucrats and all but silent in public diplomats (made more dramatic by the behind-closed-doors deliberations of the WTO). Global trade agreements are developed and put forward as if they had nothing at all to do with domestic social policies or domestic environmental protection standards. It is further asserted that nothing but good will come for wage levels, total employment, and the environment for all trading partner nations. The only visible alternative within public discourse appears to be economic protectionism, hardly the wisest choice, of course.

Moreover, the International Tropical Timber Organization has done almost nothing to protect global forests. The North Atlantic Fisheries Organization has been largely ineffective in protecting fish stocks in international waters. The last international agreement on climate warming prior to Kyoto in 1997 was an abysmal failure with the Kyoto agreement itself in jeopardy because of America's lack of support under the Bush administration. These are some of the more unfortunate instances where the focus of international organization attention has been environmental. As well, trade disputes with environmental implications do not involve open public hearings, nor are they widely reported in the press. There the environment has also fared rather badly more often than not. This is not to say that international environmental treaties should not be pursued or that environmental matters should be excluded from trade disputes. The former may be the environment's best hope in globalizing political economy, and the latter are simply impossible to avoid. But trade panel hearings with important environmental or social implications should be open and nongovernmental organizational funding provided.

The first political analyst I know of who pointed to a possible threat to democratic functioning in elevating more of the domestic issue agenda to the international level was Michael Kidron.[18] Writing more than thirty years ago, Kidron discussed the closed nature of diplomatic undertakings and the ease with which political leadership could hide behind international necessities, and the widely accepted need for secrecy in such matters. Few within the public know what goes on at that level and the media keep their distance voluntarily.

The most extreme example of internationalization of the domestic political agenda of many nations occurs whenever the International Monetary Fund (IMF) intervenes. Here decisions about employment and wage levels, interest rates, banking rules, and the like are imposed or all but imposed by officials unelected anywhere and essentially answerable to no one. At present, the IMF has supplanted the autonomy of seventy-one national governments with more than one-fifth of the world's population as a condition of emergency loans.[19] The IMF does not frequently suggest openly that environmental protections stand in the way of lifting the sanctions imposed on desperate nations, and may well not do so even in private. However, it acts most often when debt is out of control and/or when currency values drop suddenly and sharply, imposing a process which sees to it that resources can be exported more cheaply, and—normally in these situations—foreign currency will be sought at virtually any price (and environmental protection in such emergency contexts is rarely given a second thought).

With or without the intervention of the IMF, unpopular domestic political decisions can sometimes be taken, with seeming regret, within a thoroughly internationalized politics. Promises can then be made that today's environmental, social, and economic pain will lead to longer term gains, and any later failure to deliver can be chalked up to failures elsewhere, in other nations, and outside one's own responsibility and control. The wealthy can gain relative ground domestically, and no one in office has to pay a political price because the changes are explained as necessary to avoid losing ground internationally and to avoid an even greater price in terms of unemployment and plant closures. In the midst of this, the environment can lose whenever and wherever there is, out of economic desperation, resistance to further losses of this sort.

Perhaps the best response for the North American and European environmental movements within this new context is to internationalize their efforts even more rapidly (like the worldwide movement protesting the WTO). There is an urgent need now, in comparison to 1989, to create and support international nongovernmental organizations, including especially those that have grassroots support and/or are operating within oppressive regimes, and to focus as much on excessive and inappropriate consumption (in a word, sustainability) within rich nations as on the protection of the domestic environment. The environmental movement, to its credit, has been adapting in these directions. Were I writing *Environmentalism and the Future of Progressive Politics* today, I would put far greater stress on this need than I did at that time.

New Approaches to Environmental Politics and Policy

The other transformation since 1989, perhaps as much possibility as actuality thus far, is the growing focus on sustainability, the integration of economy, and environment and market-based environmental policy tools. Some of this change has been, of course, highly suspect—for some "the integration of environment and economy" is but another way to force environmental values onto the economic playing field where dollar-based values usually win because dollars are the only measure in the game. But this is not a necessary outcome of such integration. Nor need it be the case that market-based environmental policy tools are necessarily less effective than so-called command and control regulation. The outcome depends in part on whether the new tools are supplements to regulation, or replacements for regulation. Regulation is, in fact, best suited to a quite narrow range of environmental problems, and market-based tools, such as taxes, user fees, subsidies, and subsidy removal, can be used with powerful effectiveness. I did not see this as clearly in 1989 as I do now, and I did not then see very clearly the many ways in which these tools could be related to the political and economic themes that I discussed in my book.

Sustainability requires considerable transformations, but transformations comprised of millions upon millions of modest everyday decisions. There is some role for regulation inducing these changes, as in requiring minimum recycled content in certain products or in establishing fleet average fuel efficiency standards for automobiles, but for the most part market-based tools make more sense. It is in the small decisions made within the market and in everyday life that sustainable behaviors can be rewarded and encouraged and nonsustainable behaviors discouraged. Nonsustainable choices are rarely so dangerous in and of themselves individually as to warrant the relatively heavy hand of regulation. More modest market-based interventions are essentially a matter of getting the price signals right, as often as not by removing subsidies to nonsustainable economic activities and putting in place user fees for nonsustainable goods or services.[20]

Nonetheless, the release of toxic substances into the environment still demands firm and effective use of regulation. There are flaws in the regulatory system, but there also are strengths; in this I agree with some of the assessments made by Davies and Mazurek.[21] As well, many land use issues still need to be resolved directly through the use of the clear and strict intervention of government. Government also needs to escape the constraints of those who would have it that in all cases all playing fields must be level in dollar terms. This is the same as saying that there are no values but dollar values. It is one thing to say that environmentally, morally, or socially doubtful activities should not be disadvantaged in the marketplace. It is quite another to say that a society or a government does not have the right to provide some modest level of advantage in some circumstances. All that said, there are many market-based tools that could work very well to advance North American society toward sustainability, including compliance with the Kyoto agreements and better understanding on the question of climate warming with little, if any, economic damage other than perhaps the profit levels of some very profitable firms.[22]

There are many possible examples of policies which could advance both equity and sustainability simultaneously without necessarily restraining economic capacity—that is, redirecting more than limiting economic activity. Some of the tax burden could gradually be shifted from low incomes and/or payroll taxes (which can dampen employment as presently configured) to energy and raw materials. Selected road toll increases could be used to provide additional fare subsidies for energy efficient public transportation. The provision of employee parking might no longer be tax deductible by firms, but cash payments in lieu of free parking could be nontaxable benefits in the hands of employees. Taxes on nonrefillable containers, without recycled content, could help to provide temporary tax incentives to firms buying new recycling equipment. (This has been introduced in some North American jurisdictions, but not others.) The set of incentives and rules grouped as demand-side management in the electric utilities should be continued and broadened, instituted on a national or even international scale, and designed so that they emphasize the needs of the poor and elderly.

The point here is that many of the public policies that advance sustainabiliity are nonregulatory in character and many could be structured in ways that improve the economic and social situation of disadvantaged groups in North American society. Some could be developed in forms that could be incorporated into international trade regimes. Such initiatives, whether domestic or international in design, oppose the political agenda and emphases of globalization and neoliberalism. So did the central thrust of writing *Environmentalism and the Future of Progressive Politics.* The cold war is behind us and much has changed since 1989. Both the environmental movement and progressive politics have had difficult times since, but such difficulties are the best argument for renewed efforts at finding common ground and new efforts at searching for international allies.

6

Industrialism and Deep Ecology
Andrew McLaughlin

Where are we with respect to nature? Have human activities already stressed the rest of nature to the point that some sort of environmentally driven social collapse is inevitable? Or are we still within the time when corrective actions can stave off social breakdown?

The chance that we have *already* overshot the earth's carrying capacity for industrialized society may seem preposterous. Since industrial activity and the human population expands daily, how could we have overshot the planet's capacity for humans? But this is too simple. There are several ways a population can go beyond the carrying capacity of its place in nature without suffering immediate consequences. One nation can overshoot the carrying capacity of its territory by collecting resources from other places, enabling a particular population to live beyond its means. This does not show that humanity *as a whole* may have exceeded the earth's capacity. However, collecting can span time as well as space. The use of fossil fuels, for example, is a collecting of resources from the past, as is the use of other nonrenewable resources. Such collections are necessarily temporary. Somewhat less obviously, industrial activities may use up the ability of the planet to absorb pollution, while the negative consequences of such practices may only be realized in the future. The burning of fossil fuels and the resultant increase in atmospheric carbon dioxide is one example. Further, renewable resources can be used at a rate that exceeds the planet's capacity to regenerate them—overfishing, for example. William Catton estimated that freeing ourselves from dependence on the collection of fossil fuels from the past "would require an increase in contemporary carrying capacity equivalent to ten earths—each of whose surfaces was forested, tilled, fished, and harvested to the current extent of our planet."[1] It is thus *possible* that we have already gone beyond the carrying capacity of the planet, and we do not yet know it.

We do know some things. The ozone layer in the stratosphere has declined over the past few decades, increasing ultraviolet radiation (UV) at the earth's surface. This increase will have consequences, such as more skin cancers and the suppression of the immune system in humans, increased cataracts in creatures with eyes like ours, decreased crop yields, and reduction of phytoplankton, which is the base of the aquatic food web. Many nations, regarding this problem as serious, entered into international agreements to reduce or phase out many chemicals which tend to deplete the ozone layer. However, since these chemicals can take decades to reach the stratosphere and can be active in depleting the ozone layer for much longer, no one can know *now* whether these treaties were timely or too late to avert major consequences. The depletion will get worse before it gets better. In Australia weather reports include the UV levels for the day, and Australian laws require special precautions for reducing school children's exposure to sunlight when there are high UV levels. On December 9, 1997, *The New York Times* reported that most embryos of long-toed salamanders in the Cascade Mountains, where they had lived for thousands of years, were now dying from exposure to UV radiation.

Perhaps we have not gone beyond the carrying capacity of the planet for industrial civilization. Maybe overshoot will occur next Tuesday or a few decades from now. The fact that we do not—and cannot—know is unnerving, for a lot is at stake. To get off this collision course, profound changes are necessary in our relations to the rest of nature, and real solutions are not under serious consideration.

What makes the situation bleaker is that present global trends involve the expansion of market economies and industrial production to nearly everywhere. A metaphor may help. Imagine that we are all passengers on a train heading south toward general environmental and social destruction. Many environmentalists and others, alert to the dangers, have been earnestly walking north inside the train for several years. As they move from car to car, they think they are making progress. Some laws have been passed and a few international agreements have been signed. But when they pause to look out the window, they can plainly see that all of us are now much further south. Despite their best efforts, they have been unable to reverse the direction of travel. We need to ask ourselves some fundamental questions: What fuels the locomotive? Who, if anyone, is in control? What drives us on so relentlessly? What will it take to change direction?[2]

The tracks are the determination of social and political policies through economics. Today, economics is the dominant factor in determining industrial societies' interactions with the rest of nature. Capitalism is the engine that drives a truly radical transformation of humanity's relations with the rest of nature, a transformation at least as profound as the agricultural revolution (as Pirages has written about in this volume). The depth and breadth of current ecological problems have arisen out of changes that began with the explosion of European cultural and economic imperialism in the seventeenth and eighteenth centuries and matured with the industrial revolution. Although the process has continued from that point, it was the industrial revolution that laid the foundations of a global economy. Upon this foundation was developed an integrated world economy with global markets now linked by nearly instantaneous communication.

Although the capitalist global economy of industrial civilization is one important determinant of humanity's relations with the rest of nature, brief mention should be made of a number of other factors. Certain basic assumptions are embedded within humanity's current relations with nonhuman nature and often are not given critical examination. One such assumption is that nature can be owned. This possibility is denied by many other cultures, and they are cultures that have adapted rather more gently to their places. Industrial peoples further assume that nature is appropriately regarded as simply resources to be used for whatever ends humans happen to have. It is further assumed that science reveals the true nature of nature, and that what is revealed is lifeless matter in motion. This vision of the nature of nature enables and reinforces the assumption that nature is nothing more than resources. Industrial peoples also presume that they can control nature, forgetting that they are a part of nature and that, ultimately, a part cannot control the whole of which it is a part.[3] Thus, there is nothing in our understanding of nature that places cultural barriers to the exploitation of nature. We have collectively lost any sense of the sacred in the natural world. Even the depth of this loss of the sacred is often unnoticed.

Nevertheless, it is the capitalist economic system that is the most obvious force driving us to energetically expand our industrial form of life without regard for the rest of nature. A global economy allows ecologically unsustainable forms of life to not only endure but flourish. In the past few centuries we have changed from ecosphere peoples to biosphere peoples, to use Raymond Dasmann's terms.[4] Ecosphere peoples derive their livelihood from the ecosystems within which they exist. If they arrive at sustainable forms of life, they do so by developing economic and cultural ways that enable patterns of interacting with nature that do not destroy the ecosystems within which they exist. They are attuned to feedback from their ecosystems which allow them to effectively coexist with them. Their effective adjustment to their ecosystems was not necessarily rational nor intentional. Rather, it may be effected through culturally enforced myths, stories, or patterns of religious beliefs that restrain them from ecologically destructive practices. Thus, Roy Rappaport persuasively argues that the ritual activities of groups living in the interior of New Guinea help "to maintain the biotic communities existing within their territories."[5] The feedback loops within which they exist are relatively short, which facilitates social learning about mistakes (as Milbrath discusses in his chapter in this collection). If ecosphere peoples fail to find such ways of coexisting with their ecosystems, they perish or migrate.

By contrast, biosphere peoples collect portions of their livelihoods from distant ecosystems. Instead of being constrained to coexist with their local ecosystems, biosphere peoples take resources from outside their ecosystems and export their wastes. By greatly enlarging feedback loops, they easily can fail to notice their ecological mistakes, avoid the consequences for a long time, and then displace their errors onto other societies. Even worse, the flourishing of biospheric economies fosters the appearance that their modes of interaction with nature are better than primitive ways of ecosphere peoples.

Capitalism

As dramatic as the impact of capitalism has been on the relations between humans and nature, it is not at all easy to define its essence. The problem of defining capitalism arises from the difficulty in univocally naming a changing creature. Should one understand mercantile capitalism as the same as industrial capitalism? Is a highly competitive market capitalism the same as an oligopolistic or monopolistic capitalism? Is a market system with extensive state regulation still capitalist? Is competitive market capitalism linked by an internal developmental logic to an evolution toward oligopoly? Or is oligopoly a preventable backsliding from the competitive marketplace capitalism? These conceptual problems need not be resolved here.[6]

Capitalism is an economic system in which the production and distribution of economic goods is typically effected through competitive markets. These markets are the arenas within which social decisions are created. A capitalist system, to simplify, is a collection of producers linked together by markets wherein exchange rates are determined by unregulated auction, that is, prices. Some producers only are in a position to sell their labor while others own or can effectively dispose of the products that are produced by those who sell their labor.[7] Further distinctions could be introduced, but a finer analysis of the conditions of production is not necessary. The point is that people under capitalism typically confront various markets that regulate significant dimensions of their lives. This is a fact for laborer, bureaucrat, and corporate manager.

All participants encounter markets that set the prices of the elements of production that they must purchase in order to produce, and they face another market that sets the price at which their products can be sold. Thus, workers do not control the costs of food and housing, and capitalist producers typically do not control their costs for raw materials. Workers do not control the wages they are paid, and capitalists do not control the prices at which their products can be sold. The collection of such markets, it is said, leads to the best possible mixture of what is produced in society at the lowest possible cost. Thus, Adam Smith's famous invisible hand, a metaphor for the theory that producers acting only in their own interests leads to a socially optimal result, guides us all toward general prosperity without anyone explicitly intending such a result. Markets determine what otherwise might have to be decided by tradition or explicit decision.

The regulation of social life by market mechanisms has ramifications in all dimensions of human life, ranging from the nature of family life and schooling to the way people live out their lives as workers or owners. Markets tend to generate selfish behavior and discourage cooperative behavior. Typically, the participants in these markets act to enhance their welfare without regard to others. In short, they are self-regarding. This is the ordinary pattern of behavior within capitalist markets and is not a reflection of human nature, but is merely the kind of behavior rewarded by the system. Participants within a capitalist market who do not attempt to enhance their economic position tend to suffer unpleasant consequences. For example, if those who manage centers of material production fail to maximize profit, they may be unable to attract investors to modernize their systems of production. This makes them less able to compete successfully with other producers. They then lose their position in the market.

It is the imperative of growth within capitalism that inexorably propels the train southward. This imperative is absolutely central in understanding the profundity of our ecological plight. Capitalist economies *require* the continual expansion of production—a capitalist system cannot stand still. This is due to the role of competition in the dynamics of capitalism. Producers are vitally interested in their profit. One way to increase profit is to sell products at a lower price than others sell the same or similar products. This can be done by lowering the costs of producing such products. Cheaper labor, perhaps to be found somewhere else by paying lower wages, is one way of lowering costs. Another historically effective way of reducing production costs is devising ways of producing the product (or one similar to it) by a less costly process. Such innovations typically involve the use of more elaborate machinery to producer larger quantities of goods with less labor per unit. Thus, the successful producer finds a cheaper and faster mode of producing something, enabling that producer to come to the market with a cheaper product.

This confronts competitors with the problem of finding some innovation themselves or being driven from the market by cheaper goods. In this process, more is produced with less labor. If wages are the dominant form of income, the increase in the productivity of labor threatens to generate unemployment. But increased unemployment means fewer consumers able to purchase what is produced. There is, therefore, a systemic need for expanding consumption, typically by finding new consumers, increasing each person's consumption, and encouraging governmental purchases. This cycle of increased productivity of labor requiring increased consumption of nature repeats itself again and again. It is called economic growth and it is widely regarded as truly good.

The process of capitalist production involves winners and losers—wealth becomes concentrated in fewer and fewer hands. When political power can be purchased, this concentration of wealth allows the wealthy to dominate political decisions. If communications media can be purchased, then those media will tend to reflect the interests of those who own them. There is, then, little controversy over whether economic growth is truly good.

The continued expansion of economic production bodes ill for nature. Growth accelerates the process of converting more and more of nature first into resources and somewhat later into waste. The necessity of selling what is produced (in order to realize a profit), in later stages of capitalism, fosters a consumer culture where people are encouraged to conceive of the good life as the maximum consumption of things. The inner psychic life of people becomes a focus of attention, with continual attempts made to convince people to appraise their worth in terms of how much they own. But this way of achieving a sense of self-worth becomes a source of dissatisfaction when affluence becomes widespread and does not serve as a socially recognized mark of being better than one's neighbors.[8] Thus, the treadmill toward increased material consumption does not lead to satisfaction but to an unending quest for more. This may be a partial explanation for the fact that Americans now have far more material possessions than they did four decades ago, yet consistently report lower levels of happiness than in 1957.[9] *The point is not that material consumption is irrelevant to human happiness, but that material consumption, beyond a certain level, does not increase human happiness.*

This process of expanding production will not be endless—signs of its end are on the horizon. But since this process is an essential part of the logic of capitalism, changing it involves a transition to another form of economy. It is hard to be optimistic that this will happen soon.

To appreciate better the necessity for the expansion of production under capitalism, consider the conditions under which the requirement of growth can be avoided. In particular sectors of the economy producers may establish monopolies. By exerting conscious control over markets, they can avoid the dynamics of growth generated by competitive markets. Occasionally participants are successful in this, but monopolies tend to generate political regulation.[10] If the whole economy of a society becomes one huge monopoly, the imperative of growth could be avoided, but such a society would no longer be capitalist. Replacing markets as the mode of social decision making amounts to a transition to some form of state capitalism, technocracy, or socialism.

The alternative to capitalism that leaves existing relations of advantage and domination in place involves retaining control through the manipulation of politics, appearing as a regulation of the economy in the common interest, but actually leaving the fundamental structures in place. Such a publicly controlled monopoly economy would amount to a mammoth bureaucratic state capitalism. The path from an unregulated economy to a public controlled capitalist economy raises a host of problems with its associated legitimating belief systems.[11] It means the loss of the ideological justification for present inequalities. Those who suffer from (at least relative) deprivation in a capitalist society must give up their hopes for rising in the economic order. The loss of competitive markets would end the moral arguments offered for capitalism, which involve the claim that markets are the fundamental condition for human freedom. It is an open question as to how far people can be cajoled, bribed, and/or coerced into leaving control of the economy in the hands of those who profit without any compensating ideology promising that they also are free to enter the market as owners and get ahead. I assume that there is *some* limit to the extent to which people will tolerate such a situation, although I do not know where that limit is.

A managed capitalist economy might find it difficult to survive the decline in living standards that may arise from ecological constraints. Such contractions and their associated suffering, within a publicly managed economy, appear as the responsibility of politicians presumed to represent the interests of all citizens, rather than appearing as results of the blind forces of the marketplace:

> The division of gains which [poor people] accepted on the way up will not be the division of losses which they will want to accept on the way down. . . . Passing (say) $2,000 annual income per head on the way up, a society may be very unequal; passing the same figure on the way down it is likely to be more equal, or more bloodstained, or both. Even if growth merely slows or stops without actual losses, equality may suddenly seem more important.[12]

Calls for the regulation of the economy in the interests of all members of society, not simply the few who happen to own the productive apparatus, will have increasing appeal when economic growth is no longer possible. Quelling such demands for the social control of the means of production would likely involve suspending political democracy and/or fostering mass irrationality, where the citizens surrender their material interests and sacrifice them to some symbolic higher good, such as race, *volk*, or flag—plausibly the description of some form of fascism. Thus, while capitalism requires economic growth as a condition of its existence, ecological considerations indicate the impossibility of such growth continuing indefinitely. Avoiding the imperative of growth requires abolishing capitalism for some form of fascism if existing relations of inequality are maintained. To the extent that equality is fostered, the transition toward political regulation is socialist.

Socialism

Socialism can, in theory, avoid the problems capitalism faces in arriving at an ecologically sustainable form of life. Socialism provides for the conscious political control of those processes of interacting with nature that are left to unconscious market processes under capitalism. This control allows for humanity's relations with the rest of nature to be governed by conscious decision, instead of by blind markets. It makes possible a society that could regulate itself in accord with a plan. Precisely how such a plan is arrived at is an issue of profound significance for the people living in a socialist society. Indeed, various forms of socialism can be distinguished by their mode of arriving at such social plans. The extent to which these plans are arrived at through democratic processes is the major determinant of the degree of democracy within such a socialism.

In whatever form, socialism theoretically holds greater promise for ecologically sound relations between humanity and nature. The blind processes of market-based decisions can be avoided. Social plans could fully account for future generations and take account of the rhythms of ecological systems. Further, there is no *necessity* for economic growth within socialism. A socialist society could decide that growth is a mistake and devise instead a social system based on a steady-state economy.[13]

Profound changes in humanity's current relations with nature could be adopted. Within socialism explicit decisions could be made to respect nature, ceasing to treat nature as merely a collection of resources to be developed. Wilderness could be preserved without the need to appeal to utilitarian justifications. There is no inherent necessity for a socialist society to adopt an exclusively exploitative orientation to nature. It is possible for socialism to be ecologically sound.

This possibility, it must be acknowledged, was not realized in the history of the Soviet Union. Although there were many interesting and significant attempts at nature conservation in its first few decades, the ecological damage by industrialism in the USSR parallels that of the capitalist systems. For a variety of reasons, the paramount goal of the USSR was industrial production, not the development of sustainable and ecologically sound relations between humanity and nature. Nature was viewed as a resource to be exploited for human welfare. Decision makers in the Soviet Union retained the assumption that nature can be managed through science and technology and that it should be managed solely with the aim of human welfare. This attitude toward nature was exemplified by one Soviet scientist's view of the largest (by volume) freshwater lake in the world:

> The industrial significance of Lake Baikal lies in the fact that it represents a huge purifier of water. . . . The lake should be exploited, but so as not to disturb its life processes or interfere with its water purifying properties. We must therefore know how and to what extent Baikal may be polluted so that it may continue to process dirty water and yield clean water.[14]

This image of Lake Baikal as a huge water filter exemplifies the human centered orientation of industrial societies East and West. The East may be praised for its interest, in its best moments, in human welfare, but there is little difference between markets and socialism in terms of their exclusively instrumental relations with nature.

What are the ecological prospects of a Soviet-style socialism where the intention, at least, is to administer the economy of an industrial society? The goal of increasing industrial production is difficult to give up for both administrators and the administered. Clearly, a decent human life requires that people have a certain amount of material production. Beyond that, it seems clear that people within industrial cultures desire far more material production than what is necessary for a decent life. More things make more obedient citizens. Thus, socialist leaders may find the ideal of economic growth as justified both in terms of human welfare and for maintaining their political control and their own material advantages. Expanding production thus makes existing patterns of inequality more tolerable. For these reasons, socialist leaders are highly likely to direct the administrative apparatus of society toward economic growth rather than ecological sustainability. This pattern is being followed in contemporary China. It is not implausible to think that they are doing what the people want in expanding material production, particularly when that expansion is in the consumer section of the economy. Once they start down this path, their continued power seems to depend absolutely on economic expansion.

The significant difference between capitalism's and socialism's relation to economic growth is that the compulsion to growth within capitalism is absolutely fundamental to the capitalist economic system. In contrast, the roots of the ideology of economic growth within socialism lie in the desire of industrial peoples for material consumption and the leaders's need for social control. This implies that socialism could change from a growth-oriented industrialism far more easily than could capitalism. Indeed, if people living under a socialist regime came to desire a steady-state economy, perhaps out of a respect for nature, effectively realizing this desire could become a source of political power within socialism.

In the near-term future, a general desire among people for a steady-state economy does not seem likely. Equating the good life with material possessions is one of the few compensations left once mass society becomes the dominant form of life, wherein each person's lot is to labor at the direction of others for purposes set by others, and whose only return for that labor is money, useful only to buy things and services. *The maintenance of inequalities of social power is closely tied to the maintenance of a materialist consumer culture.* The promise of more goods is a powerful tool used by those who wish to maintain their positions in the upper reaches of the hierarchy. Peoples in industrial societies have become helpless and mostly passive victims of systems that they neither understand nor control. There seems to be a developmental connection wherein industrialization leads to a mass society, which leads to passive and helpless humans.[15] Lacking any form of transcendent meaning, lacking a sense of being effective in public life, lacking meaningful participation in community life, they must find such satisfactions as they can in material consumption. Industrial people literally surround themselves with concrete, effecting and reflecting a psychic and sensual numbing. The daily nature within which industrial peoples live, being itself a technological product, cannot but make nonsensical the claim that nature itself must be respected.

Industrialism

Industrialism is *both* a process of material production and the development of a consumer culture. Without consumerism, industrialism's increase in the production of labor would lead to either vast unemployment or a shortening of the working day. The central problem is, thus, industrialism as a social totality encompassing both the external development of ways of producing things and services *and* the subjective desire always for more.

It is the close interlocking between industrial production and the development of consumerism that, I think, requires that industrialism be taken as a central category for an ecologically based social analysis. Tradition and older forms of satisfaction in community and labor are dissolved as societies industrialize. The distinction between need and desire is lost, and people come to feel deprived, no matter how extensive their material possessions.

It seems simply fantastic to imagine that human societies are going to voluntarily shift from industrialism to some other social formation by choice. Recent events in Eastern Europe show that people, when they can grasp a chance for material abundance, will do so. Industrialism, urbanism, alienation from nature, the division of one's life into work and leisure, seeing nature as a mere resource, and the resultant consumerist orientation to life seem to all hang together as a social formation that most modern societies strive to realize.

There are some signs of transformation. The spell cast by the prospects of yet another round of material abundance does not catch everyone, and the spell itself may have become less enchanting. Many people, out of concern for their fellow humans, other animals, and the environment, willingly, even eagerly, adopt less ecologically destructive ways of living. Increasingly, people identify themselves as environmentalists, and this concern is being felt in the political systems of industrial countries.

The fact that consumerism is not deeply satisfying is itself hopeful. This implies that moving beyond consumerism might not be so painful. Increased material consumption simply fails to provide corresponding increases in happiness. *Within* societies, the richer express more satisfaction than do the poorer, but *between* societies one cannot find overall higher levels of satisfaction expressed in wealthier societies. The absolute level of material consumption, beyond some point passed long ago in industrial societies, is irrelevant to satisfaction. Instead, the degree of satisfaction experienced seems to depend on one's economic position relative to others in one's society, rather than what one actually has.[16] Indeed, there is a pervasive *feeling* of deprivation which permeates the psychology of consumers, despite the incredible level of affluence they (don't actually) enjoy.[17] This decline in satisfaction opens the door to the possibility of change.

Can humans be satisfied with a modest level of material consumption? From an anthropological perspective, the answer is obvious—many societies are free from the striving for material abundance. As Marshal Sahlins put it, "There are two possible courses to affluence. Wants may be easily satisfied either by producing much or by desiring little."[18] Many such societies have existed outside of the sphere of industrialism. They have found ways of existing in harmony with their environment and at least some observers have portrayed their lives as rather more pleasant than the average industrial life, involving less labor, less stress, pleasant social interactions, and freedom from the insecurities that plague most industrial people's lives.[19] It is, of course, implausible to think that industrial peoples can become hunter-gatherers, and I am not suggesting that we can or should. The question is whether we can move forward toward a society that chooses a course of affluence by desiring *less* or whether we are compelled to continue the fruitless search for satisfaction through the relentless pursuit of industrial products. The latter course is ecologically unsustainable.

This question is of considerable importance for any green politics. If one assumes that there is no way of transcending industrialism, then some accommodation must be made. But such an accommodation assumes that the level of material consumption presently enjoyed by industrial peoples can be maintained. This simply writes off the lesser developed economies of the world, since the present levels of material consumption in the industrial world cannot be generalized and achieved by *all* peoples of the world. Consider only one factor, the output of carbon dioxide:

> If past trends continue, developing countries will be emitting 16.6 billion tonnes of carbon annually by 2025—over four times as much as developed countries today. Assuming industrialized nations manage to stabilize their emissions per person at current levels, the total output per year would be 21 billion tonnes—*three times the present level.*[20]

Thus, to accommodate industrialism, realistic as it may seem in terms of political change, seems to implicitly advocate the continuing dominance of the industrial nations or a totally unrealistic image of an ecologically unlimited biosphere. Neither is likely. The current wave of economic globalization entails that industrial production is spread around the globe and the people in lesser developed countries are being enticed into the world of the modern consumer.

In summary, both capitalism and socialism have a systemic need for economic expansion, although the systems' needs are not based in the same place. Capitalism *economically* requires, while socialism *politically* requires, growth. This political requirement is tied to the need for legitimization and the production of consumer goods. Thus, the key similarity is that both systems are based on industrial modes of production and both require growth. They are both forms of expansionary industrialism.

Can the industrialism that steadily extends to all parts of the planet be justified? Is industrialism worth it? Has industrialism made a better world for humans? At least beyond a certain point, the dissatisfactions of consumerism and mass society may outweigh the gains. There is nothing within the logic of industrialism that allows a consideration of whether we already have too much. The pressures for growth spread throughout the whole system, with all sectors of society seeking more and more, yet still finding happiness elusive. If so, is the hazard worth the risk? The magnitude of the hazard need not be belabored. Suffice it to note that we have altered the global atmosphere, with largely unknown consequence, and the ozone layer is thinning. The list could be much longer. Is it worth it?

Anthropocentrism

This seemingly inexorable expansion of industrialism raises moral questions. By what right can the human species, however unwisely it seeks its own welfare, elbow aside countless species in their pursuit of resources? We already have fallen off the precipice of a spasm of species extinctions. We have encircled wilderness and we threaten all rain forests. Perhaps we have ended biological history by stopping the speciation process for large animals. We now stand ready to embark on the alchemical project of manufacturing new forms of life in the pursuit of profit. By what right do we presume to try to remake the rest of nature according to the desires of humanity?

Anthropocentrism is the assumption that humans are the only beings with ultimate value. All else, it is assumed, has value only in its usefulness to humans. It is this assumption that legitimates industrialism. If we shed our anthropocentrism bias, the expanding human population, especially when coupled with environmentally destructive forms of production, appears as a vast aggression against the rest of nature. The possible loss of the *majority* of species in the next century is a biocide of a magnitude so great as to require morally urgent radical social change toward a harmony with nonhuman nature.[21] Once industrialism is viewed from a nonanthropocentric perspective, then it *obviously* is a horrendous crime against the rest of nature.

Within industrial culture, the anthropocentric assumption is so deeply embedded that it can be hard to bring it to light. Neil Evernden offers a trenchant illustration of the problem. Imagine being at a meeting about some proposed highway that will pave over the habitat of some endangered creature. In trying to question this, you try to advocate for the interests of that creature. The likely response by man is "what good is it?" How can the anthropocentric assumption buried within that question be questioned? The temptation is to meet it in a way that will simply reinforce it, such as saying, "perhaps the creature will turn out to cure cancer." Evernden's suggested response, which should be used cautiously, is to reply, "What good are you?"[22] This response brings out the anthropocentric assumption that other forms of life have to be justified by their human usefulness, which underlies "what good is it?"

Anthropocentrism is even embedded within the way many environmentalists conceptualize the human situation. One current definition of "environment" is "all the physical, social and cultural factors influencing the existence or development of mankind."[23] Leaving aside comment on the sexism of "mankind," this definition reflects an expansive and welcome inclusion of social and cultural factors into "the environment." But it also is thoroughly anthropocentric. It fails to reflect an understanding that the very concept of environment must be relativized to the entity or species for which the rest of nature constitutes an environment. I am part of the squirrel's environment, as it is part of mine. Each center of activity has its own environment; there is no such thing as *the* environment, unless one remains stuck within an anthropocentric bias.

Deep Ecology

What would society be like if we collectively moved beyond anthropocentrism? Clearly, it would involve ending expansionary industrialism, which is risky, unsustainable, unsatisfying, and immoral. But exactly what would emerge is harder to see. Such a transformation would be like the metamorphosis of a caterpillar into a butterfly, hard to visualize in advance. Utopian novels can offer a variety of images of hope, but no one can really see far enough to draw up blueprints. What we can see now are signs pointing us toward the wise path. Deep ecology, I think, is one contemporary perspective that beckons us in the right direction.[24] The heart of deep ecology is its platform, which consists of a number of interrelated factual and normative claims about humans and their relations with the rest of nature. The platform is a potential basis for unity among those who accept the importance of nonanthropocentrism and understand that this entails radical social change. It is a popular statement of principles around which, it is hoped, people with differing *ultimate* understandings of themselves, society, and nature, can unite.

The platform itself consists of eight basic principles:

1. The well being and flourishing of human and nonhuman life on Earth have value in themselves. These values are independent of the usefulness of the nonhuman world for human purposes.

Essentially, this is a denial of anthropocentrism. It is an assertion that human *and* nonhuman life should flourish. Life, in this context, is understood broadly to include, for example, rivers, landscape, and ecosystems. Accepting the idea that humans are not the only part of nature that is of value is the watershed perception from which a radical and ecocentric environmentalism flows.

2. Richness and diversity of life forms contribute to the realization of these values and also are values in themselves.

This, along with the first principle, counters the often-held image of nature and evolution as resulting in higher forms of life. It involves a revisioning of life and evolution, changing from understanding evolution as progress from lower to higher forms to understanding evolution as an expression of multiple and equally extraordinary forms of life.

Instead of scaling nature as a hierarchy of beings from bottom to top, the idea of diversity lauds difference and rejects any single standard of excellence. The widespread alarm over the extinction of many species indicates that most people do value, to some extent at lest, diversity in the rest of nature. Denying the value of diversity requires some single standard of excellence. If there were such a measure, then all forms of existence, human and nonhuman, could be apprised as to the degree they manifested that excellence. Humans and other beings could then be ordered into one vast "chain of being."[25] But what single standard can one imagine that *all* humanity, much less the rest of nature, should exhibit?

The difference, both in concept and attitude, between seeking a single standard of excellence and valuing diversity is fundamental. The style of thinking in terms of some single standard of excellence is basic to much of the history of Western philosophy. One need only recall that Aristotle thought that there was one human essence, rationality, which created a standard by which all human activity could be assessed. As

Arthur Lovejoy points out, as late as the eighteenth century an integral part of the Enlightenment project was the belief that there was a single and universal standard of excellence, an ideal to which all should aspire. One monumental achievement of Romanticism was a reversal of this belief in a single standard, leading to the idea that not only are there in all aspects of human life diverse excellences, but that *"diversity itself is of the essence of excellence."*[26] Dethroning the image of one universal ideal spawned a vast and enlivening spectrum of aesthetic expression and is now a cultural basis for resisting the trends toward uniformity in the modern world.

Valuing human diversity also means leaving areas of the earth free from domination by industrial economy and culture. One should remember that the very idea of wilderness is essentially an outsider's construct. Most of what seems to us to be wilderness has been steadily occupied or traversed by indigenous peoples for eons. Preserving such areas from the sphere of industrialism is not only protecting wilderness, but also is preserving the cultures of indigenous peoples. Thus, the struggle for wilderness is both for biological and human diversity.

3. Humans have no right to reduce this richness and diversity except to satisfy vital needs.

The key point in this claim is the implied distinction between vital and other needs. This distinction is denied by the consumerism inherent in industrialism. To lose sight of it is to become trapped within an endlessly repeating cycle of deprivation and temporary satiation. Making the distinction opens the possibility of more enduring forms of happiness and joy. Of course, the distinction cannot be drawn precisely, since what is a vital need in one context may be a trivial want in another. There is a real difference between an Eskimo wearing the skin of a seal for warmth and wearing one for social status in an affluent society.

4. The flourishing of human life and cultures is compatible with a substantial decrease in human population. The flourishing of nonhuman life requires such a decrease.

Once recognition is given to other forms of life, then it is clear that we humans are too many already. We have already jostled many species out of existence, and the near future promises an expansion of such extinctions. The continuing increase in human numbers also condemns many humans to a life of suffering. Parents within industrial societies easily recognize that many children means slimmer life prospects for each, and voluntarily limit themselves to fewer children, hoping to give each a better life. So, too, we should collectively recognize that an increase in human numbers is not in the best interest of humans, much less the rest of life.

It is to the credit of the deep ecology that it clearly gives priority to human population as a problem and calls for a gradual decrease. This does not imply misanthropy or cruelty to presently existing humans. In fact, there is considerable evidence that the best way of moderating and then reversing the growth of human population is to find ways of providing a decent life for all.

5. Present human interference with the nonhuman world is excessive and the situation is rapidly worsening.

This directs attention to current trends and claims that current levels of interference with the rest of nature is excessive. There are at least two sorts of such interference that need to be addressed. One sort of interference is the destruction of existing areas of wilderness, such as old growth forests and rain forests. This is irreparable within any moderate time scale and is wrong. In fact, the guiding principle should probably be the continuation of biological history, creating large enough wilderness areas to allow for the continued speciation of plants and animals. This does not mean the elimination of indigenous peoples who have found ways of living within those ecosystems without destroying them.[27]

The other form of interference is based on particular forms of technology. Many forms of interacting with the rest of nature disrupt natural cycles far more than is necessary. For example, agricultural practices involving large-scale monocropping create expanding needs for fertilizer and pesticides, as crops diminish fertility and pests develop immunity to previous pesticides. Such practices interfere with ecosystems more than is necessary. Multicropping, integrated pest management, and a variety of organic farming techniques interfere less with natural cycles and can enhance fertility of soils.

Noting differences of degree of interference between various forms of technology also points to an important dimension of the population problem. Although most population growth is now projected to take place in the lesser developed countries, the populations in industrial countries have a far greater impact per person on the biosphere. The poor of lesser developed countries who scour hillsides for wood to cook their food certainly create serious problems, such as increase in flooding and deforestation. But industrial peoples driving automobiles generate large quantities of carbon dioxide each year. In thinking about such problems, it is essential to remember that industrial forms of life generally impact the biosphere much more profoundly than do those of the poor of the world.

To note that the situation is rapidly worsening understates the case.

6. Policies must therefore be changed. These policies affect basic economic, technological and ideological structures. The resulting state of affairs will be deeply different from the present.

The scope of the changes needed is great. Rethinking economy in terms of its role in sustaining human communities leads away from industrialism toward more satisfying forms of life.[28] The interconnectedness of economies, technologies, and ideologies makes the problem large, but the very same interconnectedness implies that real change in any of these areas may facilitate change in the others. Although it is hard to see the exact shapes of the new societies emerging after industrialism, it is clear that we must devise economies that do not addict us to growth.

7. The ideological change is mainly that of appreciating *life quality* rather than adhering to an increasingly higher standard of living. There will be a profound awareness of the difference between big and great.

This point is especially important for industrial peoples enmeshed within an ultimately unsatisfying consumerism. With a focus on quality, people can see that existing patterns of labor and consumption are not satisfying, but rather involve chronic dissatisfaction. Moving toward an appreciation of the *quality* of life, instead of quantities of things, leads to an *increase* in happiness, not a decrease. This is quite fundamental, since people are more apt to change when they experience change as improvement, rather than grudging submission to necessity. As long as environmentalism seems to require only denial and sacrifice, its political effectiveness will be lessened. As Bhikkhu Bodhi writes, "Unable to envisage any alternatives to the aims of industrial society . . . the basic presupposition at the root of the whole ecocrisis is allowed to stand unquestioned; namely, that the means to achieve human well-being lies in increased production and consumption."[29] Emphasis needs to be placed on the fact that the changes sought are an increase in the quality of life. Radical ecocentrism implies a more satisfactory way of living, an increase in vitality and joy.

8. Those who subscribe to the foregoing points have an obligation directly or indirectly to try to implement the necessary changes.

Although this is clear in claiming that we must begin to act, it is vague in not indicating *particular* priorities. At this point in history, priorities cannot be made more specific. No one now knows *exactly* what positive changes are necessary nor how they will come to pass. The problems with economic growth and the emptiness of consumerism are clear enough, but they do not show just what needs to be done now. People who accept the deep ecology platform will continue to disagree about what is most urgent, and there are many ways to attempt the needed changes. In the light of the value of diversity, such differences should be respected and not become occasions for sectarian squabble.

The platform, then, is a proposal for a set of general agreements among radical ecocentrists, a common ground for those who value *all* nature. Deep ecologists have, I think, done a valuable service in bringing such a platform to the fore. The time is late; the tasks are daunting—we who agree on the platform should get on with the project of education and social reconstruction.

Perhaps the most distinctive and important contribution of deep ecology to the prospect of radical change is its vision of a joyful alternative to consumerism. This seems paradoxical because deep ecologists have been the strongest critics of anthropocentrism, so much so that they have often been accused of misanthropy. Although some who accept the deep ecology platform may have a misanthropic streak, deep ecology is actually vitally concerned with humans realizing their best potential. Arne Naess remarks, near the beginning of his major work on deep ecology, that his "discussion of the environmental crisis is motivated by the unrealized potential human beings have for varied experience in and of nature: the crisis contributes or could contribute to open our minds to sources of meaningful life which have largely gone unnoticed or have been depreciated."[30] Even though Naess's ecosophy recommends that people transcend their isolation from the natural world and identify with the rest of nature, his view is, in some sense, centered on humans. The reasons for this apparent paradox is that deep ecology embodies a recommendation about how *humans* should live, and it recommends that they identify with all life, that they live nonanthropocentrically! "The change of consciousness referred to consists of a transition to a more egalitarian attitude to life and the unfolding of life on earth," writes Naess. "This transition opens the doors to a richer and more satisfying life for the species *Homo sapiens,* but not by focusing on *Homo sapiens.*"[31] Deep ecology's focus on helping us to become better, and its conviction that this is a path toward a more joyful existence, is an important and distinctive contribution toward any movement that would change society. This emphasis on an alternative to consumerism changes the fundamental message of radical ecocentrism from deprivation into one about a more satisfying way of being.

A second contribution of deep ecology platform is an emphasis on the critique of human needs. Certainly deep ecologists are in the company of many other social theorists when they distinguish between vital human needs and wants of lesser or trivial importance. One of the moral insights of social progressives is the evil of a society where some have much and others have so little. Although the rich and the poor each have unmet *needs,* there is a fundamental difference between the relatively trivial dissatisfactions of the rich and the absolute deprivation of the poor. This sense of injustice, a wider identification with the suffering of the downtrodden, was a strong element in the now dormant socialist project. As Paehlke put it, "With an emphasis on this perspective, environmentalists might restore the cutting edge to socialism, restoring a sense of the absolute perceptions of deprivation."[32]

A third contribution is deep ecology's focus on the process of identification. This is strategically critical in unraveling the knot of consumptive materialism. One of the driving forces of consumerism is the loss of traditional ways of forming one's identity and their replacement by acquiring self-identity through material possessions. Deep ecology emphasizes an alternative mode of creating one's identity through an expansion of identification. In focusing on the issue of personal identity and identification, it goes to the very core of one of the engines driving industrialism. An expansion of personal identification to *all* humans is the basis of a powerful rejection of consumerist impulses in a world of desperate unmet human need. It also is a strong basis for rejecting militarism. A further expansion of identification to some or all the rest of nature is an even more vigorous basis for rejecting consumerism and other social practices tied to the destruction of other forms of life. If one identifies with the perhaps never seen rain forest, a mahogany table, beautiful in texture, grain, and craftsmanship, becomes ugly and offensive as a part of the rain forest within which other peoples and a multitude of species once abided.

Deep ecology's emphasis on the *joyous* expansion of identification reveals other ways of being human, ways that carry an experientially based rejection of consumptive materialism. The message is not that we must give up some of what we want. Rather, the claim is that consumptive materialism could be rejected, and that is a *gain* in human well-being. The aim is a good quality of life, not material consumption. The dominance of economic ways of talking and thinking about happiness fosters the illusion that consumption and happiness are equivalent. The *experience* of an expansion of identification, along with critical reflection, shows that they are not. Such an expansion of identification is an increase in vitality and sensitivity.

It is worth noting, in this context, that the expansion of identification and the ensuing reduction of the urge to consume would be helpful in alleviating some of the suffering in the lesser developed countries. If one accepts the reasonable hypothesis that overconsumption and militarism are two of the fundamental causes of the degradation of the environment, then, as David Johns points out, deep ecology provides the most fundamental critique of each of these causes. The very concept of overconsumption changes when it is placed within the context of deep ecology. Within any human-centered social perspective, overconsumption "is primarily seen as a social relationship, a problem of distribution between the wealthy and the poor, a problem of economic ownership." On the other hand, when nonhuman nature is taken as part of the moral community and valued for its own unfolding, "then human consumption which disrupts it is wrong; it would constitute overconsumption."[33] Stemming the consumerist impulse in industrial countries would slow the transfer of wealth, both in the form of material and in human life as cheap labor, from the poor of the world to the industrial nations. If industrialism were to slow down and reverse itself, there would be much more economic and cultural space for lesser developed countries to find their own proper way of unfolding.

Finally, the first plank of the platform calls for the flourishing of all life, human and nonhuman. If the idea of letting *every thing* flourish is powerful when applied to nature, it is even more so applied to human societies—let *every* person flourish. This fundamental norm is continuous with the ideals of all progressive social movements, going beyond them by including nonhuman life. Implicit in this ideal is the goodness of each human developing to their fullest. It would be hard to overestimate the impact of this ideal of human development in progressive social change. It is at the very root of political democracy and calls for economic democracy. Socialism and anarchism stand resolutely for the right of each person to realize their best potential. Thus, what is wrong with capitalism? Would there be anything wrong with it if it were successful in bringing home the bacon for everyone? Yes. Capitalism promotes a systematic and deepening inequality, both economically and, more profoundly, in terms of human dignity. Karl Marx observed that the increase of wages for the worker is "nothing but *better payment for the slave,* and would not conquer either for the worker or for labour their human status and dignity."[34] Naess, too, notes the evils of economic class, noting that most of the people in industrial countries are a "global upper class" and that the core of class suppression is the repression "of life fulfillment potentials in relation to fellow beings."[35] Imperialism and colonialism promoted a systematic inequality among humans of differing countries and inequality within each of those countries. Racism promotes a systematic inequality of equals. Sexism promotes a relationship of domination and inequality between men and women. In each of these—capitalism, racism, and sexism—the victors are degraded in their victory, as they lose their full human potential in enacting the role of oppressor. So, too, with humanity and nature. The domination of nature presumes the moral irrelevance of the rest of nature, and this "victory" diminishes humans.

The real problem is the behemoth of industrialism ever expanding its grip around the globe, within the earth, and into the skies. The seeds of an effective and radical egocentrism are those who somehow awaken to the exhilaration of being human in harmony with the rest of nature. Some may choose to stand for the forests, and that is good. Others reach out to the oppressed of the world and build bridges between the poor within the industrial world and those at the periphery. This requires political organization and action—another essential path.

One can easily find grounds for despair, as they are all around, but it is important also to see the grounds for hope. The environmental movement has broadened and deepened with astonishing rapidity. The green movement is a significant presence in the national politics of many countries. Environmental groups supporting direct action, such as Earth First!, Sea Shepherd, and Greenpeace, often have significant support from the general public. Feminism, both in theory and in practice, has become an important force for social change, and ecological feminism will probably increase in importance within feminism.

It is hard to know, at this stage of the struggle, whether such movements can gain sufficient strength in numbers to force a reversal of the structure of industrialism. We really do not know how much time we have. We may be in a transitional epoch and not the closing hours of industrialism—no one knows. If there is time, then building an effective radical ecocentric movement founded on the desire for community, a rejection of social domination and sexual oppression, an empathy for other animals, and a love for all of nature may be possible. Perhaps such a movement can effectively challenge and restructure industrialism.

We recently have taken a few steps back from the nuclear abyss. Should demilitarism spread, as it can if citizens continue to press for a real peace, this will release massive social resources for social and ecological reconstruction. The cost of reforestation, stopping desertification, controlling and reversing population growth, developing energy efficiency and eventually getting off the use of fossil fuels, stopping the loss of rain forests, expanding wilderness, ending the human extinction of animal and plant species, protecting the ozone shield, dealing with climate change, and the many other tasks must somehow be funded. Since the world military budget is some $800 billion each year, the financial resources are there if we can demilitarize society. The point is not that it is easy but it is possible. The struggle is lifetimes long, and it is important to live in a way that enables one's spirit to flourish.

Humility, humor, and compassion are necessary to stay on the path. Mistakes are part of the way, and results are often ambiguous. While the search for purity is admirable, its attainment is not possible, and the results of action are uncertain. Such an understanding can sustain us through the hard times with a joy in existence and an appreciation of our fellow travelers, both the hawks and the field mice.

7

A Green Theory of Value

Robert E. Goodin

As rightful heirs to the 1960s counterculture, contemporary greens affect a certain studied looniness.[1] An American green once offered me the recipe for placenta soup, to be served at our newborn's naming ceremony. That sort of thing, together with hugging trees and communing with the Great Chain of Being, gives greens a bad name. It makes their views easily—in my view, all too easily—discountable when it comes to serious policy discussions.

That plays, in turn, into the hands of mainstream parties keen to marginalize greens. They want to treat them as just another quirky, single-issue interest group. Such groups inevitably have a point but, being monomaniacal, they inevitably make too much of it. Self-styled "responsible parties of government" say therefore that they may—indeed, that they must—borrow judiciously from single-interest agendas, taking on board some but certainly not all of what those single-issue groups say.

A prime case in point is the Australian government's recent consultation document titled *Ecologically Sustainable Development.*[2] Its title reveals what its text tries to obfuscate. The goal in view is fixed by the noun, "development." "Ecological sustainability" serves as a mere modifier, a mere side constraint on economic development, rather than as an end in itself. And if what we are seeking is as much economic development as ecological constraints will permit, then our aim is not really the preservation of the environment so much as its efficient destruction. The *conservation* here in view just amounts to "the saving of natural resources for later consumption."[3]

Resource economists confess that fact freely.[4] Politicians, naturally, have to be a bit more cagey. At many points, the text of that consultation document is at pains to deny that the Australian government intends any such thing. Be the government's ultimate intentions as they may, I think we can, nonetheless, see in that document a characteristic response on the part of mainstream parties to their new green challengers. They will always at least pretend to take their point. But they will invariably do so only in part, and quite possibly in ways counterproductive to the ends that greens hope to serve.

I think that the green agenda actually deserves more respect than is manifested by such piecemeal borrowing.[5] Setting flaky advice about personal lifestyles firmly to one side and fixing our focus instead on the greens's public policy demands more narrowly, we find there a coherence that is rare in party political manifestos.[6] All of the items on the green political agenda are arguably informed by a single moral vision—one and the same green theory of value—in a way those of other, more mainstream political parties certainly are not.[7]

If I am right in thinking so, then the green political agenda would form something more akin to an all or nothing package than we are ordinarily accustomed to seeing in party political appeals. It would be an all or nothing proposition, just because accepting the validity of any given theory of value for some purposes but not for others would be simply incoherent. A theory of The Good holds true regardless of context. We must give the same considerations equal weight in all circumstances in which they are equally implicated. Theories of The Good do not flicker on and off like some faulty light switch.[8]

Such is the practical point of the present exercise—to force mainstream parties to face up to some pretty uncomfortable environmental choices and to face them squarely rather than picking and choosing proposals just as they please off the larger green agenda. I make no apologies for that frankly political aim, nor would I care to disguise it.

Still, there is only so much that can be done within the confines of a single essay.[9] So, having given fair notice of the larger purposes to which this analysis will eventually be put, I shall be concentrating here more narrowly on the philosophical preliminaries that are so crucial to the success of that larger project.

Theories of Value

Let us start, then, with the general notion of a theory of value or, in philosophically more standard terminology, a theory of The Good. Such a theory should tell us both *what* is to be valued and *why*. It should tell us which things are good and which are not, and in respect of what attributes those things are supposed to be good.

A theory of The Good is not necessarily all there is to moral evaluation, of course. Notions of The Right as well as of The Good have a role to play.[10] But the theory that I shall be discussing is, undeniably, one particular sort of theory of The Good. And how important a component of overall morality it will be therefore depends, at least in part, on how important you think considerations of The Good ought to be in the final moral mix more generally.

There seems little danger that they will be utterly without a role, though. Virtually no one—not even the fiercest critic of consequentialism—really would want to assert that any action is right or wrong, literally *whatever* the consequences. Virtually everyone concedes a place in moral evaluation to considerations of The Good and to the calculations of consequences that derive from them.[11]

Where philosophers talk of a theory of The Good, economists tend to talk instead of a theory of value. I take those terms to be absolutely equivalent, or nearly enough so for present purposes. Where the one talks about what is good and why, the other talks about what is valuable and why. It is a distinction without a difference, so far as we are here concerned.[12]

Or, rather, the difference is a purely practical one. Economists simply seem to feel more comfortable with—and consequently more threatened by—arguments couched in terms of value than in terms of The Good.[13] And, of course, connecting with the discourse of economists is crucial in environmental contexts.

It is economists who are, intellectually, the most direct targets of green political movements.[14] The dominance of a particular and peculiarly economic theory of value is, green theorists would say, what leads us to overvalue material prosperity and to undervalue all that is sacrificed in pursuit of it. So, if talking about a theory of value rather than a theory of The Good helps us join issue more directly with economists, then little will be lost and much gained by transposing our argument into those terms.

A Taxonomy of Theories of Value

Approaching the problem of The Good from this vaguely economistic angle, there are essentially three distinct bases on which we might ground a theory of value—consumer satisfaction, labor inputs, or natural resource inputs.[15] These options correspond, roughly, to capitalist theory of value, a Marxist theory of value, and a green theory of value, respectively.

Those latter labels are adopted purely for expository convenience, and I should warn at the outset that they may be misleading. In particular, they may make the options to which they refer seem more mutually exclusive than they actually are. In the end, we may want to—in the end, we may have to—concoct some mixed theory of value drawing upon all of these theories, and perhaps more besides. Even if we do end up mixing and matching the theories, though, it is nonetheless important to see clearly from the start the character of each of the distinct components that are being intermixed.

First, then, we have the capitalist—or, if you prefer, neoclassical welfare economic—theory of value. This is essentially a consumer-based theory. It traces the value of things to values which people derive in the course of partaking of them.

There are myriad variations on that basic theme. Some crudely link value to subjective mental states, like happiness. That is the Benthamite version. Others link it, less crudely, to satisfaction of subjectively felt desires where there is no assumption that want satisfaction necessarily equates with happiness. Others link it, less crudely still, to the capacity of something to satisfy desires which are, or will be, or otherwise would be subjectively felt.[16]

There are important differences between all these alternative ways of filling out the basic logic of that consumer-based theory of value, of course. Much philosophical ink has been spilt debating their relative merits. Happily, we can afford to skirt those issues here, though, since our present concern is simply with the common theoretical core that all of those variations share. At root, all are consumer-based theories of value—that category that forms our first broad class of value theories.

A second broad class is the Marxist—or, if you prefer, Ricardian— theory of value. This is a *producer-based* theory. Its distinctive feature is that it traces the value of things to values that people impart to these things in the course of producing them.

In principle, these values might derive from any number of different attributes displayed by producers or by their productive activities. In practice, though, this sort of theory almost always amounts to a labor theory of value. Certainly, that is its most familiar form, anyway, both in its Marxian and in its more general Ricardian-cum-Lockean forms.

Here again, there are myriad variations on the basic theme. The root idea is that value of an object corresponds to the amount of labor time invested in producing it. But more subtle versions of the theory might differentiate between skilled and unskilled labor time, between the amount of time actually spent producing a thing and that which is socially necessary to produce it and so on.[17] Again, though, the many and subtle variations should not blind us to what all of them have in common: These theories are, at root, all producer-based theories of value.

Third, and nowadays far less familiar, is the third class of value theories that I associate with the green theory of value. This is a natural resource-based theory of value. Its distinctive feature is that it links the value of things to some naturally occurring property or properties of the objects themselves.

There are, once again, countless variations on this basic theme, depending upon what exactly it is about naturally occurring properties of objects that is said to give them value. Some variations on this theme point out, disingenuously I think, to objective attributes of objects themselves—the hardness of diamonds, and such like.[18] Another variation on this theme, one which is perhaps historically the most famous, is the physiocrats's claim that land alone has the capacity for producing value.[19]

The green answer that I shall be sketching later in this chapter constitutes yet one more way of filling out the same basic formula. I happen to think that the green formulation is the most satisfactory way of filling out a natural resource–based theory of value at this point. But I should emphasize at the outset that it is only one among many possible ways of explicating what exactly it is about the naturally occurring properties of things that gives them value.

In any case, it ought to be tolerably clear by now how a natural resource–based theory of value, of which the green theory of value is an instance, is to be distinguished from the others. It differs from producer-based theories of value insofar as it insists that value imparting properties are natural, rather than being somehow artifacts of human activities. And it differs from consumer-based theories of value insofar as it insists that value imparting qualities somehow inhere in the objects themselves, rather than in any mental states (actual or hypothetical, now or later) of the people who partake of those objects.

Of course, the hard-line proponent of each sort of value theory will naturally try to discredit the others or reduce them to his own preferred analysis.[20] Such refutations and reductions may work well, or they may work badly. Or, more likely, they may succeed but only partially—thus forcing us to tell a rather more nuanced story about value.[21]

I do not want—or need—to contend that the particular theory of value that I am investigating here is correct utterly to the exclusion of all others. I merely shall be insisting that it has a legitimate place (alongside others, perhaps) in any larger, mixed theory of value.

Natural Values

Taxonomies are not arguments. The taxonomy just produced is even less of one than most. It has merely served to situate the green theory of value in relation to other, more familiar ones. The green theory of value is a particular instantiation of the "natural resource-based theory of value," tracing the value of a thing to some attribute of the natural resources comprising it rather than to any facts about the people who have produced or will consume it.

Nothing I have said so far specifies what exactly it is about natural resources that makes them valuable. There are many ways of filling out the more general theory at that point. According to the distinctively green variant, what it is that makes natural resources valuable is their very naturalness. That is to say, what imparts value to them is not any physical attributes or properties that they might display. Rather, it is the simple fact that they have a history of having been created by natural processes, rather than by artificial human ones.[22]

History and Process As Sources of Value

The green theory of value thus shows itself to be an instantiation of yet another pair of other more general theories of value—a process-based theory of value on one hand and a history-based theory of value on the other.[23]

Such theories tend to suffer guilt through their association, in recent social philosophy, with Robert Nozick's historical entitlement theory of justice.[24] For Nozick, a distribution is just if everything within it was originally acquired justly by its first owner and was subsequently transferred justly from each owner to the next.

That is, at least potentially, a deeply conservative theory of justice. Many take strong exception to it. Those who do often let their repugnance for Nozick's conclusions spill over to his general methodology as well. But, of course, that is a mistake. While Nozick's theory of justice certainly is one example of a process-based, history-based ethical theory, his is hardly the only way of fleshing out such a theory. Those who are appalled by the use to which Nozick puts such methods ought not necessarily be put off by that whole larger class of theories in consequence.

In light of those potentially unfortunate associations, then, it is particularly important to recall that in various other connections it seems perfectly familiar, natural, and plausible to suppose that process-based and history-based considerations are indeed crucial in fixing the value of things. Consider, for a first example, the role of process-based considerations in imparting legitimacy to the outcomes of political deliberations. Decisions devoid of substantive merit (and, indeed, brimming with substantive defects) are standardly reckoned to be nonetheless worthy of respect, just so long as they have arisen through the workings of the democratic process. Similarly, administrative actions are typically deemed socially acceptable, to a surprisingly large extent regardless of their substantive merits or demerits, just so long as the canons of due process have been respected in reaching them.[25] In both connections, the only reason we prefer outcomes with less value but the right history is, presumably, that we attach some *independent* value to the process producing those outcomes.

For another very different example, consider a problem from aesthetics. What value ought we to attach to fakes, forgeries, replicas, reproductions, and restorations? The answer is easy, the explanation less so. Of course, we standardly suppose that fakes, forgeries, and so on are less valuable—not merely contingently but necessarily less valuable— than the originals which they replicate. But why?

Surely it is not just a matter of copies being bad copies. For we can imagine (even if we can never make) an absolutely perfect copy, one that reproduced all the observable features of the original absolutely perfectly. I think that most of us would still suppose that even a perfect replica of the *Pieta* would be less valuable than the masterpiece that sits in St. Peter's.

Supposing that it really is a perfect replica, though, there can be none of the standard aesthetic grounds underlying that judgment. All of the replica's observable features—its color, texture, line, shape, and so on— are *ex hypothesi* identical to those of the original. So if the replica is less valuable, that can only be so on account of its history, for *ex hypothesi* that is the only respect in which it differs from the original.

The one particularly potent value impairing feature of the Vatican *Pieta* which no other *Pieta* can ever hope to replicate is, of course, the fact that it was created by the hand of Michaelangelo. Similarly, the *Mona Lisa* has the peculiar value it does because of the history of who painted it. If the copy hanging in the Louvre turned out to be a Napoleonic-era forgery, the image would remain the same, but the significance of the painting would nonetheless have altered. It would have lost the value it once had for us as a manifestation of Leonardo's genius.[26]

In aesthetics and in politics, then, history and process impart value. An original was created by a master's hand—and necessarily so, for that is what it means to be an original. The fake, forgery, or replica was not—and necessarily so, for that is what it means to be a fake, forgery, or replica. And it is necessarily having that history that, in turn, appears to be crucial in making the one sort of object necessarily more valuable than the other.[27]

Naturalness As a Source of Value

All of that is merely by way of working up some intuitions for the plausibility—and, more to the point, undermining intuitions about the implausibility—of attaching value to a thing by virtue of the history of the process by which it has come about. Nozick notwithstanding, there is nothing outrageous about that as a general proposition about values.

That said, however, the question remains why we should attach special value to the particular sort of history which greens identify as a source of value. What is so especially valuable about something having come about through natural rather than through artificial human processes? In the words of one memorable title, "What's Wrong with Plastic Trees?"[28]

We might make a start on this question by assimilating it to the problem of fakes and forgeries. The title just mentioned refers to events that are real, not merely feared or fantasized. When the city fathers discovered that real trees could no longer survive the polluted air of the Los Angeles freeways, they tried planting plastic ones alongside them instead. When they found that those plastic trees kept being chopped down, they professed genuine surprise?[29] If so, I suspect they were just about the only ones to be surprised, though.

Most of us, confronting schemes involving the destruction of some especially unique bit of the natural landscape, would surely leap almost automatically to protest its loss. But the sponsors of such schemes have a response that comes almost as automatically. As Doug Anthony—then deputy prime minister of Australia—remarked apropos of schemes for sand mining on Fraser Island, such protests would subside if only we would "become more informed and more enlightened as to what reclamation work is being carried out by mining companies nowadays."[30]

So let us imagine the best-case scenario. Let us suppose—*per impossible*, perhaps—that the developers can offer an ironclad, legally binding promise to recreate the landscape exactly as it was, once they have finished. Let us suppose that they provide detailed plans for how they propose to go about doing so. Let us suppose that we find those plans absolutely convincing. In short, let us suppose that we have no doubt whatsoever that the landscape will indeed look just the same after they have finished as it did before they began.

Still, I think, we would be inclined to object to the proposal. Even if we are convinced that the landscape will *look* the same, it will not really *be* the same. Previously, it has been the work of nature. Afterwards, it will have become the work of humanity. However talented restorationists the developers' landscape architects might be, the one thing that they cannot possibly replicate is history. They might be able to restore something perfectly in every other respect, but the very act of restoration itself necessarily and irrevocably alters a thing's history.

Just as a particularly talented forger might replicate the *Mona Lisa* perfectly, so too might particularly skilled landscape architects replicate nature perfectly. But that amounts to faking nature.[31] Fakes might look the same as the originals, but they cannot possibly be the same, for they have different histories and different origins. And insofar as the history and origins of the original are what matter to us, neither is it possible for those fakes to have the same value for us.

Putting the point in terms of fakery rather begs the question, of course. By pretending to be something that they are not, fakes necessarily concede their own inferiority. The things that they pretend to be somehow must be superior to what they actually are, or else there simply would be no point in the pretense.

But it is not just the element of fraud that makes fakes, forgeries, and counterfeits less valuable. The same is true (to a lesser but nonetheless significant extent) of restorations, reproductions, and replicas, where the element of fraud is absent. It is the very act of copying something that, in the end, crucially concedes the superiority of what is copied.

What is the point of copying if you could have done better by yourself starting from scratch?

The developers in our hypothetical example thus can ill afford to accept faking nature as a description of what they propose. That much was probably obvious from the start. The more surprising implication of the observation just offered is that it is not merely the pejorative description which the developers must shun. If they are to avoid conceding the necessary inferiority of the landscape they will leave, as compared to what they have destroyed, they must not even try to recreate the original. They must instead assert that they will create something different from and better than—or, anyway, of a worth that is incomparable to that of—the natural landscape which their handiwork will replace.

Landscape architects themselves may well suffer just such hubris. They may well regard that claim, however immodest, as being nonetheless perfectly true. Still, few firms proposing to despoil the natural environment would be willing to take any such stance publicly. Of course, that does not necessarily mean that they think it is untrue. They might merely regard it as being impolitic to say so. But even for such a claim to be impolitic, it must necessarily be the case that it is seen as untrue—indeed, untrue to the point of outrage—in the eyes of the population at large.

Why should that be so? Ultimately, I think we are driven to say that what is especially valuable about the products of natural processes is that they are products of something larger than ourselves.[32] No questions, I hope, are being begged by the word "larger." That is the standard way of putting the point, to be sure; but for my purposes, it would do equally well to say that the processes in question are things "outside" of ourselves. The point is merely that such natural processes, and our relation to them, serve to fix our place in the external world.[33] In Margaret Manion's phrase, they serve to "locate the self."

To say they "give meaning to our lives" would be to skate dangerously near thin theological ice. I wish to remain explicitly agnostic as regards any metaphysical load that such arguments might be asked to bear.[34] There may or may not be any *meaning* or *purpose* underlying the larger natural order. Nonetheless, there is undeniably an order to nature, operating independently of us—and increasingly, in spite of us. Furthermore, people undeniably derive deep satisfaction from seeing their lives set in some such larger context.

How all of this would impinge upon arguments for respecting nature should be clear enough. Suppose that what people value about nature's creation is that it was produced by processes larger than (or merely outside of) human actions. Then an object loses that value-imparting property once it has been restored, replicated, or recreated through human interventions.

Restoration still may be preferable to the alternatives. Restoring as best we can a once "wild and scenic river" to its former glory may well be better than devising a new and wholly artificial watercourse. Reclaiming waste land to create a new forest, rather similar to the old one that used to stand there, might be better (especially after several decades of letting nature take its course) than planting a wholly artificial ornamental garden on the site. Letting clear-cut lands revegetate might be better than letting cattle or sheep continue to graze them to the ground. Nonetheless, a restored or even a seminaturally regenerated bit of nature is, on this green theory of value, necessarily not as valuable as something that has been literally "untouched by human hands."

The Place of Humanity in Nature

Two related sets of objections can easily be anticipated at this point. Because they are so easily anticipatable and so substantively important, it is worth sketching in advance my general response to each. Far from being a purely negative exercise of parrying attacks, though, responding to these challenges actually enables me to extend my own positive analysis in some practically important directions.

Both of the objections I have in view here pertain to the larger question of the place of humanity in nature. The second objection, which I shall address shortly, queries the artificiality of any separation between humanity and nature. People are a part of nature, too, this argument insists—and, I think, rightly so. I think that I can concede that point and still sustain all the arguments that I really want to be making here. Before addressing that issue, though, let me consider an even more predictable complaint coming from self-styled deep ecologists.

Values and Valuers

The most stinging form that that objection might take would be to assert that, on the account of it just given, the green theory of value would reduce right back to the neoclassical welfare economic one. That complaint is all the more stinging for being partially true. Both the neoclassical welfare economic theory and the green theory of value as I have presented it link the value of nature to the satisfaction that consumers derive from it, in one way or another.

But when I say that people derive deep satisfaction from seeing their lives being set in some larger context, "deep" satisfaction ought not be read simply as "great" satisfaction. The point of calling it deep is that all other sorts of satisfaction are somehow parasitic upon this sort, in turn. People must be able to see some sense or value in their own lives if they are to be able to see sense or value in any other more specific project they might pursue as part of their own larger life plans. And that, in turn, presupposes that their lives form part of something outside of themselves, individually or collectively.

Even if it does not reduce back to the neoclassical welfare economic theory of value, though, that formulation still seems to come down decisively on the shallow side of the deep ecology debate. The question at the center of that dispute, recall, is whether natural objects have value in and of themselves or whether they have value in relation to people and their purposes.[35]

The green theory of value, on my analysis of it, would seem to deny the former and affirm the latter. It traces the value of nature to its value to human beings and the place it occupies in their lives. That shallowness runs contrary to the self-conception of most greens—certainly, at least, to the self-conceptions of the most vociferous and dedicated among them, who most assuredly see themselves as the deepest of deep ecologists.[36]

Let us not allow the terms of this debate to polarize too sharply too quickly, though. Most of all, let us not allow the debate to be decided by cheap rhetorical tricks. Surely, the naïve might say, anyone who genuinely cares about the environment should be a deep ecologist. Surely *shallow* ecologists are simply lacking in moral fibre; they are just insufficiently committed to the cause. All of that might seem to follow straightforwardly from the sheer meaning of the terms "shallow" and "deep," respectively. Or at least so greens suppose, I suspect, in signing so unanimously and so firmly onto the principles of deep ecology.

But if that is all there is to the argument, then it is an argument that works through persuasive definitions alone. Were the description of each respective position actually warranted, then the conclusion that true greens should shun shallow ecology would indeed follow straightforwardly. After all, who would embrace a shallow view of any subject one cares about, when a deeper view is available?[37]

The question, though, is whether or not the description really is warranted. Implicit in the shallow/deep dichotomy is, in effect, an assertion that the deeper view of the matter contains all the truths of the shallower view, plus some additional ones as well. The truth of the matter is, of course, otherwise. The shallow view is in no sense a proper subset of the deep one. Rather, the two are simply different views. Which is the right view is, therefore, a genuinely open question. And I see no reason in principle why greens themselves, having overcome the prejudicially loaded language, should not be prepared to consider shallower versions of the deep ecology creed.

I have cast that phrase in comparative terms quite deliberately. In assessing these issues, it is important to realize that, here as elsewhere, there are a great many gradations of shallowness and depth. The deepest ecology, perhaps, would be one which claims that things have value quite independently of the existence of any conscious valuers. Thus, the deepest ecologists would say, it would be wrong for the last man left on earth to push the button to destroy all nonhuman creation as he was himself about to expire.[38] Conversely, the shallowest ecologist—an economist perhaps—would say that things can have value only in relation to human uses, and things should be saved (if at all) only for possible subsequent human use. In between those extremes a variety of intermediate positions are possible.

The green theory of value that I have been advancing here is one such halfway house. It does indeed entail the proposition that things can only have value in relation to us, but that is very different from the proposition, urged by the shallowest ecologist-cum-economist, that things can only have value to us or for us.[39] Saying that things can have value only in relation to us is very different from saying that the value of nature reduces purely to human interests.[40]

The proposition I am advancing asserts that: (1) values presuppose valuers, that valuing presupposes consciousness; and perhaps slightly more tendentiously, (2) human beings are the only beings on Earth with a sufficiently sophisticated consciousness for this purpose. That being so, it is necessarily the case that human beings figure essentially in deriving value from nature. But to say that The Good of nature can be realized only through interactions with human consciousness is not to say that nature is good merely because it is, in some crassly material way or even in some deeply spiritual way, good for the human beings involved.[41]

So much for distinguishing my view from that of the shallowest ecologist. Now, let me suggest more positively how my view might be regarded as at least moderately deep. Contrary to the claims of the most shallow ecologists, it is not my view that values are all in people's heads. The existence of people, as valuers, may be crucial in imparting value. But there is some feature of nature existing independently of human beings that is crucial in this process, also. Just as you cannot reduce the value of nature wholly to natural values (as the deepest ecologists might attempt), neither can you reduce the value of nature wholly to human values (as the shallowest ecologists would wish). There are two separate and quite independent factors at work here.

On my analysis, natural objects have certain value imparting characteristics. They actually create value when—only when—in the presence of (human) consciousness. But the characteristic of nature that, on my analysis, is crucial in imparting value is the characteristic of its "being part of something larger than or outside of ourselves." That characteristic, by definition, must necessarily be separate from and independent of humanity. Hence, those value imparting properties (if not the values themselves) exist independently of humanity. That, I submit, is sufficient to qualify mine at least a moderately deep ecology.

Humanity As Part of Nature

So much for the first easily anticipatable objection to my analysis of the green theory of value. Let us now consider a second objection, still very much a variation on the general theme of the place of humanity in nature.

One way of describing the green theory of value which I have been advancing is to say—as I have myself been saying, as a kind of convenient shorthand—that it attaches special value to those parts of natural creation that have been untouched by human hands. But human hands, it might reasonably be objected, are part of the natural order, too. When someone insists that some bit of the landscape should be untouched by human hands, that is not to insist that nature be kept separate from something unnatural. Rather, it is to insist that one part of nature be kept separate from another.

The problem, notice, is not the relatively trivial one of how definitionally to distinguish humanity from nature. We might easily enough follow John Stuart Mill carving out a sense of nature according to which the term would refer "only to what takes place without the agency, or without the voluntary and intentional agency, of man."[42]

The challenge is not to draw some such distinction between the results of human and of nonhuman (stipulatively natural) processes. The challenge is instead to justify attaching any moral importance to the distinction, thus drawn. According to the green theory, it is the naturalness of the process that imparts value. But if so, then why is the sort of voluntary, intentional agency associated with processes of human nature any less natural—or hence valuable—than other aspects of the natural order?

Only those with a very strong sense of humanity's very special place in the order of creation could fail to feel the force of this objection. Yet, the objection, if allowed free rein, might have most unwelcome consequences. If "human nature cannot help conforming to Nature," as Mill says, "then everything we do is part of nature . . . in that primary sense," as one noted contemporary philosopher has inferred.[43] The upshot would be to license wanton human destruction of (other parts of) the natural environment, on the grounds that anything that humans do is natural, too. That, clearly, cannot be right. Clearly, I think we ought to be seeking some middle ground in this dispute.

One form this middle ground might take is to say that if we respect and value the products of natural creation, then we ought to take steps to protect that natural creation from destruction—even by natural forces. We should, on that account, dam the Colorado River above the Grand Canyon so that it does not undo through future flooding all the wonderful work that it has done through past erosion. We should artificially reinforce the lip of Niagara Falls so that the Niagara River does not eat away at the perfect horseshoe falls that its cascading waters have created through past erosion.[44]

That line is not altogether appealing, though. For one thing, it attaches evaluative significance to a distinction between creation and destruction in a way that seems wholly unwarranted, even within its own theoretical terms.[45] On the green theory of value, what imparts value to an outcome is the naturalness of the historical process through which it has come about. On that account, two outcomes that have come about through equally natural processes ought to be equally valuable. There seems no room, within that model, for making further distinctions between outcomes that are constructive or destructive, between ones that result in some object's coming into existence or ones that result in some object's disappearing or disintegrating or increasing in entropy.

In an unjustifiably neglected essay on "Nature," John Stuart Mill poses the problem for us in an unusually stark form. Either humans are part of nature, too—in which case the results of human interventions are as natural as the state of things before humans intervened—or else whatever humans do to nature necessarily counts (from the human perspective, at least) as an improvement upon nature. Mill's own words on the subject are worth quoting at length:

> If the natural course of things were perfectly right and satisfactory, to act at all [to improve upon nature] would be gratuitous meddling. . . . [But] everybody professes to admire many great triumphs of Art over Nature: the junction by bridges of shores which Nature has made separate, the draining of Nature's marshes . . . the dragging to light of what she has buried at immense depths in the earth; the turn away of her thunderbolts of lightening by lightening rods, of her inundations by embankments, of her ocean by breakwaters. But to commend these and similar feats, is to acknowledge that the ways of Nature are to be conquered, not obeyed. . . . All praise of Civilization, or Art, or Contrivance, is so much dispraise of Nature; an admission of imperfection, which it is man's business, and merit, to be always endeavoring to correct or mitigate.[46]

Now, I suspect that the automatic first response of greens, or of anyone else, to Mill's dilemma would be to deny its second premise. There is no reason to believe that every human intervention improves the world. There is not even any compelling reason—in logic, still less in recent experience—to suppose that all human interventions taken together make for a better world than would have existed in the absence of any such interventions. Nor can we even be confident that any given intervention will have had consequences that are on balance beneficial when all is said and done, given the various knock-on effects that any action will inevitably have into the distant future.

Thus, we can easily enough avoid being impaled on the horns of Mill's dilemma by pointing out that there is a third possibility Mill has missed. That amounts to admitting that human interventions are not natural—but then going on to point out that contrary to Mill's supposition, being nonnatural does not necessarily ensure that they will constitute improvements on nature, either.

That argument is true and important. And it is, in itself, more than enough to defuse Mill's dilemma. But there is another way of evading Mill's dilemma that is even more in keeping with the green theory of value that I have been developing here. Where the reply just given queries the second of Mill's premises, this alternative reply queries the first.

Greens might say that humans are part of nature. But, greens might go on to point out that not everything human beings do—not all forms of human society, not all forms of human activity—are equally natural. Some may be more natural than others. And if so, then some forms of human society and human activity would actually be more valuable than others, purely on the basis of a green theory of value that assigns more value to the natural over the artificial.

That is the version of the argument that I want to explore here at more length. It is important to recognize that humanity is part of nature and that human interventions are natural, too. But surely it is wrong to leap from that to treating all human interventions as if they were equally natural. We want to make—and, if I am right about it, the green theory of value allows us to make—some important distinctions between different modes of human intervention.

As a start, let us consider a problem safely far from home: English hedgerows. Groups like the Council for the Protection of Rural England are much exercised to prevent hedgerows from being plowed under to merge small fields and make them more amenable to modern, mechanized farming methods. But those hedgerows, like many of the other aspects of the natural environment that conservationists most cherish, are not, in fact, purely the work of (nonhuman) natural forces.

The thing to notice, in the context of the present argument, is that that intrinsically valuable aspect of the countryside is in no sense a natural part of the countryside. Hedgerows are human artifacts—not only in the weaker sense of being the residual by-products of where humans have chosen to plow and where not to plow, but also in the stronger sense of being quite deliberate, intentional human creations. Hedgerows and the peculiar habitats associated with them simply did not exist before the humans got to work. They were created, intentionally, as part of a deliberate policy of clearing the primordial forests and of carving up and fencing in the medieval commons. So what hedgerow conservationists today are wanting to preserve as a quintessential part of the English environment is not the product of nature but rather of past phases of English society.

The same obviously can be said in trumps for various other aspects of English villages—ancient churches, old houses, and such—that conservationists would also want to preserve. They might not phrase those demands in terms of "protecting the environment" perhaps (although the phrase *built environment* is indeed in common currency, among these groups as much as among center-city architects). But the arguments given for preservation of the surrounding hedgerows are obviously of a cloth with the arguments given for preservation of the village green and surrounding structures.

Ancient monuments of that sort obviously can qualify for protection on account of the historical value. They might qualify for protection on account of their ethnographic value, as representative of dead or dying cultures. The question before us is to what extent can they qualify for protection on account of value derived from their being part of nature, somehow construed.

These things were all shaped by human hands rather than natural forces, to be sure. So they do not, on the face of things, qualify for the strong sort of special status described by the green theory of value above. People cannot set their lives in the context of something larger than themselves, if that context is merely one which they have themselves created.

That argument might move a little too fast, though, in sliding between individual and group levels of analysis. If the issue is merely one of setting your own life in the context of something larger than yourself, then setting it in the context of any history larger than your own personal history can conceivably qualify. The history of your group—your race, club, nation, or species—could count.[47] Hence things that have value on account of their (purely human) history might well derive that value from a source *akin* to, if not strictly identical to, that imparting value to naturally occurring objects in the nonhuman world.

There is, then, a case to be made for the conservation of things in general on account of their history, whether human or natural. That provides an argument that is both intellectually important and politically powerful, for the preservation of ancient monuments and historical landmarks.[48] I do not want to say anything here to undermine that case. Rather, I want to supplement it with yet another.[49]

The distinction that will prove crucial for this further argument is between forms of human society in which people live broadly in harmony with nature and ones which attempt to impose upon and tyrannize over nature.[50] An example of the former is the human-scale, close to the land culture of the medieval English cultivator, as represented by the English village, its church, cottages, manor house, and hedgerows. An example of the latter is Los Angeles: a megalopolis of several million souls, so inappropriately sited on such a semiarid plain that it can provide its citizens with adequate water only by piping it in from hundreds of miles away (as Milbrath discusses above).[51]

The temptation at this point is, of course, to say that the one mode of life is simply more natural than the other, and on the green theory more valuable in consequence. In attempting to give the flavor of this response to Mill's challenge, I have as a kind of shorthand been speaking this way myself. But in the end, I think a slightly more nuanced response rally is going to be required.

Certainly English village life requires less—though, in the end, nonetheless considerable—human intervention into various natural processes in order to sustain it. But if humanity is to be regarded as part of nature, then there can be no grounds for disparaging as artificial the interventions required to sustain civilization (if it can be called that) in Los Angeles. Human interventions are required, to be sure: The natural rainfall, river flow, and water table are not adequate to meet the demands of the population now resident there. But, on this analysis, there is nothing artificial about such human interventions. They are part of nature, too.

What we still can say, I think, is this. People who live more in harmony with nature—as in traditional English villages, rather than postmodern Los Angeles—are living to a greater extent in a context that is outside of themselves, individually and collectively. Even those of us who merely visit them from time to time are reminded by the existence of such places of that larger context in which we might see, if not actually live, our own lives. Places and peoples embodying such down to earth lifestyles are well worth preserving and conserving (or creating or recreating, if lost), as a means of providing everyone, whether directly party to them or not, this larger perspective on their own lives.

All that can be maintained without claiming that St. Mary Mede is more natural than Los Angeles or that hedgerows are more natural than freeways. What is at issue is not the naturalness of their creation, since humanity is part of nature and its creations are therefore natural, too. What is at issue instead, on this account, is the modesty of the creation. It is not that, in the one case, nature is "in better balance."[52] It is rather that, in the one case, humanity does not ride roughshod over other parts of nature. And that allows humanity to derive satisfaction from reflection upon its larger setting, in a way that it cannot were that larger setting more exclusively of its own creation.

Saying that the small-scale English village is more in harmony with nature is simply to say that it represents a form of life that is better, from the green perspective sketched here, than a postmodern megalopolis which is dramatically not in harmony with nature. But saying "better" is, of course, very different from "best." If our choice is between St. Mary Mede or Los Angeles, then the former is clearly the option to be preferred. And that is typically the form in which the choice is presented to us, of course. It should go without saying, though, that there is nothing in this argument to suggest that if faced with a choice between preserving pristine nature and tearing it down to build even the most harmonious small-scale village we should prefer the former to the latter option in that pair.

Conclusion

That last set of propositions, though developed by reference to safely distant examples, have more than passing relevance for environmental debates. Up to this point, I have intentionally cast them in European terms, in part to remain faithful to these debates themselves, and in part to avoid raising local hackles prematurely.

In closing, though, let me apply those propositions to the Australian case. To do this, recall the tale of the great debate over the damming of the Franklin River. Environmentalists cherished that part of the Tasmanian rain forest as genuine wilderness—a primordial part of the Australian landscape untouched by human hands. But it turned out that the best way to protect that wilderness was to produce evidence of very early human habitation there.

Where prehistorians produced such evidence, their findings were greeted with considerable ambivalence among members of the Wilderness Society. At one and the same time, those environmentalists recognized the pragmatic importance of demonstrating human habitation on the site—but they also wished that it were not so. There was a side of them that said that, insofar as the site really is not pristine nature after all, to that extent it is not so very much worth preserving.

I suspect that there is probably a similar side to almost every environmentalist. Most, I suspect, would be tempted to equate "unspoiled nature" with "that part of nature that literally has been untouched by human hands."

The moral of this Franklin Dam story is not merely that insisting on that would be to set the standard too high, that there virtually is nowhere about which we can say that with any confidence. More important, to insist on that would be to set the standard unnecessarily high. If what we value about nature is that it allows us to see our own lives in some larger context, then we need not demand that that nature literally be untouched by human hands. We need demand merely that it be touched only lightly or, if you prefer, lovingly by them.

Some cultures, including earlier periods of our own culture, manage to live in harmony with nature rather than try to dominate it and bend it and subordinate it to their will. Those cultures still shape nature, in various ways, through their interactions with it. But they do so respectfully, and in ways that allow nature to retain some real independence from humanity. And that, in turn, allows nature to retain its valued role for us.

This conclusion is particularly important in a setting—like Australia —where so much of the case for environmental preservation is couched in terms of respect for the attitudes toward the land held by the original aboriginal inhabitants and their contemporary heirs. Suppose, for the sake of argument, that there is not an inch of the continent that is without contact with and meaning for the original Australians.[53] That would come as desperately bad news to environmental purists, who would infer from that fact that there is not an inch of the continent where nature is pristine and untouched by human hands. But recalling the attitude that the original Australians took toward the land that they knew so well, there is no need to see the land as having been somehow contaminated by their touch—in a way it may well have been by the hands of more domineering subsequent settlers.[54]

8

On Reconciling Progressivism and Environmentalism

Michael E. Zimmerman

Ever since heady speculation about the practical power of early modern science led European savants to renovate the ideal of historical progress, that ideal has faced resistance from groups who have felt threatened by such progress, and has undergone crises stemming from unexpectedly untoward consequences of attempts to make political and economic progress. Especially since the 1960s, many people have asked whether the modern ideal of progress retains validity when confronted with ecological problems that may undermine the crucial progressive goal of overcoming scarcity.[1] The environmental crisis has generated such questions as: Is an arguably finite planetary ecosystem compatible with the capitalist and socialist goal of using instrumental rationality to produce an infinitely expanding quantity of material goods? Will "ecological scarcity" finally block humankind's efforts to overcome material scarcity? Must freedom from want be purchased at the expense of ecological stability? Can democratic societies long survive if rapidly growing Third World populations bring about vast ecological changes in pursuing the same level of material prosperity already achieved in First World countries? Will ecological problems become the central national security issue of the twenty-first century?[2] Such questions form the background for this essay, which examines whether progressivism and radical environmentalism can be reconciled in terms of an evolutionary teleology that is consistent both with nondual spirituality and with contemporary science.

My book, *Contesting Earth's Future,* was motivated by a similar concern about the sometimes antimodernist and antiprogressive attitudes of environmentalism. Having once attempted to read Martin Heidegger's philosophy as consistent with deep ecology, I was forced to rethink that position after 1987, when evidence surfaced demonstrating that Heidegger's infamous relation with national socialism was deeper and longer lasting than many commentators had supposed.[3] If Heidegger's thought was at least in some ways compatible with German national socialism, I asked myself, to what extent is deep ecology compatible (perhaps unwittingly) with ecofascism? In a subsequent essay, I again attempted to warn radical environmentalists of the potential dangers of ecofascism, while also promoting a progressive reading of environmentalism.[4] The present essay encourages radical environmentalists in particular to tone down antimodernist rhetoric and to embrace the constructive dimensions of modernity, even while continuing to criticize its weaknesses, including heedless environmental destruction.

Human cultures always have generated ecological perturbations, including some so great that they may have eradicated the mega fauna of North America and others that may have destroyed ancient Near Eastern civilizations. *Ecological changes induced by modernity, however, dwarf anything in previous human history.* Modernity may be defined roughly as the recent epoch in which humanity has attempted to gain intellectual, political, and religious freedom, and to liberate itself from the crushing burden of material scarcity (see Kassiola's contribution in this volume for other aspects of modernity). Modernity always has had its dissenters, especially those who condemn its instrumental rationality, which objectifies human life and turns nature into a stockpile of resources. But many more people have accepted modernity's goals, even though not always with great enthusiasm. As Robert Pippin writes, precisely by depriving nature and human life of mystery and transcendent purpose, and by reducing to the status of merely private beliefs the traditional worldviews that once formed the basis for community, modernity has forced many people to conclude that "the narrow confines of strategic and instrumental rationality" are "the best concrete, realizable hope we have got for [social] coordination."[5] Even though instrumental rationality marginalizes the practical realm, undermines civic virtue, atomizes human community, destroys traditional social formations, and causes vast ecological damage, then, such rationality seems to be the only attitude consistent with modernity's widely accepted view that "most of if not all human misery was scarcity (a new and quite controversial claim) and that scarcity was a solvable technical problem."[6]

Contemporary critics of instrumental rationality include deconstructive postmodernists and radical environmentalists, who represent the somewhat conflicting tendencies of the counterculturalism of the 1960s. Though sharing some concerns with such counterculturalists, Pippin insists that we cannot adequately understand the implications posed by the limitations of instrumental rationality (including ecological and social problems), unless we develop an adequate answer to the following question: *Why did the modern idea that misery arises from eliminable scarcity triumph over the premodern idea that misery has additional causes that are more difficult to correct?* Pippin is right, I believe, in asserting that modernity's project of overcoming scarcity through the mastery of nature cannot be adequately understood simply as a technically more proficient way of accomplishing what premodern people already had been doing.

Despite retaining important links with the past, European modernity involves a novel conceptual and experiential horizon in which humanity gradually came to define itself and its relation to nature differently than before. To exploit the extraordinary productive potential of insights produced by natural science, modern "man" (here and elsewhere, I use this masculine term to emphasize the patriarchal dimension of modernity) develops a new mode of subjectivity, egoic rationality, and a related ideology, anthropocentric humanism, which portray man as the source of value, the standard for truth, and the master of nature. Modern individual man asserts his freedom, both from illegitimate political authority and religious dogmatism. He defines truth not as revelation, but rather as the product of rational inquiry, including scientific method. He assumes that modern science, combined with the energies of free men, will make possible the conquest of nature, thereby ending material scarcity. Within a few centuries, the whole planet had been transformed by the institutions, ideology, and subjectivity that arose within the audacious modern horizon.

Contemporary people operating from within this seemingly all-encompassing horizon presuppose that scarcity is humankind's major ill, and that scarcity can be vanquished by rational deliberation and advanced technology. Socialists and market liberals alike usually conclude that continued scarcity and its attendant suffering result from misguided political economies. Socialists argue, for example, that if only the means of production were collectively owned, humankind would achieve the mastery of nature needed for material abundance. Critics of modernity, including radical environmentalists, do not deny that scarcity is an important ill, but maintain that there are important problems other than scarcity, and that a number of those problems arise from reckless efforts to overcome it. Indeed, they argue not only that attempts to generate infinite abundance will fail, because they will undermine the ecosystems on which human life depends, but that superfluous abundance in consumerist societies blocks fulfillment of other human needs. Suspecting that the tragic myth of Daedalus, not the defiant myth of Prometheus so favored by Marx, should be used to interpret modernity's effort to control nature, most radical environmentalists agree that modernity's continued reliance on technological fixes will not work in the long run, since purported solutions to yesterday's problems (e.g., using nuclear fuel to overcome a scarcity of electricity) create even greater problems (e.g., safely disposing of a surplus of nuclear waste). In other words, modern society cannot dig itself out of its ecologically poisoned hole by using the same conceptual and practical tools employed to dig that hole in the first place. Instead, in order to behave in ecologically viable ways, humankind must enter into a postanthropocentric conceptual and attitudinal horizon.

Although often only grudgingly, many progressives have gradually concluded that industrial economies must reform their practices in order to minimize those environmental problems that threaten human well-being. Many of those same progressives, however, also suspect that radical environmentalists are socially regressive at best and ecofascist at worst, because they refuse to concede that overcoming scarcity justifies virtually any treatment of nonhuman beings. Demanding that humans conform to an allegedly more "natural" way of doing things, and proclaiming the need for a mystical reunion with nature, some radical environmentalists ostensibly promote an antihumanism that—in a way similar to deconstructive postmodernism—is inconsistent with progressive views of history.

I begin this chapter by focusing on an incident of industrial pollution in Bogalusa, Louisiana, to bring out aspects of the conflict between radical environmentalists and progressives. Then, I examine more closely the contention of many modernists, that radical environmentalism has affinities with nature worshipping, reactionary movements earlier in this century. Next, I briefly show that deep ecology and ecofeminism can be read as having a "progressive" dimension, despite their criticisms of modernity's efforts to dominate nature. Finally, I analyze transpersonal theorist Ken Wilber's attempt to reconcile the best features of radical environmentalism, which accuses modernism of a mortality-denying arrogance stemming from a fear of nature and the body, with the best features of modern progressivism, which accuses radical ecology of social and psychological regressiveness, antihumanism, and blindness to the fact that human well-being inevitably requires the control of nature. Acknowledging the validity of modernity's quest for freedom from religious dogmatism, political oppression, and material want, Wilber also agrees with those radical environmentalists who argue that a renewed spirituality is necessary to transform society in the ways needed to avoid ecological catastrophe. For Wilber, however, such spirituality will result not from an ostensibly regressive union with Mother Nature, but instead from a progressive development of consciousness and the social institutions needed to support such development. Convinced that a new narrative is needed to inspire and to guide humankind in this difficult age, Wilber develops an evolutionary story that synthesizes contemporary science, developmental psychology, and nondual spirituality. As we shall see, however, environmentalists and modernists alike are suspicious of Wilber's narrative.

In what follows, the term "progressives" will refer both to liberal capitalists and socialists; "radical environmentalists" will refer to counterculturalists who believe that capitalism and socialism must be replaced before they produce global "ecocide," but who also retain something in common with progressives (e.g., the belief that the current situation can be improved, or that natural science generates objective truth); and "deconstructive postmodernists" will refer to counterculturalists who are unsparing in their critique of modernity, and who generally refuse (unlike most radical environmentalists) to offer an alternative and superior worldview, since they fear that in so doing they would become complicit in justifying yet another system of domination.

The Bogalusa Incident: A Microcosm of the Progressivism Versus Environmentalism Dispute

Let us move toward our necessarily limited examination of this complex nest of issues by analyzing a specific instance of industrial environmental contamination. On October 23, 1995, in Bogalusa, Louisiana, about sixty miles northeast of New Orleans, a railroad tank car imploded, spewing out large quantities of a poisonous chemical, nitrogen tetroxide, manufactured at the local Gaylord Chemical plant. Horrified city officials ordered the evacuation of thousands of people near the implosion site. Almost overnight, lawyers swarmed in seeking clients for class action suits against Gaylord Chemical. At the end of the week, several black leaders charged that racism had dictated evacuation procedures: Allegedly, black neighborhoods were evacuated only after white neighborhoods were cleared out.[7] Such accusations led a Baton Rouge attorney to invite Johnnie Cochran, one of O.J. Simpson's attorneys, to establish a legal "dream team" to represent black clients in class action suits. Although calling for an inquiry to see if racial preference had influenced evacuation patterns, Cochran chose to not exploit the potentially incendiary accusation that racism influenced rescue efforts. Instead, he remarked: "In the country right now, we're going through a great racial divide, with the Million Man March and the [O.J. Simpson] verdict. I encourage you not to let this further divide this community. That plant out there may be the culprit."[8]

The Bogalusa implosion and Cochran's remarks about it touch on many issues related to the crisis in modernity's progressive vision. During the past fifteen years, the ideas of environmental justice and environmental racism have emerged as potent forces demanding changes in the production and disposal of toxic substances. Louisiana, where I live, is a national leader in the amount of toxic chemical emissions.[9] The petrochemical corridor stretching from Baton Rouge to New Orleans is nicknamed "Cancer Alley" by environmentalists convinced that pollutants harm the health of nearby residents, many of whom are both poor and black. As blacks and other minorities have found venues in which to express their long-standing concerns about the unhealthy consequences of industrial pollution, and to charge that their communities are disproportionately affected by such pollution, they also have forced changes in the mainstream environmental movement. Long criticized for failing to include more blacks and minorities in their organizations, and accused of being more concerned about wilderness areas than about the environmental well-being of the poor and minorities, environmentalists have had to ask whether their environmental goals are compatible with progressive political aims.

Johnnie Cochran came to Bogalusa shortly after the end of the O.J. Simpson trial, where the racially polarizing verdict revealed that racial friction continues to plague American life, despite the achievements of progressive politics in the 1960s. Today's Balkanizing, identity-based politics is antithetical to progressive universalism. Despite being an exponent of cultural diversity, Cochran knows that the civil rights movement succeeded by affirming universal human rights, and that many members of that movement couched their demands for rights in the language of Biblical justice. In court, Cochran himself borrows the rhetorical style of black Baptist preaching in order to demand justice for his clients. Even though religion has played an important role in various progressive movements, progressives have unfortunately ceded the religious domain to cultural conservatives.

In my view, developing an adequate spiritual sensibility is crucial for encouraging the emergence of new forms of subjectivity and new institutions that will take into account the concerns of progressives and radical environmentalists, even while surmounting their limitations. It is well known, of course, that many commentators have viewed the modern ideal of progress as a secular version of Biblical eschatology. Religious people and progressives alike assume that human history will eventuate in a New Jerusalem, although the former expects that this new world will come about through divine intervention, while the latter pins its hopes for an Earthly heaven on human reason and effort. A defiant anthropocentrism characterized some Enlightenment thinkers, but others conceived of progress in broadly spiritual terms, as the development and dissemination of rationality, which could lead to moral perfection and technical power.[10] Enlightenment thinkers generally agreed, however, that church and state had to be separated, since the latter was so often in league with conservative social forces.[11]

Becoming increasingly atheistic, many modern people adopted scientific naturalism, including Darwinism, which professed to have no need of theological or teleological principles to explain natural phenomena. Scientific socialists, following Marx's lead, were particularly critical of religion, but retained a teleological view of history. Though political considerations led liberal capitalists to be more cautious in their treatment of religion, their embrace of secular economic theories and practices left little doubt about where their real loyalties were to be found. Unfortunately, in jettisoning the spiritual insights forming the core of traditional religions, progressives may have thrown out the baby along with the bath water. Renouncing divinity as nothing more than a magnified projection of human traits, as did Feuerbach and Marx, displays an immature understanding of authentic spiritual experience. Such understanding encouraged an overestimation of humanity's place in the cosmos. Indeed, many of the social and ecological disasters of the past century may be attributable in part to progressive modernity's paradoxical

ideology of naturalistic humanism, which involves both human self-assertion and self-abnegation. On one hand, modern humankind proclaims its
uniqueness and independence by dissociating itself from a meaningless
nature below and an allegedly absent divinity above. On the other hand,
modern humankind conceives of itself as an insignificant part of the mechanical world system, in which human consciousness is merely a puzzling
epiphenomenon of material processes, though an epiphenomenon that proves
useful in the hairless ape's struggle for survival.

Today, however, as mechanistic materialism is being displaced not
only by quantum theory but by developments in the sciences of chaos,
there emerges the possibility of a worldview that affirms the achievements of rational subjectivity, including its skepticism about the claims
of revealed religion and its suspicion of the political motives of such
religion, but that also interprets such subjectivity as a phase within an
evolutionary process leading to a higher, more integrated level of awareness. Such a worldview, which interprets consciousness as a basic, not
an accidental, feature of a teleological cosmos, holds that humankind
can evolve toward appropriate relationships with nature and divine, after having gradually dissociated itself from both. As we shall see in our
discussion of Ken Wilber's work, however, such a worldview would be
viewed with suspicion by modernists and environmentalist alike.

Let us return for now, however, to Cochran's remark that the chemical plant itself may be the culprit. This remark allows for several readings. As an attorney, Cochran was trying to focus attention on the
corporate entity that will be the object of legal action. As a political
agent, he was trying to pacify the community by unifying it against a
common enemy: wealthy capitalists operating their plant in ways that
risks the lives of thousands of people, white and black, in a small Southern city. As a person long exposed to nightmarish scenarios about human-
made ecological catastrophe, he also may have been questioning the
wisdom of modernity's commitment to technological mastery over nature. Cochran may believe that human well-being cannot be achieved
without a healthy natural environment, but like many other Americans
he probably also believes that ecological health can be achieved without
drastically altering the personal lifestyles and economic institutions allegedly necessary for economic growth.

Years ago, when the Gaylord Chemical plant was built, many community leaders—white and black alike—were probably convinced that
the plant promised improved material conditions, a better educated work

force, and eventually healthier social and political relations. Indeed, the civil rights movement made its greatest gains not only because it appealed to the nation's conscience, but also because unprecedented economic prosperity allowed people to act generously. During the past two decades, however, as real wages have shrunk and as conservative politics have become the rule, racial tensions have been increasing. Although diminishing incomes have resulted less from ecological problems than from structural economic changes, including the loss of industrial jobs abroad, many people—including those who need a growing economy for their own employment—wonder whether an expanding global economy is ecologically sustainable in a time of enormous human population growth. Recognizing the deleterious long-term economic and public health consequences of the petrochemical industry, but also needing gainful employment, even Louisiana's poor and poorly educated populace now questions the facile either/or: either jobs (i.e., furthering material and social human well-being) or environment (i.e., protecting nature in ways that block progress).

Long before taking environmental matters seriously, progressives—including many union leaders—supported some version of this either/or, for they presupposed that economic exploitation of nature would have only beneficial social effects. Ecological problems, including polluted air and water, were treated as economic externalities and as acceptable trade-offs for material abundance. Only in the late 1960s did some progressives begin taking seriously the environmentalists's claim that heedless "development" of "natural resources" was threatening human health and undermining the biosphere on which the continued production of material wealth depends.[12] Today, despite a conservative political trend, most American politicians portray their views as being environmentally sound. Democratic liberals, contending that systemic reform will bring about the changes needed to avert ecological calamity, recommend a mix of governmental regulations and market mechanisms. Because improved environmental indicators demonstrate that such reforms have worked, most Americans have criticized the Republicans in Congress (and now the White House after the election of 2000) for trying to dismantle those reforms.

Socialists, of course, have little faith in the long-term consequences of such liberal market reformism. They maintain that because most ecological problems result from capitalism, such problems only can be solved by first gaining public control of industrial facilities, and then by running them in ways consistent with human well-being. Neoclassical liberals, in contrast, insist that many environmental problems result from government control over natural resources and markets; hence, privatizing governmental holdings and rescinding restrictions that currently skew market processes would have positive ecological consequences. Elsewhere I have argued that free market environmentalism can contribute significantly to the goals of environmentalism.[13] From the viewpoint of progressives, whether socialist or free market, changing control over the means of production changes everything. Radical environmentalists argue, however, that socialists and market liberals—far from being opposites—are both anthropocentric humanists who regard nature solely in instrumental terms. Thus, changing control over the means of production would generate social changes, but not basic changes in attitudes about the status of nonhuman beings.

Progressives reply that in portraying humankind as no more important than any other strand in the "cosmic web," radical environmentalists promote antihumanistic views that are all too compatible with reactionary politics. Turning our attention once again to Louisiana, we recall that racial animosity—fueled by reactionary politics and by economic fears—led many white voters to support David Duke's campaign for governor in 1991–1992. Duke gained most of his support by using a racist analysis to explain the real economic fears of many white voters, but the neo-Nazi Duke also claimed to be an environmentalist. During his campaign, he did not emphasize his belief that there is a link between pure land and pure blood. Contemporary neo-Nazis in Germany, however, also playing on widespread economic concerns, are far more explicit about resurrecting the Nazi motto of *Blut und Boden*: The pure blood of the German Volk is inextricably tied to and dependent on healthy land.[14] Demanding the expulsion of foreigners who supposedly take away jobs and land from Germans, and who allegedly pollute the blood of Germans by marrying them, reactionary groups are resurrecting the "green" themes that were part of Nazi ideology.[15]

Aware that national socialism was both antimodern and in some ways ecofascist, progressives have traditionally been wary of the antimodernist sentiments among radical environmentalists. Progressives exhibit merely prudential concern about how humans treat nonhuman beings, not only because progressives believe that control of nature is necessary to overcome scarcity, but also because they usually believe that humanity's rational faculty sharply differentiates humans from (other) animals. Modern social theorists denied that the cultural domain could be understood in terms of natural causality. As Michael Redclift and Ted Benton write:

> In one move, the opposition between nature and culture (or society) made room for social sciences as autonomous disciplines distinct from the natural sciences, and undercut what were widely seen as the unacceptable moral and political implications of biological determinism. The firm categorical opposition between nature and culture has, of course, been subsequently reinforced by the twentieth century's continuing experience of biological determinism in practice—in eugenic projects of "racial hygiene," in successive waves of resistance to women's social and political demands, and, most infamously, in the rise of European Nazism.[16]

Many progressives fear that radical environmentalists, in emphasizing the interdependence between humans and other life forms and in demanding "rights" for nonhuman beings, are undermining the humanity-nature distinction, which serves as an impediment to racism and biological determinism. As Jeffrey Herf has pointed out, however, the political terrain here is complex.[17] In pre-1933 Germany, for example, concern about the industrial impact on nature had been the province primarily of nature romantics and political reactionaries (the two groups having some overlapping members), but the catastrophic consequences of Nazism and its "religion of nature" led many reactionaries in the postwar era to adopt a mildly, if resignedly, promodern, proindustrial stance. Curiously, however, by the 1960s the ecological and social consequences of industrialism led many critics, including some with progressive ties, to conclude that modern technology (whether capitalist or state socialist) is inherently domineering. Such a conclusion contradicts Marx's faith in the emancipatory promise of industrial technology.

How Criticism of Modernity Influences Environmentalism

Since the emergence of modernity, there have been many attacks on it and revolts against it, some completely antimodern, others with a more nuanced attitude toward modernity. The influential critical theory of Max Horkheimer and Theodor Adorno is an example of the latter. Writing during World War II, these theorists concluded that the humanity-nature distinction which constituted one aspect of progressivism had been marginalized by another aspect, namely, scientific naturalism. The same science that enabled the technological control of nature also allowed modern society to conceive of human beings simply as intelligent animals that could be controlled like other animals. Increasingly, the emancipatory struggle to overcome scarcity degenerated into the quest to control everything sheerly for the sake of control. As the culmin. tion of the dialectic of enlightenment, modernity leads not to human emancipation, but rather to ever more cunning forms of social domination and in ecological devastation.[18]

Second-generation critical theorist Jürgen Habermas concedes that instrumental rationality has overstepped its legitimate boundaries, by colonizing the ethical and aesthetic domains that in modern times are supposed to exercise their own legitimate kinds of reason, but he insists that instrumental rationality rightly seeks to establish the scientific truths and to develop the technological means needed to overcome scarcity by mastering nature. Habermas is concerned that Horkheimer and Adorno's critique of modernity too closely resembles that of Heidegger, who infamously used it to support national socialism. Nazi ideology was reactionary in part because it sought to de-differentiate what modernity had distinguished: natural science, ethics and politics, and aesthetic judgment and experience. Rejecting modern humanism's distinction between the domains of history and nature, many Nazis adhered to a version of scientific naturalism, according to which humans are one organism among the many competing for survival. In the Nazi *Gleichschaltung,* all elements of society—scientific, ethical-juridical, and aesthetic—were united and coordinated in support of this life and death struggle. Individual rights were sacrificed to the communal good. As social Darwinists and antisemites heavily influenced by eugenics theories, the Nazis also sought to purify German blood by methods that culminated in the "final solution."

Despite giving allegiance to national socialism, however, Heidegger retained the modern distinction between the historical and natural domains. Explicitly disagreeing with Nazi ideology, he insisted that humans are more than clever animals. Nevertheless, he condemned modernity for making material productivity the central human goal, and for defining freedom as self-assertive, self-grounding human autonomy. According to Heidegger's "anti-humanism," humanity is an important element in a transcendent, but nonteleological, nonprogressive process that discloses the ontological horizons (i.e., demarcates what it means for things "to be") of various historical epochs. Rejecting Biblical eschatology and its modern secular variations, Heidegger denied that there is any "reason" in history, and concluded that the very search for such reason (foundation, ground) culminates in the control obsessed era of modernity. Indeed, in the end he portrayed capitalism, socialism, and the "historical reality" of national socialism as variations of naturalistic humanism, which views humans as animals struggling to maximize their fitness at the expense of other living beings.

For Heidegger, Western history constitutes a nihilistic degeneration from the early Greeks' encounter with the being of entities. Instead of existing as the pre-Socratics did, namely, as ontological openness in the service of the self-manifesting of entities (plants and animals, gods and mortals), Western philosophy soon became the search for an ultimate ground or foundation for entities. Following Aristotle's lead, but as corrupted by Roman and Christian doctrines, modern humanity eventually conceived of itself as an animal whose rationality enables it to understand and thus to control entities. Descartes's philosophy emphasizing the ideal of self-grounding rationality brought to its climactic phase the West's metaphysical search for an ultimate ground or foundation for entities. Technological modernity is simply the working out of the claim that for something to be it must be the object for the autonomous, self-grounding human subject.

Along with Nietzsche's critique of Western efforts to gain absolute truth, Heidegger's deconstruction of Western foundationalism influenced the French counterculturalism of the 1960s, which may be roughly described as deconstructive postmodernism.[19] Such postmodernists, like many radical environmentalists, maintain that colonialism, suppression of cultural difference, two world wars, the Russian Gulag, the nuclear arms race, political authoritarianism, and ecological destruction form the dark side of modernity's "emancipatory" project. The postwar liberation movements, including feminism and civil rights in the West and revolutionary anticolonial movements in the Third World, helped to promote deconstructive postmodernism's claim that the allegedly "universal" truths of Western humanism are simply ideologies, that is, power-enhancing perspectives of white, male, industrial, Western elites (communist and capitalist), who strive to mold the world in their own image. Alhough largely agreeing with deconstructive postmodernism's critique of humanism, linear-progressive history, instrumental rationality, cultural homogeneity, and ecologically destructive technology, many radical environmentalists resist deconstructive postmodernism's moves of deconstructing truth and portraying "nature" as a social construct. Moreover, environmentalists fear that deconstructive postmodernism's suspicion of grand narratives undermines efforts to devise critical analyses that have sufficient breadth to grasp the global complexity of multinational capitalism, which is destroying indigenous cultures and local ecosystems. Although many radical environmentalists insist that people must develop local (bioregional) narratives that give voice to interactions between humans and non-humans, others insist that far more encompassing narratives about the entwinement of human and natural evolution are needed to offset the disenchantment of the world brought about by modern science.

Many environmentalists call on natural science to support their contention that technological modernity is destroying the biosphere, but they also recognize that science has become part of the instrumental rationality contributing to such destruction. Environmentalists' faith in scientific truth claims was greater earlier in this century, when scientific ecology used metaphors such as the "balance of nature" and "biotic communities" to describe environmental phenomena. Such metaphors were consistent with environmentalists' demands that humans were overstepping their boundaries and upsetting the balance of nature. In the past few decades, however, ecosystem ecology has been largely displaced by population dynamics, which uses metaphors like chaos, unpredictability, imbalance, and competition to describe natural processes.[20]

In part because of such changes in scientific ecology's representation of natural phenomena, a number of authors—including progressives and former environmentalists—have contested the validity of scientific "facts" used by environmentalists to support predictions of ecological calamity. These authors contend that the ecological "crisis" is not as bad as it has been portrayed. Of course, the scope of ecological damage remains hotly contested. Nevertheless, according to critics, environmentalists run the risk of crying "Wolf!" once too often.[20] When I was in college during the late 1960s, predictions made by leading environmentalists convinced me that by now the planet would be uninhabitable. The failure of such predictions does not mean that other doomsday forecasts will not pan out. The point here is that environmentalists use scientific "facts" and rhetorical strategies to advance their own goals. However much environmentalists may strive to represent a "general" interest, one that includes the concerns of all life, their assertions also reflect interests that call for critical scrutiny.

Environmentalists, then, must not ignore postmodernists who question the status of all truth claims, including those made by environmentalists and by natural scientists, and who maintain that nature is a social construct, for any encounter with nature is mediated by human categories, images, and concepts. Yet some radical environmentalists not only insist that humans can directly encounter nature in wilderness, defined as pristine nature that has been largely untouched by human hands, but also believe that people can generate truth claims that have universal validity. Many scientists and progressives share this belief. Steven Vogel, however, a sympathetic critic of critical theory, argues that progressives must affirm that nature—understood both as an economic resource and an object of scientific investigation—is a social construct, because human experience of nature is always socially mediated. According to Vogel, there is hardly anything on the planet that has not been influenced by human activity.[22]

Conservation biologist Michael Soulé agrees that there is no "pristine" nature. Hence, he warns that environmentalists have played into the hands of developers by maintaining that wilderness—pristine nature—is the only nature worth protecting.[23] If there is no such pristine nature, environmentalists would be forced to conclude that there is nothing worth protecting! Soulé maintains, however, that there still are relatively wild areas that are worth protecting, but largely because they contain a variety of endangered species, not because they show no traces of human intervention. Even though conceding that there is no untouched Nature that forms the Other to humankind, Soulé joins many progressives and radical environmentalists in resisting the current idea, inspired by a certain interpretation of Nietzsche's perspectivalism, that scientific truth claims are little more than the expression of unexamined conceptual prejudices and personal and institutional power interests. In a world where truth amounts to the victorious power perspective, radical environmentalists and progressives fear that there would be no rational basis for preferring one assertion to another. Social critics and natural scientists presuppose that some assertions more adequately represent states of affairs than do other assertions.

Donna Haraway, an environmentally concerned progressive with postmodern sensibilities, concedes that truth claims are always partial and perspectival, but also insists that some truth claims have more validity than others.[24] Empirically well-founded scientific assertions are not arbitrary pronouncements, although they cannot help exhibit some biases. A number of feminist epistemologists have argued that scientific assertions may become more reliable to the extent that they arise from self-critical scientific communities with members who represent diverse groups and interests.[24] Modern science is unavoidably inflected by various (often hidden) interests, but—charitably regarded—it promotes in principle the infinite task of objectivity. In my opinion, however, natural science must be distinguished from the ideology of scientific naturalism, according to which humans are animals competing with other species for survival and power. Scientific naturalism hides its normative perspective behind the mask of scientific "truth." Somewhat surprisingly, variations of this ideology are used by progressives to support economic practices that environmentalists claim are ecologically suicidal, and by environmentalists to support political agendas that progressives regard as socially regressive.

Progressives often blend the antithetical vocabularies of anthropocentric humanism or humanistic exceptionalism (humans are unlike and superior to animals) and scientific naturalism (humans are merely clever animals) into a naturalistic humanism, which depicts humankind as having the "right" to dominate all other animals in the quest for security. Such naturalistic humanism justifies attempts to "dominate" nature. Radical environmentalists often appeal to scientific naturalism to emphasize the similarity between humans and other animals. As is the case with other species, so we are told, the human population can so rapidly increase that it "overshoots" its natural resources. To prevent species suicide, some deep ecologists call for drastic population reduction. In reply to the complaints of progressives and many ecofeminists that this view represents either a new Malthusianism or an obsession with controlling women, deep ecologists insist that unless population reduction occurs now in as humane a manner as possible, Draconian measures will likely be necessary in the future.

Even though condemning anthropocentric humanism and favoring scientific naturalism, many radical environmentalists subscribe to their own paradoxical version of humanistic exceptionalism. Among all life forms, humans alone are expected to curb their territorial expansiveness. Held to be morally wrong for pursuing the goals that other animals pursue naturally, humans are sometimes regarded by environmentalists as behaving "unnaturally." Indeed, one environmentalist has described humans as "natural" aliens.[26] Scientific naturalism presupposes, however, that humans are clever animals struggling for survival. Such naturalism would seem to have no place for normative judgments of the sort that humans ought to curb their drive to become ever fitter, though naturalism does allow that this drive succeeds best if humans take prudential measures to avoid fouling their own nest. Having little patience with such a viewpoint, progressives often conclude that radical environmentalism is simply incompatible with modernity's emancipatory aims, and is thus reactionary. A brief examination of deep ecology and ecofeminism, however, will demonstrate that things are not so simple, for progressive themes can be discerned in both these branches of radical ecology.

Progressive Dimensions of Two Branches of Radical Environmentalism: Deep Ecology and Ecofeminism

Proponents of modernity sometimes represent radical ecologists as irrational nature worshippers seeking a return to cave dwelling. Fortunately, this caricature fits few radical environmentalists. Consider one of the most articulate radical ecologists, Arne Naess, who bases his version of deep ecology, Ecosophy T, on the notion that all living things strive for self-realization.[27] For humans, self-realization means not egoistical self-assertion, but rather development of the intrinsic capacity for compassion, defined as taking active interest in the self-realization of all beings. To achieve genuine self-realization, people must widen and deepen their sense of identity beyond the ego, body, family, and friends, so as to embrace all forms of life. Just as self-interest leads me spontaneously to take care of my own body, so a wider identification with plants, animals, and even ecosystems will lead me spontaneously to care for them. The notion of self-realization as a wider sense of self reflects the ecological intuition that all phenomena are interrelated or at least somehow reflective of one another. Acknowledging the possible uniqueness of humankind's self-reflective capacities, Naess maintains that such gifts impose great responsibilities.

Although recommending an "ecocentric egalitarianism" according to which all beings have an equal right to flourish, Naess recognizes that humans must not only kill other beings in order to live, but insists that one should avoid taking any life except for fulfilling "vital" human needs. Recognizing that there always will be disagreement about what constitutes vital needs, Naess makes clear that consumerist society generates many nonvital needs. Hence, he calls for significant social and economic changes, though he believes that such changes must be shaped by, as much as they shape, humanity's capacity for achieving a wider identification with all life.

Naess's idea of self-realization may have something in common with the progressive teleology of thinkers like G.W.F. Hegel, though whereas Hegel focused on the self-realization of spirit through humankind, the former emphasizes the self-realization of all beings. In this regard, Naess shows the influence of Mahayana Buddhism, Advaita Vedanta, and Gandhi. Modernist in recognizing the universal character of the striving for self-realization, but nonmodernist in extending the legitimacy of such striving beyond the human realm, Naess would seem to have a melioristic perspective: Things can improve if humankind realizes its potential for compassion.

Affected by nondual spirituality, Naess would answer Pippin's question—Why did modern Europeans decide that scarcity was the major ill?—as follows: The quest to eliminate scarcity was motivated not merely by justifiable concerns about human want, but also by ignorance both about other (nonmaterial) factors that generate suffering and about the interdependence of all beings. According to Buddhism, suffering is generated by craving, especially the craving to exist. Since the ego structure and body are mortal, the craving to exist ultimately will be disappointed. Greed for possessions beyond those needed for a decent life indicates that one is gripped by this insatiable craving. Naess also agrees with the Buddhist view that because humankind is interrelated with other forms of life, one cannot promote the long-term well-being of the former by exploiting the latter.

Ecofeminists, especially Susan Griffin and other radical feminists, have their own answer to Pippin's question. Early modern European man decided that scarcity was the major ill not only because of widespread hunger and deprivation, but also because he was experiencing an intensification of the patriarchal mode of subjectivity, according to which reason and soul (the masculine) are immortal, whereas emotions and body (the feminine) are mortal. During the Middle Ages, the idea of nature as a good, bountiful mother had restricted man's exploitation of nature.[28] With the rise of mercantilism and rationalism in early modern times, however, and with the separation anxiety associated with the emergence of disembodied Cartesian subjectivity, Western man began portraying nature either as lacking in reason altogether, or else as an irrational and baneful female.[29] This view of nature as radically other than and threatening to rational mankind invited what many ecofeminists have described as a technological assault against nature. The quest to end scarcity by dominating "mother nature," then, was a symptom of the death denial associated with a heightened egoistic subjectivity that was dissociated from the body, emotions, the feminine, and nature.

For many ecofeminists, the primal form of domination is the domination of women by men. Hence, patriarchy can be present even in a socialist society, in which class structure has been eliminated. Modern man's exploitative treatment of nature is an extension of his domination of woman. Man justifies dominating woman because he regards her as inferior to him; allegedly, she is endowed with less of the rationality that sets humans apart from all other creatures. Less rational than man, woman is supposedly more akin to nature. This analysis enables ecofeminism to shed light on environmental racism. Karen J. Warren maintains that just as alleged intellectual inferiority justified male domination of women, and just as the greater inferiority (nonrationality) of natural beings justified technological dominion over nature, so the purported intellectual inferiority of poor, ignorant, and nonwhite peoples justifies their domination at the hands of white elites.[30] Just as women in patriarchal societies are expected to deal with bodily wastes, so racially inferior, ignorant, and/or poor people are expected to put up with having their neighborhoods, homes, and bodies polluted with industrial wastes.[31] Even as downtrodden Louisianans gradually gain the political muscle needed to prevent toxic wastes from being dumped in their state, however, those wastes are being shipped to Third or Fourth World countries, whose people look very different from the families of those who own and run First World industries.

Although criticizing modernity for continuing the patriarchal attitudes that cause social and ecological damage, many ecofeminists attempt to appropriate and to redefine the emancipatory aims of modernity. In including nonhuman beings within the field of entities to be emancipated, however, ecofeminists transcend the conceptual limits of modern liberation movements, and have thus sought inspiration drawn from diverse sources, including goddess religions, Eastern thought, and native American traditions. This spiritual interest distinguishes ecofeminism from secular progressivism, according to which nothing (except perhaps humankind) is sacred. Although supposedly this-worldly in orientation, modern man contradicts this tendency by dissociating himself from and seeking to transcend nature, body, and woman. In this way, he arrogates to himself the transcendent features of the deceased Biblical God. Because progressive teleologies are so tainted by the dissociate, nature-dominating patriarchal narratives of self-worshipping modern man, many ecofeminists develop narratives calling for people to reconnect with what has been lost or forgotten: spontaneity, intuition, deep natural harmonies, and the sacred immanent in nature.

Social ecologists such as Murray Bookchin, however, have criticized deep ecologists and ecofeminists for refusing to embrace a progressive teleology, and for seeking an allegedly regressive spiritual reunion with divine nature. However innocent may be the intentions of those who promote the idea of such a reunion, according to Janet Biehl, such ideas are often uncomfortably consistent with ecofascism, which maintains that humankind must enter into communion with and conform its behavior to divine Nature. Bookchin's insightful cosmic narrative maintains that human historical activity is a development of the revolutionary-teleological activity at work in nature.[32] Unfortunately, Bookchin also engages in *ad hominem* attacks that distort the views of his "spiritual" opponents. Bookchin's atheism apparently compels him to see only regressive tendencies in discourse about the sacred, despite the fact that the two philosophers on whom he relies most heavily for his own progressive teleology, Aristotle and Hegel, reserved important roles for the divine in their thought.

Ken Wilber's Attempt to Reconcile Progressivism and Environmentalism

Ken Wilber has developed an even richer teleological narrative that defends the achievements of modernity, acknowledges the intrinsic worth of nature, and restores the role of the divine in cosmic evolution. Constructing an unabashedly grand narrative in the face of postmodern deconstructivists' suspicion about such narratives, Wilber assumes that only a progressive narrative—informed by contemporary science and a nondual spirituality—can generate the speculative vision capable of reconciling many of the concerns of progressives and environmentalists. Although recognizing the force of deconstructive postmodernism's critique of objective truth, Wilber insists that absolute nondual awareness provides an infinite context capable of containing the moves that occur when modernists and postmodernists attempt to outcontextualize one another, as when Marx tried to outcontextualize capitalism, and as when deconstructive postmodernists try to outcontextualize Marxism and other progressive views of history. Only an infinite context can simultaneously admit that because all views are relative there is no historical "progress," and that such progress is nevertheless discernible in cosmic, terrestrial, and human history as the realization of divine potential. Of course, not everyone is willing to go along with Wilber's contention that the universe unfolds within such an infinite context.

In *Sex, Ecology, Spirituality,* Wilber affirms that modernism and environmentalism both have important insights about humankind and its relation to nature.[33] Environmentalists are right that industrialism is threatening the ecosystems on which all life depends; progressives are right in seeking political freedom and in trying to liberate humankind from material scarcity. If progressives discount humanity's relationship with the biosphere, however, environmentalists fail to grasp that human consciousness transcends the biosphere even though also depending on it. Despite attempting to be evenhanded in his analysis, Wilber's sympathies clearly lie with progressivism, not least because he uncharitably represents deep ecology ("ecomasculinism") and ecofeminism as being more regressive than they are.[34] Despite oversimplifying his account of radical environmentalism, Wilber clarifies important issues about the appropriate relationship of progressivism and environmentalism.

In his earlier book, *Up From Eden*, Wilber answered Pippin's question—Why did modernity focus on scarcity and its elimination?—in a way similar to Arne Naess and a number of ecofeminists.[35] *According to Wilber, overcoming material scarcity became important for modern man not only because it prevented starvation, but also because it symbolized that rational egoic subjectivity could control nature, thereby overcoming death.* Death denial, then, led modern man to dissociate himself from his body, from the female, and from nature. Whereas many critics depict modern man's quest for immortality, the "God project," either as an act of hubris or as a huge mistake, Wilber argues that this quest inevitably arose in connection with the progressive evolution of human consciousness over the ages. From the dim and magical awareness of tribes many thousands of years ago, humankind evolved varieties of group consciousness during the rise of urban civilization, until individual awareness began arising first with certain Egyptian pharaohs and later with individuals in Greece, India, China, and elsewhere. Each stage of greater separation from other people and nature (i.e., each stage of individuation), brings with it heightened death anxiety, which people deal with in ways consistent with their cultural practices and material circumstances.

In Western history, unfortunately, the important process of differentiating from nature turned into an unnecessary process of dissociating from body, nature, and female. Hence, otherworldly religions called for mortification of the flesh as a way of freeing the soul from its corporeal imprisonment. Later, as a greatly heightened separate self-sense emerged during the Renaissance and early modern times, dissociative tendencies generated both the witch trials and the quest to dominate nature. *The noble goal of ending material scarcity, then, was part of an all-encompassing project of denying death both by controlling natural forces, and even more important by generating the wealth to which men cling as a hedge against death.* Although ultimately an ineffective substitute for immortality, modern individuated subjects remain so attracted to it that socialism has little chance of working in the way envisioned by its proponents.

In the process of dissociating himself from nature, modern man also gradually dissociated himself from the divine. The emergence of modern science's mechanical worldview, along with the idea that human freedom involves rational self-law giving without interference from any outside force, be it human or divine, led progressives to conclude that God is either a nonintervening creator or else altogether absent. Alone as the only form of consciousness in an inert cosmos, stricken with the anxiety that accompanies modern egoic subjectivity, dissociated from his feelings, his body, nature, and the divine, and alienated from other people, audacious European man colonizes the planet, subjecting native peoples to his will and transforming entire mountain ranges into industrial raw materials.

Without denying modernity's drawbacks, Wilber argues that it has brought genuine progress. In many places, democratic institutions have replaced despotic regimes, the right to own property has become recognized as an important dimension of owning oneself (i.e., of being a person), scientific knowledge enables us to understand both the fact of and the causes for today's ecological problems, and extraordinary productive forces have ended scarcity for vast numbers of people and could in principle end scarcity for all. *The task for an authentic "postmodern" humanity is to further the evolution of consciousness, the next stage of which involves reintegrating what has been dissociated: body and nature "below" and divine "above."* Such integration does not mean giving up the gains associated with individuated selfhood, anxiety ridden though it may be, by regressing to earlier stages of consciousness and collective-authoritarian social formations. Instead, integration involves an *Aufhebung,* in which the individuated selfhood of rational egoic subjectivity is both included and transcended in a more comprehensive form of awareness that is open both to nature and divine.

Wilber argues that the achievement of rational bourgeois selfhood living in constitutionally governed societies is only one stage of human history, not its culminating moment. Humankind is only about halfway along in a lengthy and often painful evolutionary process. Although emphasizing the importance of reintegrating the divine into human life, Wilber nevertheless insists that the greatest possible contemporary revolution would be the worldwide achievement of responsible personhood, constitutional democracies, and market economies, since grave social and ecological problems arise in countries where premodern, autocratic ways impede the material productivity and social institutional change necessary for the rise of modern individuals. In other words, only when the positive political and economic achievements of modernity are consolidated on a planetary basis can large numbers of people begin exploring the next, integrative phase of human history. There is a dialectical relation between material circumstances and consciousness development. Scarcity prevents people from developing their human potential, yet regressive social structures impede the development of the productive forces needed to overcome scarcity.

In *Sex, Ecology, Spirituality*, which focuses on the clash between progressivism and environmentalism, Wilber offers a somewhat different account of modernity. De-emphasizing his earlier claims that science contributes to modern man's dissociation from nature, he argues instead that during the Enlightenment era science portrayed humankind as a clever animal in the vast, all encompassing, mechanical cosmic system, which is devoid of purpose, value, and consciousness, except for its virtually inexplicable appearance in humans. In concluding that consciousness can be nothing more than a by-product of physico-organic processes, natural science follows its basic assumption that the cosmos in general has no "interior" dimension, no "subjectivity," and nothing that includes but transcends physico-organic reality. In thus lopping off the higher levels of the Great Chain of Being, natural scientists become ontological "flatlanders" for whom reality is limited to the material (physico-biological) planes. According to Wilber, progressives and environmentalists are both flatlanders, because they accept natural science's powerful, but constricted account of reality. For such flatlanders, humans are clever animals that can relate to nature in two possible ways: either they can dominate it to maximize fitness (progressivism), or they can merge with it to overcome the pangs of separation from the mother ground (radical environmentalism). Neither approach is adequate, for the former leads to ecological catastrophe, whereas the latter leads to regressive psychological and social formations, possibly including ecofascism, the ecological consequences of which could be horrendous.

To avoid this unacceptable choice, Wilber inverts the naturalistic cosmology, shared by modernists and environmentalists alike, which holds that the "noosphere" (consciousness) is contained within the biosphere. Wilber maintains, however, that the biosphere is contained within the noosphere, in the sense that self-reflective consciousness both includes and surpasses the structures that previously evolved on the physical and organic planes. Consciousness constitutes a different level of reality that cannot be deduced from or understood in terms of physico-organic processes. Rejecting eliminative materialism, which reduces consciousness to the status of physico-organic events, Wilber maintains that consciousness is an emergent phenomenon that must be understood on its own terms. In attempting to reenchant the world by affirming that cosmic evolution is teleological, Wilber also valorizes the political and scientific achievements of modernity, including its critique of revelation-based religions. Unfortunately, in the process of freeing reflexive, self-grounding rationality from the interference of dogmatic religions, moderns went too far, for they denied altogether the transcendent dimension represented (however inadequately) by those religions.

Influenced by Plotinus, Wilber's claims that matter-energy, which arose through the Big Bang, is a manifestation or emanation of nondual, absolute spirit. Matter-energy arises from such spirit, not the other way around. Absolute spirit, which is both immanent in all things and transcends all things, acts as a "strange attractor" luring things to surpass their existing conditions, to bring forth something new. Wilber believes that contemporary science supports his contention that the emergence of life and self-conscious life are inevitable processes. Life did not have to emerge on Earth, but it necessarily occurs on many planets in the universe, because matter-energy tends to generate ever more complex, differentiated modes of being. Terrestrial life and human evolution are only local instances of intergalactic processes that will culminate in the greatest differentiation consistent with the attainment of absolute nondual consciousness.

Wilber's teleological narrative supports the emancipatory aims of modernity, but recognizes that such aims cannot be achieved by trashing the biosphere. Beyond saying that prudential considerations require better treatment of the biosphere, he concedes that environmentalists rightly intuit that the biosphere deserves respect, admiration, and care. He criticizes the neopagan revival of nature worship, however, because it allegedly exhibits a flatland ontology, which fails to recognize that the divine is both immanent in creation, but also transcends it. Wilber fears that certain forms of neopaganism will undermine the achievements of modernity, including personal individuation and political universalism.[36]

Neopagans reply that in *Up From Eden,* Wilber's own characterization of the emerging level of consciousness ("centauric," representing the reintegration of body and mind) has important similarities to states reported by people involved in neopaganism. Denying that they simply are regressing to earlier stages of consciousness, some neopagans assert that they are attempting to do what Wilber himself has called for: reintegrating what modernity has dissociated (body, emotions, female, nature) both by exploring a higher (more integrative) level of consciousness, and by redefining modern categories in a way that transforms dissociation into the differentiation needed to retain the positive achievements of modernity, including greater economic prosperity, personal individuation, and democratic institutions based on universal human rights.[37]

Here, it is worth comparing Wilber's critique of the new paganism with the one offered by social ecologist Janet Biehl. Like Wilber, Biehl sharply criticizes the "New Right," which for her apparently includes some postmodern theorists, neofascists, and ecofascists. According to New Rightists, the ecological crisis and the suppression of national identity have been brought about by the "dualistic, homogenizing universalism" of "Semitic" religious traditions, especially Christianity along with its secularized political ideologies, liberalism and Marxism. The same universalism that led Christians to evangelize the world is at work in modernity's efforts to eliminate non-Western cultural identities. Moreover, through the unbridled technology to which it gave rise, this modern universalism is said to have perpetrated not only the destruction of nature but an annihilation of the spirit; the destruction of nature, it is said, is life-threatening in the spiritual sense as well as the physical, since when people deny pristine nature, their access to their "authentic" self is blocked.[38]

Criticizing the socially splintering tendencies of the New Right, Biehl strongly defends the universalism derived from monotheism. She rejects, however, the principal claim of such monotheism: that there is a transcendent Creator. Indeed, she would agree with those environmentalists who complain that monotheism promotes an ecologically problematic otherworldliness. Denying divine transcendence, Biehl holds that transcendence does occur both in natural evolutionary processes that give rise to greater complexity and differentiation, and in human historical activities that form a "second nature" (culture) that distinguishes humankind from first nature. In contrast, New Righters, pagans, and ecofascists not only reject monotheistic transcendence, but also human transcendence that embodies the emancipatory universalist impulse of monotheism. For Biehl, then, the spirituality celebrated by many deep ecologists and ecofeminists can only take the form of regressive neopaganism, according to which the divine is wholly immanent in nature. Allegedly, such spirituality calls on people to achieve "authentic selfhood" by submerging themselves into sacred mother earth.

Wilber joins Biehl in criticizing nature worship, but he would disagree both with her dismissal of spirituality and with her account of the divine toward which an advanced spirituality is directed. For Wilber, an adequate cosmological narrative must include the nondual divine, understood both as the primal source for the universe and as the final goal that lures creation to differentiate itself through evolutionary processes culminating in nondual awareness. For Wilber, the divine transcends nature but is also immanent in it, for nature is a manifestation of the divine. Human evolution involves the painful and exhilarating process of discovering an appropriate relationship to creation and creator, immanent divine and transcendent divine, many and one. Presumably, Wilber would concur with Rosemary Radford Ruether, who understands why many ecofeminists reject the "male monotheistic God as a hostile concept that justifies alienation from and neglect for the earth." Like Wilber, however, Ruether denies that the "god-problem" can be solved by "replacing a male transcendent deity with an immanent female one."[39] She goes on to say:

> We need a vision of a source of life that is "yet more" than what presently exists, continually bringing forth both new life and new visions of how life should be more just and more caring. The human capacity for ethical reason is not rootless in the universe, but expresses this deeper source of life "beyond" the biological. Consciousness and altruistic care are qualities that have some reflection in other animals, and indeed are often too poorly developed in our own species. To believe in a divine being means to believe that those qualities in ourselves are rooted in and respond to the life power from which the universe itself arises.[40]

Today, scientists are attempting to unlock the genetic code that makes life possible, while others are moving ever closer toward developing artificial intelligence. In technological postmodernity, we may well see the rise of cyborgs that transgress existing boundaries between human and animal, and between human and machine. Surely our capacity for care will be tested by the creative ferment that will unpredictably shape human consciousness and institutions. Cyborgs may pose a threat to human freedom and they may reinforce, rather than reduce, existing social inequities, but there is no inherent reason that such technological innovations will impede rather than develop freedom, or that they will undermine rather than contribute to the higher, more integrated forms of consciousness. Emerging technological developments may well generate forms of subjectivity and thus to personal, social, and political problems, of a sort that cannot be imagined in terms of today's conceptual categories. Some years ago, the Dalai Lama remarked that he could see himself being reborn as a computer, if by then computers had attained enough complexity to support self-consciousness. Consciousness does not have to be restricted to organic beings.[41]

Conclusion

Ken Wilber's evolutionary narrative has some drawbacks, including indiscriminate portraying of virtually all deep ecologists ("ecomasculinists") and ecofeminists as adhering to naive and misguided forms of "spirituality," which risk promoting psychologically and socially regressiveness practices consistent with ecofascism. By doing so, Wilber ignores the extent to which radical environmentalists—including social ecologists and some deep ecologists and ecofeminists—share concerns about forms of ecospirituality that promote reactionary politics and regressive personalities. Despite such problems, Wilber's cosmological narrative manages to achieve a great deal.

Wilber acknowledges that modernity has important limitations (including social alienation and potential ecological calamity) stemming from its conclusion that material scarcity is the central problem for humankind. This conclusion is related to modernity's relatively one-dimensional cosmology, according to which humans are clever animals struggling for survival and power within an all-embracing materialistic-mechanistic cosmos. Many radical environmentalists share neopaganism's intuition that this cosmology lacks the spiritual sensibility needed to reveal the sacred dimension of nature, and thus reveals nature as nothing but raw material for human ends. Yet by portraying nature itself as divine, and thus by denying the transcendent dimension of divinity in which humankind has a proportionately larger share than do plants and (most) animals, some radical environmentalists may become attracted to regressive psychological and social ideas. Wilber agrees that modernity lacks spiritual sensibility, but maintains that a spirituality appropriate for today's situation must simultaneously reject otherworldly monotheism as well as this-worldly paganism, while envisioning a divine that is manifested as immanent in nature, but also as the evolutionary process by which nature transcends the physico-biological planes on the way to ever more differentiated planes of consciousness.

Modernity has contributed to this evolutionary process by making possible greater individuation, but modernity's understandable reaction against religions based on revelation and supportive of reactionary regimes went too far. Denying the divine altogether, whether as the source of matter-energy or as the end toward which cosmic evolution strives, modernity ends up defining progress as the ever greater control of the physico-biological plane and thus as ever greater capacity for satisfying human desire, instead of as an evolutionary process that makes possible a higher, more integrated level of consciousness and the social institutions consistent with that level. *Satisfying material desires is surely important, but humanity's ultimate desire can never be satisfied, even by an infinite amount of material goods, for arguably what people really want is not more consumer goods, not more power over nature, not a longer life span, but eternity in the form of union with the nondual divine* (Compare and contrast with Hobbes's view of humanity as infinite desirer discussed in Kassiola's analysis in this volume). The consumerist culture that wreaks social and ecological chaos arises because so many people are using material goods to fill a void that such goods cannot fill. One can never get enough of what one doesn't really want.

If progressives must take environmental problems seriously, environmentalists must recognize the validity of modernity's emancipatory economic and political aims. Freeing people from material deprivation and political authoritarianism is a noble goal, but one that must be furthered in ways that enhance all life on this planet, whenever possible. Reconciling progressivism and environmentalism is central to a positive, postmodern awareness that transcends customary boundaries—physical, organic, mental, artificial—in disclosing the creative principle at work in all phenomena. A prerequisite for the rise of this more inte-grative awareness is that the majority of people need to develop modern consciousness and institutions, although such development must avoid critical damage to the biosphere. Therefore, we see the need for environmentalists and progressives to cooperate in reminding each other of what the other finds so important.

9

Questions to Ponder in Understanding the Modern Predicament

Joel Jay Kassiola

> Conditions such as finitude, fallibility and temporality
> occasion some of the most pressing questions that we ask. . . .
> In the face of questions that for twenty-five centuries have
> defined the efforts of philosophers to find demonstrable
> answers, how can we avoid intellectual despair? . . . Thinking
> provides no certain and unequivocal answers but nevertheless
> opens the way to understanding.
>
> *—Glenn Tinder*

One distinguishing characteristic of political theory, as Tinder expresses in the epigraph above (and in the volume from which this passage is taken),[1] is that it does not provide *solutions*, in the mathematical sense, to its problems, nor does political theory provide answers with certainty to its questions, even after thousands of years of efforts. Tinder and other political theorists instruct their readers that this lack of certainty in political theory should not be considered as a fault of the field or a deficiency of its members, because its questions do not admit of unequivocal answers as a result of humanity's "finitude, fallibility and temporality," in short, humanity's limited nature. Questions, problems, or issues in political theory, involving human judgments of value and their reasoned defense, can only aspire to offer supportive evidence on behalf of proposals, thereby stimulating additional political thinking with the goal of advancing human understanding; no answer to a political theoretical question can ever be totally assured of being correct, nor can it, thereby, avoid potential criticism.[2]

Even in the vaunted field of demonstrable mathematics, a field reputed for certainty, submitted solutions, when properly understood, remain open to doubt, as in all human—and therefore, limited—inquiry. Mathematician Kurt Gödel's famous proof eradicated the possibility of achieving infallible or certain knowledge in any human study, even mathematics.

> [Gödel's] proofs brought the astonishing and melancholy revelation that it is impossible to establish the logical consistency of any complex deductive system except by assuming principles of reasoning whose own internal consistencies is as open to question as that of the system itself.[3]

In political theory, value conflicts are like conflicts between different mathematical systems with different assumptions and definitions wherein the argument is really over which system (or view of the world, including values) should be adopted. In the absence of some super or higher order system that both synthesizes and reconciles opposing systems of thought, continuous debate with increased learning is the only appropriate aspiration whereby each theory's advocates engage their opponents in rational dialogue; all because the limits to the human condition preclude perfect knowledge.

Does this lack of certain and unequivocal knowledge, resulting in the need for ongoing thought and discussion, make political theory (or mathematics, or all human inquiry) worthless? The answer is, no, because while certain and perfect political solutions to political problems are impossible, greater understanding of the human condition, its political nature, and its goals *can* be advanced; progress in human understanding of political experience is possible. For this to occur, we always must keep in mind the unlikelihood of unanimity on any political theoretical question or judgment and, as a result, the likelihood of objections to a particular position. Nonetheless, just as in Western jurisprudence and legal practice, a preponderance of evidence for one view can be adduced and collectively recognized. Even with the absence of political certainty and finality, political value judgments and theories can be assessed comparatively and reasonably for the necessary practical purposes of human action.

Given the open-ended nature of all human inquiry, including political theory, one of its main aims is to raise questions for the purpose of drawing the community's attention to issues that have been taken for granted, incompletely considered, or ignored altogether, in order to provoke increased systematic social thinking about them. Tinder captures this point well.

> Regardless of any conclusions that are reached, thinking in itself helps us gain a humanity not available in any other way. We are thinking beings, and even through inconclusive thinking, we can gain access to our humanity. . . . Thinking is a summoning of the self. . . . Struggling with and living with doubt has a role in the formation of individual identity.[4]

With this understanding of political theory as background, the environmental crisis (first expressed in the 1960s by the publication and impact of Rachel Carson's *Silent Spring* in 1962), and environmental political theory, as several of the contributors to this volume note, have achieved the primary aim of political theory. This includes increasing public consciousness of the assumptions, definitions, and values of our modern society as well as forcing us to think about society's long-term ecological sustainability and even its desirability as a social order. In a word, the environmental crisis has "radicalized"—in the Greek sense of "going to the roots"—or summoned modern publics to engage in deep thinking about the nature of modernity, including its fundamental value structure and worldview as articulated in another of the crisis's products: environmental political theory.

If political theory emphasizes uncertainty, continuous thinking, and social debate, exemplified by the questions raised by the environmental political theoretical essays contained in this book, then providing the usual editor's "conclusion" to this volume would seem to be inconsistent with the uncertain and unceasing thinking spirit of such discourse. Instead, I would like to use this space to illuminate the important questions I have noted from the contributions for the readers' consideration and contemplation, thereby, according to Tinder, providing them with the means to advance their own, and civilization's, humanity. In this manner, I hope to encourage the users of this book to develop political theories about the environment so they may be able to conduct their own "explorations in environmental political theory." The recommended additional reading section provides suggestions of additional discussions to be used as guides through this difficult but rewarding intellectual voyage.

Clearly, the most central point from these readings is the normative political basis of the environmental crisis; everything about environmental political theory, as envisioned here, flows from this seminal notion. This insight and defining characteristic of environmental political theory leads to many other questions, mostly related to transforming our presently hegemonic modern society, the social order that has produced the environmental crisis. Milbrath's questions are instructive in this regard and worth pondering:

> The most important problem faced by mankind is: *How do we transform an unsustainable society into one that is sustainable?* That question raises a series of additional questions: how did we get into this predicament? Why is modern society unsustainable? What happens if we do not change? What must be changed if human society is to survive? What can we do to bring about the requisite changes?[5]

I would add to this list derived from the question of the ecological sustainability of modernity offered by Milbrath and Pirages, a quintessential question of equal concern for a just world order in addition to that of its sustainability; having clean air and water means little if people are weighed down by the miseries of injustice.[6] From the very beginnings of the modern environmental movement, concern for the natural environment and the biophysical limits to modernity's supreme value—economic growth—emphatically were *not* intended as barriers to social action to achieve greater global justice (although the public image of this literature may have overlooked this important point). Using the alarm over environmental limits and threats to human life to freeze the egregious worldwide inequality between materially rich, industrialized nations and the rest of the world was rejected, even though progrowth defenders of the status quo tried to use the charge of self-interested elitism against environmentalists. For example, the leaders of the Club of Rome who published their famous first report, *Limits to Growth*, considered to be the founding document of modern environmentalism and public awareness of the environmental crisis (along with Carson's *Silent Spring*), attempted to prevent a conservative-elitist hijacking of the environmental crisis in order to preserve undeserved privileges of the industrial rich and the unjust global distribution of wealth. They wrote in 1972 (!):

> We unequivocally support the contention that a brake imposed on world demographic and economic growth spirals must not lead to a freezing of the status quo of economic development of the world's nations. If such a proposal were advanced by rich nations, it would be taken as a final act of neocolonialism. . . .[7]

Since the inception of the environmental crisis, advocates calling for fundamental change within modernity have been accused by their

promodernity, prostatus quo, proendless growth critics of attempting to
deny the economic advancement of the poor by denying the industrial,
capitalist, modern logic of unlimited economic growth and, therefore,
of being elitist and simply protecting their self-interest.[8] To avoid this
powerful criticism that goes to the heart of the environmental crisis,
environmental political theory, and the limits to growth critique of modern industrial civilization, the concern for social justice must be considered equally with achieving ecological sustainability and avoiding
environmental disaster, as Zimmerman's contribution attempts to do with
its goal of "reconciling progressivism and environmentalism."

Milbrath's superlative characterization of the transformation of modern industrial society as constituting "the most important problem" facing humanity today is warranted according to the environmental political
theory readings included here. Recognition of this urgent social need
for transformation raises, in turn, many other profound questions, as
Milbrath notes, regarding the nature of social change, the dynamics of
the transformation of modernity, and, of course, the criterion of an alternative postmodern society that is both ecologically sustainable and socially just. These crucial issues for humanity are examined by all the
authors included in this volume. I invite the reader to ponder these questions that, at first, appear bewildering and not amenable to any progress;
however, if the radical environmentalists and environmental political
theorists are correct, the environmental crisis leaves us no choice but to
attempt to transform modernity or face catastrophe. Pirages directly
addresses this important point in his contribution regarding the ecological need for a Third Revolution, one that will create a global, sustainable (and, I would add, *just*) social order. If this collection of explorations
in environmental political theory improves the reader's ability to reflect
on this and its derivative questions emanating from the environmental
crisis, it will have achieved much of its purpose.

The question "How did we get into this predicament?" focuses on
several causes collectively referred to as "modernity" and targeted by
environmental political theorists and the contributors here. In alpha-
betical order, for lack of any systematic comparative study of relative
significance, they are: capitalism, industrialism, liberalism (or
Hobbesianism). Capitalism's economic (and political) logic necessitat-
ing unlimited and continuous economic growth; industrialism's emphasis on unlimited material expansionism and consumerism; liberalism's
(and its founder, Hobbes's) emphasis on individualism, competition for

social honor or status, materialism in an effort to deny death, and the impossibility of human satiation or satisfaction—all these are contained within modern society, where its instrumental and exploitative view of nature, anthropocentrism, materialism (driven by death denial), and technologism are all applied. This rich set of interrelated and overlapping themes may be the most enduring contribution to social thinking for the new millennium by environmental political theory. *The revolutionary political consequences that follow from this profound inquiry fill the momentous and misleading gap created by both environmental scientists and environmentalists who ignore the normative political bases of the environmental crisis.*

Perhaps the most important, yet least discussed, aspect of the overall environmental political theoretical agenda is the crucial role the denial of limits plays in modern society (see chapters by Kassiola, McLaughlin, and Zimmerman). This essential characteristic of modern industrial, capitalist, and liberal (Hobbesian) society could be the fundamental cause of the threats to the global environment and the alienation experienced by citizens of such societies. We are experiencing the modern denial of the environmental limits to natural resources and of the capacity of the natural environment to safely absorb the huge amounts and toxic nature of waste products from advanced industrial economic activities. Our modern denial is prompted by service to the demanding and unforgiving advanced industrial god of ceaseless economic growth and consumption and to maintaining a society that is dedicated to its worship. Furthermore, as some of our contributors have astutely observed, the modern denial of death—the limit of human mortality—should be added to this characteristic of modernity and underscored.

Zimmerman draws our attention to the philosophy of Ken Wilber whom he says perceived that modernity seeks to overcome material scarcity as a way of overcoming death,[9] thereby linking, in a fundamental manner, modernity's quintessential traits of death denial and consumerism. This idea, I believe, powerfully explains the preoccupation, even obsession, with consumption in late modern societies. Moderns, Wilber argues, seek wealth and consumer goods as a "hedge against death." Might the contemporary, consumer culture, now worldwide because of globalization with its "shop 'til we drop" and "you are what you own" ethos, wherein consumption is "a way of life,"[10] be a futile, misconceived, and ecologically dangerous effort to stave off what the modern social order attempts to suppress because of its inability to address it explicitly and effectively: the limit of human mortality. Zimmerman is trenchant on this most basic of issues:

> Satisfying material desires is surely important, but humanity's ultimate desire can never be satisfied, even by an infinite amount of material goods, for arguably what people *really* want is not more consumer goods, not more power over nature, not a longer life span, but eternity in the form of union with the non-dual divine. The consumerist culture that wreaks social and ecological chaos arises because so many people are using material goods to fill a void that such goods cannot fill. One can never get enough of what one does not really want.[11]

This insight demonstrates why Hobbes's limitless desirer conception of human nature that makes satisfaction impossible (a conception important to the worldview of liberalism and modernity) is central to the consumerism of modern society. It also may explain the paradox of how advanced industrial societies get materially richer without a corresponding increase in happiness.[12] It is well known that throughout his life Hobbes was preoccupied by a fear of death. This was the driving force in his view of the world and political theory and, therefore, was significant in the origins of the modern perspective and experience; Hobbes's political theory has had great influence on the modern outlook and social order.[13] This grim but paradigmatic view holds that human satisfaction is never actually achieved, and that humans are destined to seek new desires endlessly, ceasing only with death when finally, "peaceful rest" can be realized. Social theorist, Daniel Bell, provides the clearest statement of this defining, denial of limits characteristic of modernity:

> The deepest nature of man, the secret of his soul as revealed by modern metaphysic, is that he seeks to reach out beyond himself, knowing that negativity—death—is finite, he refused to accept it. Beyond the chiliasm of modern man is the megalomania of self-infinitization. In consequence, the modern hubris is refusal to accept limits.[14]

Environmental political theory will make an important impact on the understanding of ourselves and the comprehension of our social order and show us the way out of our modern predicament if it can effectively communicate this individually and socially self-destructive component of a society built on the denial of limits to the human condition. From this perspective, the environmental crisis threatening our planet today is the result of this modern hubris and its myriad consequences. It must be eliminated if we are to achieve a sustainable and satisfying life for all.

When we truly understand the nature of modernity, including its dark, Hobbesian, denial of limits side, we can identify the real contemporary doom and gloom advocates. Critics of environmentalism have attacked the focus on the environmental crisis as an unduly depressing and pessimistic position, full of doom and gloom about the future of humanity and the planet. These defenders of the hegemonic, advanced industrial social order claim that exaggerated and misguided ecological analyses are contaminated by an antimodern, anticapitalist, antiliberal, and so on, bias.[15] However, once modernity's erroneous beliefs and values are identified as the actual cause of the environmental crisis, the real doom and gloom purveyors are the hucksters for modernity and endless consumption who embody the grim Hobbesian view of the world, and thereby fail to recognize humanity's nonmaterial—or spiritual— needs and deny humanity's limits and its possible satisfaction. Our reliance on Hobbesianism and its perverse consequences is largely nonconscious because we do not discuss them in such modern social institutions as mass media or schools; therefore, they remain below the modern public's awareness. How could environmentalism be more depressing than the modern worldview itself and the social order we have built on it that defines humanity as incapable of ultimate satisfaction, continuously striving for more, competing and consuming only to cease with death? At the same time, this view endangers the Earth for all current and future living creatures.

This point raises some crucial political theoretical questions. What is the nature of human wants and happiness? How does it relate to the physical environment and other living beings? Goodin has these additional queries about the theory of human value: Is it material only? Limitless? Competitive? Superior to other beings? Environmental political theory specifically raises and addresses these questions. They are among the most important questions for society, individual citizens, and social theorists to contemplate.

As we reflect upon the causes of the potentially lethal modern predicament, we face the central question of how modern societal transformation will occur. This raises the concomitant, apparently insurmountable, obstacle of the current elite's opposition to such change in values and social institutions: How will the rich accept the lower material levels necessitated by environmental limits, and create a more just world order through a redistribution of wealth and power?

The unhappy experience and knowledge of increasing environmental degradation with threats to all planetary life should move the industrial rich to recognize the self-defeating and unsatisfactory nature of modern values and social practices. They may come to accept the necessity of a new, postmodern social order, one not so characterized by the ideologies of capitalism, industrialism, and Hobbesianism. In this new order citizens—including the rich—can have more leisure time to experience and contemplate the nonmaterial and more fulfilling aspects of the human condition, like nature. Nature's value to humans, as Goodin tells us, lies in directing humans to something "outside themselves," something "larger than themselves," that "locates the self."[16] Of course, extensive social learning will have to occur if such a radical change is to occur, but it is precisely such a type of change that is needed to realize sustainability and justice. The crucial role of such social learning to societal transformation is emphasized by both Milbrath's and Pirages's contributions.

An urgent question remains: What specific agent can transform modern society to an environmentally consistent, moral, and satisfying social order? Several contributors note the role of disappointment, or tragedy (in Oscar Wilde's sense of "emptiness after success") on the recognition of mistaken goals. We experience alienation as we work harder and longer "getting and spending" yet increase our anguish and dissatisfaction with life. Some of our authors have remarked about the Wildean tragedy, or irony, of the most materially successful society in world history having success be its downfall. However, just as Zimmerman admonishes us to preserve what is positive about modernity (for example, freedom from the shackles of feudalism and increased productivity to meet human biological needs), I feel compelled to remind the reader of Paehlke's discussion of globalization, especially as it pertains to the global industrial elites and the effective spread of their ideology of growthmania and endless consumption. These elites control the global mass media of communications and direct the expanding reach of increasingly large and powerful transnational corporations. The dynamics of how the current hegemonic rule of the industrial corporate behemoths will be undermined has yet to be written, posing a significant challenge to all environmental political theorists, environmental researchers and activists (similar to Zimmerman's unforseen "caterpillar into a butterfly" transformation analogy). As Paehlke fears, we merely may be moving forward between cars on a train as it moves backward without changing its direction! But even the most destination-minded train engineer will stop, change direction, and reassess her/his stated objective when they run out of fuel, see disastrous circumstances ahead, and realize the train's projected destination does not exist!

I would like to close these questions to ponder the chapter and this volume by noting how Milbrath's essay implores us to transform our modern society because it is ecologically unsustainable and politically (and morally) faulty. After listing the values and social policies of a postmodern society, which we should work toward creating and learning to accept, Milbrath offers the reader the following saga-cious remarks:

> Our common journey promises to be challenging and exciting, even though difficult. It will be much easier, and more likely to be successful, if we face it optimistically with a deep understanding of the pace and character of social transformation. . . . We are the only creatures that can imagine our extinction. That special gift of understanding places a unique moral responsibility on humans. Once we have contemplated the future, every decision that could affect that future becomes a moral decision. Even the decision not to act, or to decide not to decide, becomes a moral judgment. We humans, given the ability to anticipate the consequences of our actions, will become the conscious mind of the biocommunity, a global mind that will guide and hasten social transformation. Those who understand what is happening to our world are not free to shrink from this responsibility.[17]

This calls for social transformation, especially the final sentence noting the unavoidable responsibility for social transformation by those persons who understand what is happening to our world, is the para-mount recommendation from environmental political theorists for the benefit of their audience and the future of the planet. Those of us who understand what is happening to our world, ecologically, politically, morally, and socially are not free to shrink from the immense but invigorating responsibility to work toward changing it for the better. It is the goal of environmental political theory, as I envision it, and as the essays collected in this volume represent, to vastly increase the numbers of people on Earth who understand what is happening to our world and therefore to increase the numbers of people worldwide, not free to shrink from the responsibility to transform our unsustainable and unjust industrial world order.

I hope that this book has shown the nature of the questions posed by environmental political theory to be as complex, wide ranging, and profound as any dilemmas addressed in the 2,500-year history of Western political theory; political thinking and argument must continue since the quest for perfect solutions and certainty is always impossible.

I ended my previous book-length discussion of environmental political theory with a quote from Rabbi Tarfon whose words about the obligation to study the sacred Jewish text, the Torah, are especially applicable to our explorations in environmental political theory and our efforts to transform the social order that has produced an environmental crisis that threatens our world:

> The day [life] is short; the task is great; the workmen [human beings] are lazy; the reward is great, and the Master is insistent. It is not your part to finish the task; yet neither are you free to desist from it.[18]

The essays contained in this book are intended to assist readers in the urgent endeavor to understand and transform our civilization, and hasten the third sociocultural revolution to reach sustainability and the justice that we need so desperately. Rabbi Tarfon, alas, is correct: Life is, indeed, short, and the task facing us of creating a sustainable and a just world is, in fact, great. And, as I wrote earlier:

> Human beings are, indeed, lazy; we succumb easily to inertia, we fear change, and the pain and insecurity it brings. Furthermore, we are reluctant to challenge the dominant worldview and social structure of our existing social order. Our goals are difficult to formulate and intimidating to achieve. However, if enlightened . . . citizens can overcome these obstacles and meet these demanding tasks, the reward of a sustainable, just . . . world is also great. For Rabbi Tarfon, the Master was insistent. For us, the urgent, [environmental] limits-to-growth issues confronting contemporary humanity are no less compelling.[19]

Afterword

The Surprising Value of Despair and the Aftermath of September 11

Joel Jay Kassiola

The social and psychological consequences of the September 11, 2001 attacks resulting in destruction of the World Trade Center towers, a seriously damaged Pentagon, and the deaths of thousands of civilians, and their aftermath seem clear. The attacks and saturation media coverage (seventy-two hours on television without commercial interruption) of these shocking events has helped produce the following outcomes: Many Americans are still having difficulty sleeping months after the events of a day that has been proclaimed by commentators as "the day that changed everything" and "the day the world changed"; air travel has been sharply reduced; colleges and universities report decreased applications from distant students seeking admission; surveyed Americans report increased appreciation of family life and want to spend more time with relatives; security has been heightened at infrastructural installations such as bridges, power plants, public water system reservoirs, tunnels, and energy pipelines; public anxiety levels have increased, intensified by highly publicized security alerts and warnings by the FBI. When the unsolved anthrax-caused deaths and warnings of different forms of potential bioterrorist attacks with no known immunizations or cures are added, it is obvious that America as a nation, and Americans as individuals, are experiencing an emotionally traumatic and turbulent period. Our emotions have been well-documented in the various forms of communications media: anger toward the alleged perpetrators of the terrorist acts—whipped up by political leaders using the extreme rhetoric of war; sadness for the victims of the attacks and their families; and admiration for our new national heroes at Ground Zero, Washington,

D.C., and Western Pennsylvania. Nonetheless, I believe there is another collective emotion present in America that has gone unnoticed and unanalyzed despite the flood of public commentary and coverage in print and the airwaves since September 11: the emotion of despair. I would like to claim that although the emotion of despair is conventionally considered to be a negative and undesirable experience, it possesses the capacity for surprisingly great personal and social value as a catalyst for positive change.

The dictionary informs us that the word "despair" means to lose all hope, to be overcome by a sense of futility or defeat, and a sense of powerlessness or resignation. Synonyms for despair include: hopelessness, desperation, and despondency.[1] While this linguistic analysis appears to suggest that human despair is unqualifiedly grim and undesirable, there is a point of view that maintains the highly valuable aspects of despair—a perspective that we do not encounter in public discourse (or in the dictionary). It is this positive potential of despair that I wish to emphasize and attempt to clarify in relation to the aftermath of the September 11 attacks by referring to such a positive analysis of despair in connection with the environmental crisis that confronts us today.

I am an environmental political theorist who has been thinking, teaching, and writing for the past twenty-five years about the deteriorating state of our environment and its relation to our social values and institutions. The scientific literature about the global environmental conditions during this period often has been characterized pejoratively as full of "doom and gloom" by its critics because it details the depressing and ominous developments that constitute the current global environmental crisis that humans and all living creatures on Earth are confronting: extinction of species, destruction of old growth forests, water and air pollution, and various other environmental threats to the future of the planet, such as global warming and stratospheric ozone depletion. This cluster of environmental problems, and the challenges they create in advanced industrial nations like the United States, have led to what I have termed "industrial pessimism,"[2] wherein citizens of materially affluent societies have grown deeply discouraged about the viability of their industrial way of life in the face of these environmental constraints. Such pessimism is based on knowledge about the earth's environmental limits for both the natural resources required to sustain industrial life and the capacity to absorb waste products safely. The penetrating wit of Woody Allen capturing this contemporary dismal sentiment was quoted in Chapter 1.[3]

My goal in this afterword is to show that this reaction of despair to the environmental crisis may help us to understand the aftermath of the attacks of September 11. Contrary to the dictionary meaning of "despair," these reactions do not need to be hopeless, despondent, nor defeatist, even if despair is experienced. Indeed, I want to claim further that these devastating occurrences surprisingly can produce, according to the ordinary understanding of "despair," profoundly positive results that would not be possible without despair. Despair, I believe, can be an essential catalyst for the necessary social transformation to make a better society (as discussed at the end of Chapter 9), if, and only if, we comprehend the possible salutary consequences of this vital human emotion *and* cognitive accomplishment; an outcome, however, that is especially difficult to achieve given the human propensity to engage in wishful or reality-avoiding (and reality-denying) thinking and acting. I shall attempt to explain this paradoxical aspect of the human condition and the great, but largely ignored, opportunity that despair affords humanity.

Psychologist Alexander Lowen has cryptically written: "The path to joy leads through despair."[4] When one reflects on this statement, it appears paradoxical, especially when one considers the definition of "despair" discussed earlier, including feelings of hopelessness, defeat, and resignation. *How, we may ask, can the decidedly negative experience of despair lead to joy?* Lowen offers a powerful insight in his response to this skeptical question, according to social and environmental theorist Philip Slater, who interprets Lowen's surprising statement about despair leading to joy in the following manner:

> Despair is the only cure for illusion. Without despair we cannot transfer our allegiance to reality—it is a kind of mourning period for our fantasies. Some people do not survive this despair, but no major change within a person can occur without it. People get trapped in despair when this despair is incomplete—when some thread of illusory hope is still retained.[5]

According to Slater, Lowen's statement about despair and joy highlights the causal relation between despair and human illusions, resulting in the latter's elimination as a means to joy. This is of primary importance to individual mental health and flourishing; and I would add here, germane to understanding the meaning of our reactions to the September 11 events and their aftermath on the societal level. Despair, on this view, involves the recognition and admission that our fantasies are illusory, and therefore are impossible to achieve. We must then go on to replace them with more realistic values and objectives that permit their realization, and thereby transform our goals from the impossible to the realizable so that joy is within reach.

The despairing recognition is like the grief associated with the death of a loved one, except that it is the death or dismissal of our dreams, our illusions, our fantasies, and the awareness of the need to have them replaced with values and aspirations that are in reality feasible, allowing fulfillment and joy, rather than ones that are illusory and, therefore, destined to be disappointingly unachievable because impossible, when despair is complete and successful. This cure of despair for our illusions produces their death and elimination, and, this loss, in turn, results in a mourning period, as Slater explicates the phenomenon of despair; *We sadly realize that what we thought was desirable and real is neither, and thus must be given up forever!*

I propose that this understanding of the concept of "despair," and how it might apply in social life, can provide insight into the aftermath of the attacks of September 11. Moreover, the experience of despair could provide the breakthrough in consciousness necessary concerning the current environmental crisis wherein despair about industrial civilization and its foundational values and institutions, remains "incomplete," "with some thread of illusory hope being retained," as Slater puts it, allowing hegemonic and deleterious industrial delusions and social practices built upon them to continue.

How, specifically, does despair, understood here as the necessary and valuable "mourning period for our fantasies" and "cure for our illusions," apply to the terrorist attacks of September 11 and their consequences? It is well known that after 1989 Americans witnessed the fall of communism in the Soviet Union and with it the collapse of our only military competitor, and the adoption of free market principles and consumerism throughout the world, including China, Russia, and the former Soviet satellite nations. Today, thanks to global communication, virtually the entire human population seeks to live like affluent Americans. International agreement on (modern industrial) values is unprecedented in world history and could be considered one component of the important but elusive concept of "globalization."

Furthermore, the post–1989 period saw global domination by American military forces reinforced by the scintillating success in the Persian Gulf War. The serious economic troubles of our major economic rival, Japan, resulted in a similar American hegemony in the domain of the

global economy that establishes America as the world's largest and dominant economy, possessing the most stable and trusted currency, used as
the worldwide standard. All these post–1989 developments add up to a
military and economic *Pax Americana* that extends worldwide (not to
mention cultural domination through American rock music and cinema),
or so Americans fantasized. Our worldviews of superiority and invul-
nerability were reinforced every day by rabid chauvinistic and paro-
chial media. Who could blame Americans for our confident and arrogant
(but illusory) beliefs in the establishment of an American global empire
in the late 1990s, given world history since 1989 and the victorious end
to the cold war?

Military hegemony was matched economically. American economic
exuberance in the late 1990s was accurately reflected in the book title:
The Dow at 30,000. Thirty-year-old dot.com executives believed that
they could become millionaires overnight and retire at thirty-five like
the few high-tech whizzes who actually did fulfill this cultural goal of
"the new economy" based on the computer, global consumerism and
trade, technological innovation, corporate mergers, and get-rich-quick
IPOs (initial public offerings) of stock during the high-flying, mid- to
late-1990s.

Stunningly, the surprise attacks of September 11 on our national territory brought death to civilians and destruction and damage to major
cultural symbols of power and world domination. Our illusions of military and economic invincibility and global hegemony were shattered.
Despite our fantasy of military inviolability, the suicidal hijackers were
largely successful in perpetrating their hostile and violent acts (with
only one out of four commandeered jetliners crashing before it could hit
its planned target). Their plan was not anticipated—*nor envisioned,* let
alone protected against—by American security forces and leaders.

Let me elaborate on this last point. The capability and willingness of
fanatic hijackers to turn our own machines against us by transforming
fuel-filled tanks of jumbo civilian airplanes into missiles of destruction
aimed at chosen targets of great iconic value, representing the unequaled
might of American society and global domination—New York City's
World Trade Center and Washington, D.C.'s Pentagon—were not even
speculated about or contemplated as a scenario in this specific manner
by American military and political leaders. Therefore, the September 11
attacks were "surprise" attacks not only in their execution (where and
when they occurred) but *in their conception,* unlike the infamous Pearl

Harbor attack in this regard, although references to Pearl Harbor were frequent in the aftermath of September 11. *The targets of the September 11 attacks were cultural symbols representing America's economic and military fantasies of global supremacy.* The illusory belief of American territory and citizens being invulnerable to foreign attack (supported by history to that point) was reduced to rubble right before our eyes as television cameras caught the collapse of the World Trade Center towers and broadcast the damage to the command and control heart of the worldwide American military juggernaut in the Pentagon.

Our vaunted military power producing a sense of total and invulnerable domestic security from attack by foreign enemies is now experienced as illusory. We hear our national leaders admitting that it is impossible to protect completely the potential targets of terrorist attacks 365 days a year given their size, number, and geographical dispersion. There are hundreds of thousands of power plants, water reservoirs, bridges, airports, train stations, government buildings, malls, and so on throughout this vast nation. The illusory sense of invincibility and total protection from violent attack—let alone bioterrorist attack from microscopic organisms illustrated by the frustrations in solving the anthrax killings—was instantly transformed in the early hours of September 11 to deep anxiety, vulnerability, and insecurity. *Is it any wonder that Americans are despairing and mourning for our pre–September 11 illusions of safety and superiority?*

American illusions of dominant economic power also were devastated in the aftermath of the September 11 attacks. Not only did the New York and American stock exchanges shut down for days for the first time in history, and then sharply decline, but American corporations' earnings hit long-time lows. Unprecedented losses were sustained especially in the large industries of travel and tourism, culminating in an official recession. Moreover, as if to underline the economic despair after September 11, the very foundation of post–World War II American (and now global) consumer culture and economy was so seriously threatened by the post–September 11 despairing reflections and replacement values that the president of the United States and mayor of New York City, in between war preparations and counting the dead and missing, took time off to admonish Americans "to go shopping" as a patriotic act because the shopping malls were deserted!

After September 11, Americans experienced despair as a result of being shocked into recognizing and admitting our illusions about

American military and economic power. Faced with the reality of human loss, either personal or vicarious, Americans began to question the illusory and misguided nature of our values and lives, centering on material acquisition and accumulation. This is a crucial basis for restructuring social values, increasing the possibility of social change, and engaging in political theorizing about a new American social order. This is what recognizing the positive value of despair could mean if only we can learn from our environmental threats brought on by industrial social illusions.

Thus, to summarize my argument, I believe the September 11 attacks on the World Trade Center and the Pentagon graphically, shockingly, and grotesquely demonstrated that our nation was neither militarily nor economically invulnerable to disaster. These September 11 attacks and their saturation media coverage, followed by the anthrax mysteries, were accompanied by official fears and alerts of future (bio)terrorist attacks, and the admission by authorities that there is no absolute deterrent in place; this brought us to despair. *More than people were killed on September 11—our social fantasies were killed as well—and this recognition resulted in the post–September 11 national despair, and social and psychological indications with which we are still living.*

Whether it produces new airline security measures such as bulletproof cockpit doors, checked baggage inspections, shoe examinations for explosives, or federalizing and upgrading airport baggage screeners, or causes us to discover the hollowness of a life of overwork so committed to material consumption that it harms family life and other nonmaterial values, despair over the September 11 attacks has shocked Americans into recognizing and reevaluating our previous fantasy-based thinking, valuations, and actions. We are in a mourning period for our military security fantasies that has constructively stimulated major changes for the better regarding airline security and safety—with additional changes promised. But, a central political theoretical issue remains: *Can the value changes and resulting modifications in behavior, based on the supremacy of material consumption in our industrial lifestyle, have durability and a permanent social impact when so many people's livelihoods are at stake in the illusory, pre–September 11 economic status quo founded on the fantasy of everyone achieving the life of wealth and leisure?* (Consider how many tens of millions of Americans, including middle-class workers, have their retirement funds dependent on the stock markets, with serious policy proposals made to increase this dependency through Social Security reforms. Is the plight of the Enron employees who lost a lifetime of savings and retirement accounts a vision of the future for American workers if these policies are adopted?)

Here is where I believe the analogy between despair in the environmental crisis and despair in the aftermath of September 11 becomes significant. Since the 1960s and the first Earth Day in 1970, environmental scientists, environmental advocacy organizations, and their members have been attempting to convey the important message that the planetary limits will not permit us to sustain our materially wasteful, extravagant, and unjust way of life for long. Certainly these limits will preclude all 6 billion people currently inhabiting the earth, (let alone the projected 8 or 10 billion in future decades) from living like affluent Americans in our disproportionate resource use and pollution production. Owing to global communication and Hollywood movies, the world's population already has fallen prey to this dangerous industrial illusion of material wealth and prosperity for all. We must abandon this illusion if we are to avoid ecological catastrophe, natural resource wars, and the constant threat of terrorism by the poor and oppressed of the world as their only method of striking back in a world marked by gross global inequality. To be truly effective, the real "war"—or as I would prefer to express it, the real "initiative" or "social transformation"—to end the threat of terrorism must start here with these social value-based driving forces of industrial illusions.

The American illusion about domestic invincibility from foreign attack was dramatically destroyed. Likewise, I contend that our social fantasies of environmental limitlessness, ceaseless economic growth, and endless material prosperity must be exposed and discarded because of environmental finitude. The resulting experience of a mourning period for these fantasies will produce a despair that can transform our industrial way of life to one that is more consistent with reality: a postindustrial society that is environmentally sustainable and socially just.

This is where the emerging field of environmental political theory (as exemplified in this volume) can play a vital role by examining and analyzing where and why our industrial civilization is incompatible with the environmental planetary limits and to then prescribe changes that are more in line with these limits. In this manner, environmental political theory can be instrumental in saving our planet from environmental disaster. In this instance, the path to joy will lead through the political despair of our industrial fantasies articulated by environmental political theorists and the corresponding social transformation advocated by them. Could there be a more important field of study?

I think despair led us to this profound transformational political process after the September 11 attacks. I hope—unlike the pessimistic prayer options of Woody Allen—that a shock in the environmental realm equivalent to the September 11 attacks will not be necessary before a commitment to social transformation occurs. We still have time to prevent a shocking, despair-inducing environmental disaster costing tens of thousands or even millions of human and animal lives. Ominously, in the ecological domain, a "surprise" event, one that we have not even conceived of as a threat such as a global-scale environmental catastrophe like the sudden, extreme climate change with all of its threatened dimensions may not allow us the opportunity to change, or give us the time to experience despair to achieve the required social transformation by giving up our illusory socioeconomic fantasies.

Social psychologist and theorist Erich Fromm captured an important point about social illusions when he said: "One needs to destroy illusions in order to create the conditions that make illusions unnecessary."[6] Following this point of Fromm's, I maintain that despair—as illusion busting or fantasy ending—is vitally important to the conduct of political theory whereby our illusions can be burst so that a society not dependent on them and their deleterious consequences may be created. Futurist Alvin Toffler termed the challenge facing us the "awesome but exhilarating task that few generations in human history have ever faced: the design of a new civilization."[7]

My conclusion is that the path to success in this "awesome but exhilarating task" of designing a new civilization, a new civilization that is consistent with both environmental limits and social justice, must occur through the salutary experience of despair because new social values, and new social institutions based on them, are urgently needed. It is imperative, I believe, that we recognize, discard, and finally, mourn for and replace our industrial illusions that are both ecologically fatal and morally undesirable, and that have become globally hegemonic since 1989. In this essential respect, the despair of the aftermath of September 11 can prove to be a lesson of paramount importance for humankind, the planet, and all of its living species, demonstrating the surprising value and necessity of despair.

Notes

Notes to Introduction and Overview

1. *Philosophy and Social Criticism,* 8, no. 1 (Spring 1981): 87–113.
2. Albany: State University of New York Press, 1990.
3. See, Plato, *Last Days of Socrates: Euthyphro, The Apology, Crito*, trans. Hugh Tredennick (Baltimore: Penguin Books, 1954): 71–72.

Notes to Chapter 1

1. Oscar Wilde, *Lady Windermere's Fan*, in *Representative English Plays From the Miracle Plays to Pinero*, 2d ed., eds. J.S.P. Tatlock and R.G. Martin (New York: Appleton-Century-Crofts, 1938): 863.
2. See the introduction to Wilde's play by Tatlock and Martin, ibid., 843.
3. Ibid., 843–44.
4. Henry Kissinger, CBS Television Network, October 13, 1970, quoted in L.S. Stavrianos, *The Promise of the Coming Dark Age* (San Francisco: W.H. Freeman, 1976): 165.
5. Albert O. Hirschman, *Shifting Involvements: Private Interest and Public Policy* (Princeton, NJ: Princeton University Press, 1982):16, emphasis in original.
6. Nicholas Rescher, "What is Value Change? A Framework for Research," in *Values and the Future: The Impact of Technological Change on American Values*, eds. Kurt Baier and Nicholas Rescher (New York: Free Press, 1971): 74, emphasis in original. See p. 82 for Rescher's use of the term "realization erosion."
7. Joan Davis and Samuel March, "Strategies for Societal Development," in *Alternative to Growth I: A Search for Sustainable Futures*, ed. Dennis L. Meadows (Cambridge, MA: Ballinger, 1977): 225.
8. Thomas Hobbes, *Leviathan*, Part I, Chapter XI, See *Leviathan, Parts I and II*, Library of the Liberal Arts Edition, ed. Herbert W. Schneider (Indianapolis, IN: Bobbs-Merrill, 1958): 86.
9. For more on Hobbes and modern political theory from this point of view, see Chapter 8, "Materialism and Modern Political Philosophy," in my book, *The Death of Industrial Civilization* (Albany: State University of New York Press, 1990): 125–42. The current chapter draws upon much of the research done in connection with this publication.
10. Jean-Jacques Rousseau, "Discourse on the Origin of Inequality," in *The Social Contract and Discourses*, ed. Jean-Jacques Rousseau, trans. G.D.H. Cole (New York: E.P. Dutton, 1950): 270.
11. Hobbes, Part 1, Chapter 13, 107.
12. Alfie Kohn, *No Contest: The Case Against Competition* (Boston: Houghton

Mifflin, 1986): 111. The first emphasis is mine, while the second is in the original. The source for the Super Bowl comment is George Leonard, "Winning Isn't Everything, It's Nothing." *Intellectual Digest* 4 (October 1973): 46.

13. See Abram N. Shulsky, "Economic Doctrine in Aristotle's Politics," in C.B. Macpherson, (Compiler), *Political Economy and Political Theory.* Papers from the annual meeting of the Conference for the Study of Political Thought (April 1974): 20–24.

14. Woody Allen, quoted in Robert Byrne, *The 637 Best Things Anybody Ever Said* (New York: Athenaeum, 1982): 79.

15. Kurt Vonnegut Jr., "Only Kidding Folks?" *Nation* 226 (May 13, 1978): 575. Vonnegut is referring to the science fiction works of Stanislaw Lem.

16. While space does not permit a full discussion of the environmental crisis, I would direct the reader to the annual editions of *The State of the World*, produced by the Worldwatch Institute and published by W.W. Norton, and the biannual *World Resources: A Guide to the Global Environment*, produced by the World Resources Institute, the United Nations Environment Programme, the United Nations Development Programme, and the World Bank, and published by Oxford University Press. Also, the recommended additional reading section at the end of this volume provides additional sources on the environmental crisis.

17. Erich Fromm, *To Have or To Be?* (New York, Harper and Row, 1976): 1–2.

18. Donella H. Meadows, Dennis L. Meadows, Jorgen Randers, and William W. Behrens III, *The Limits to Growth: A Report to the Club of Rome's Project on the Predicament of Mankind*, 2d. ed. (New York: New American Library, 1975). For a sample of the huge limits to growth literature this volume has inspired, see Kassiola, Chapter 1, footnote 5, 219–20, and the recommended additional reading section at the end of this volume.

19. Jean-Jacques Rousseau, "A Discourse on the Origin of Inequality," 197.

20. Adam Smith, *An Inquiry into the Nature and Causes of the Wealth of Nations*, Modern Library Editions, ed. Richard F. Teichgraeber III (New York: Random House, 1985), Book 2, Chapter 3, 147.

21. Ibid., Book 1, Chapter 12, 15.

22. Herman E. Daly, "Introduction," in *Toward a Steady State Economy*, ed. Hermann E. Daly (San Francisco: W.H. Freeman, 1973): 281, emphasis in original.

23. For the ancient Greek view where it is asserted that "the Hellenic impulse always emphasized limits," and the *polis* was always limited by what the Greek could take in "at a single view," see Murray Bookchin, *Toward an Ecological Society* (Montreal: Black Rose Books, 1980): 143. For the first Greek political theoretical attack, upon the "unlimited acquisition of money" as "overstepping the boundary of the necessary," see Plato's *Republic*, 372d–373d, 49–50 of the translation by Allan Bloom (New York: Basic Books, 1968). For a general history of the Western opposition to unlimited acquisition, see John Sekura, *Luxury: The Concept in Western Thought, Eden to Smollet* (Baltimore: Johns Hopkins University Press, 1977).

24. Peter L. Berger, Brigitte Berger, and Hansfried Kellner, *The Homeless Mind: Modernization and Consciousness* (New York: Random House, 1973): 185.

25. Walter W. Weisskopf, "Economic Growth versus Existential Balance," in Daly, 242. We should note the similar logic of criticism of Smith by Weisskopf here and Hobbes by Rousseau: Both charge their opponents with a misreading of human

nature as a result of a faulty generalization from one particular historical period of society, modernity, to humanity's basic nature per se.

26. See Thorstein Veblen, *The Theory of the Leisure Class: An Economic Study of Institutions* (New York: New American Library, 1963).

27. See Fred Hirsch, *Social Limits to Growth* (Cambridge: Harvard University Press, 1976).

28. Albert Camus, *The Rebel: An Essay on Man in Revolt*, trans. Anthony Bower (New York: Alfred A. Knopf, 1956): 11.

29. In addition to *The Rebel*, ibid., I would recommend the nonfiction essay, *The Myth of Sisyphus and Other Essays*, trans. Justin O'Brien (New York: Alfred A. Knopf, 1955), and fictional works contained in *Caligula and 3 Other Essays*, trans. Stuart Gilbert (New York: Vintage Books/Random House, 1958), especially the play, *The Just Assassins*.

30. Camus, *The Myth of Sisyphus*, Ibid., 3–8.

31. Ibid., 2.

32. Daniel Bell, *The Cultural Contradictions of Capitalism* (New York: Basic Books, 1976): 49–50.

33. Lewis Mumford, *The Myth of the Machine*, 2 vols., (New York: Harcourt, Brace Jovanovich, 1967, 1970), vol. 1, 203. Once again, with Mumford's last sentence, we confront the criticism of modernity's inconsistency with nature and its mistaking modern humanity's real, limited condition. Compare this to Rousseau's critique of Hobbes and Weisskopf's of Smith.

34. Camus, *The Myth of Sisyphus*, 2.

Note to Chapter 2

1. Albany: State University of New York Press, 1989.

Notes to Chapter 3

1. These kinds of measures of efficiency are proposed in Herman Daly, *Steady State Economics* (San Francisco: W.H. Freeman, 1977), Chapter 4.

2. The dominant social paradigm concept is derived from the work of Thomas Kuhn, *The Structure of Scientific Revolutions* (Chicago: University of Chicago Press, 1962). See also Dennis Pirages and Paul Ehrlich, *Ark II: Social Response to Environmental Imperatives* (New York: Viking Press, 1974).

3. Willis Harman, *An Incomplete Guide to the Future* (New York: W.W. Norton, 1979).

4. Paul Ehrlich, *The Population Bomb* (New York: Ballantine Books, 1968). A good account of the course of environmental activism is provided by John McCormick, *Reclaiming Paradise: The Global Environmental Movement* (Bloomington: Indiana University Press, 1989).

5. Donella H. Meadows, Dennis L. Meadows, Jorgen Randers, and William W. Behrens III, *The Limits to Growth: A Report to the Club of Rome's Project on the Predicament of Mankind* (New York: Universe Books, 1972).

6. Dennis Pirages, *The Sustainable Society: Implications for Limited Growth* (New York: Praeger, 1977).

7. Herman Daly, *Steady State Economics*, Chapter 1.

8. World Commission on Environment and Development, *Our Common Future* (New York: Oxford University Press, 1987): 43.

9. Walter Corson, "Measuring Sustainability: Indicators, Trends, and Performance," in *Building Sustainable Societies: A Blueprint for a Post–Industrial World*, ed. D. Pirages (Armonk, NY: M.E. Sharpe, 1996).

10. Postmaterialism is explored in Ronald Inglehart, *Modernization and Post–Modernization: Cultural, Economic, and Political Change in 43 Societies* (Princeton, NJ: Princeton University Press, 1997).

11. Figures are from the World Bank, *World Development Report 1995* (New York: Oxford University Press, 1995), Table 1.

12. Figures taken from Population Reference Bureau, *1997 World Population Data Sheet* (Washington, DC: Population Reference Bureau, 1997).

13. Daniel Bell, *The Coming of Post-Industrial Society* (New York: Basic Books, 1973).

14. Clifford Cobb, Ted Halstead, and Jonathan Rowe, *The Genuine Progress Indicator* (San Francisco: Redefining Progress, 1995).

15. Organization for Economic Cooperation and Development, *Aging Populations: The Social Policy Implications* (Paris, France: OECD, 1988): 32.

16. Figures derived from World Resources Institute, *World Resources 1996–97* (New York: Oxford University Press, 1996).

17. Thomas A. Wathen, "Trade Policy: Clouds in the Vision of Sustainability," in *Building Sustainable Societies*, ed. D. Pirages (Armonk, NY: M.E. Sharpe, 1996).

18. See Joel J. Kassiola, *The Death of Industrial Civilization* (Albany, NY: State University of New York Press, 1990), and his chapter in this volume.

19. See the evolutionary argument made in Duane Elgin, *Awakening Earth: Exploring the Evolution of Human Culture and Consciousness* (New York: William Morrow, 1993).

Notes to Chapter 4

1. Krishan Kumar, *Utopianism.* (Milton Keynes, UK: Open University Press, 1991): 27–28.

2. Ibid., 27.

3. Bryan Norton. *Toward Unity Among Environmentalists* (New York: Oxford University Press, 1991).

4. Kumar, 1991, 29.

5. Donella Meadow, Dennis Meadows, and Jorgen Randers, *Beyond the Limits: Global Collapse or a Sustainable Future* (London: Earthscan, 1992): 8–9.

6. Ibid., xvi.

7. Lyman Sargent, "The Three Faces of Utopianism Revisited." *Utopian Studies* (n.d.): 6.

8. Kumar, 29.

9. Kumar, *Utopian and Anti-Utopia in Modern Times* (Oxford, UK: Basil Blackwell, 1987): 103.

10. P. Bunyard, and F. Morgan-Grenville, *The Green Alternative: Guide to Good Living* (London: Methuen, 1987): 71, my emphasis.

11. Edmund Burke, *Reflections on the Revolution in France* (Hammondsworth, UK: Penguin Books, 1790/1968): 119–20.

12. Kumar, 1987, 103.

13. Kumar, 1991, 29.

14. Kumar, 1987, 100.

15. Ibid.

16. Ibid., 405.

17. Kumar, 1991, 106.

18. Kumar, 1987, 110.

19. John Gray, *Beyond the New Right: Markets, Government and the Common Environment* (London: Routledge, 1993), Chapter 4, 124.

20. Kumar, 1987, 100.

21. William Ophuls, *Ecology and the Politics of Scarcity: A Prologue to a Political Theory of the Steady State* (San Francisco: W. Freeman, 1977).

22. By, for example, Kropotkin, *Fields, Factories and Workshops* (London: Hutchinson, 1899).

23. Given the arguments over whether there is such a thing as a natural condition, "Natural" might be better here.

24. R. Bahro, *Building the Green Movement* (London: Heretic Books, 1986): 90.

25. R. Bahro, *Avoiding Social and Ecological Disaster: The Politics of World Transformation* (Bath, UK: Gateway Books, 1994): 306.

26. Small experiments "doomed to failure," according to Marx's assessment of utopian schemes outlined in the Communist Manifesto in L. Feuer, *Marx and Engels: Basic Writings on Politics and Philosophy* (Glasgow, Scotland, 1976): 79.

28. E. Goldsmith, *A Blueprint for Survival* (London: Tom Stacey, 1972).

29. Kumar, 1991: 3–4.

30. E. Goldsmith, *The Way: An Ecological World-View* (London: Rider, 1992): 353.

31. William Ophuls, "The Politics of a Sustainable Society." In *The Sustainable Society: Implication for Limited Growth*, ed. D. Pirages (New York: Praeger, 1977).

32. André Gorz, *Ecology as Politics* (London: Pluto Press, 1987): 47.

33. Ibid., 9.

34. Tim Hayward, *Ecological Thought: An Introduction* (Oxford, UK: Polity Press, 1995).

35. Hayward criticizes this stance, and makes a sustained argument for the enlightening of ecology and the ecologizing of Enlightenment.

36. Kumar, 1991, 100.

37. John Dryzek, "Green Reason: Communicative Ethics for the Biosphere." *Environmental Ethics* 12 (1990): 195–210.

38. John Dryzek, *Discursive Democracy: Politics, Policy and Social Science* (Cambridge, MA: Cambridge University Press, 1990): 15.

39. See, for example, Julian Simon, *The Ultimate Resource* (Princeton, NJ: Princeton University Press, 1981).

40. Albert Weale, *The New Politics of Pollution* (Manchester, UK: Manchester University Press, 1992).

41. Ibid., 76.

42. See the conclusion in A. Dobson, *Green Political Thought: An Introduction.* 2d ed. (London: Routledge, 1995) for a detailed description.

43. Peter Christoff, "Ecological Modernization, Ecological Modernities." *Environmental Politics* 5, no. 3 (1996): 476–50.

Notes to Chapter 5

1. Robert Paehlke, *Environmentalism and the Future of Progressive Politics* (New Haven: Yale University Press, 1989).

2. Robert Paehlke, "Eco-History: Two Waves in the Evolution of Environmentalism." *Alternatives: Perspectives on Society, Technology and Environment* 19 (September/October 1992): 18–23.

3. Barbara Jancar-Webster, "Eastern Europe: Environmental Problems." In *Conservation and Environmentalism: An Encyclopedia*, ed. Robert Paehlke (New York: Garland, 1995), pp. 187–92; Philip R. Pryde, "Former Soviet Union." In *Conservation and Environmentalism: An Encyclopedia*, ed. Robert Paehlke (New York: Garland, 1995): 294–96.

4. *Our Common Future: The Report of the World Commission on Environment and Development*, ed. Gro Hartem Brandland, chair (New York: Oxford University Press, 1987).

5. Mathis Wackernagel and William Rees, *Our Ecological Footprint: Reducing Human Impact on Earth* (Philadelphia: New Society, 1996).

6. Marina Fischer-Kowalski and Helmut Haberl, "Tons, Joules, and Money: Modes of Production and Their Sustainability Problems," *Society & Natural Resources* 10 (1997): 61–85.

7. William Greider, *One World, Ready or Not: The Manic Logic of Global Capitalism* (New York: Simon & Schuster, 1997).

8. Jeremy Rifkin, *The End of Work* (New York: G.P. Putnam's Sons, 1995).

9. See, for example, Bron R. Taylor, *Ecological Resistance Movements: The Global Emergence of Radical and Popular Environmentalism* (Albany: State University of New York Press, 1995).

10. Benjamin R. Barber, *Jihad vs. McWorld* (New York: Random House/Ballantine Books, 1995).

11. George Soros, "The Capitalist Threat." *Atlantic Monthly* 279 (February 1997): 45–8.

12. James Goldsmith, *The Trap* (London: Macmillan, 1994).

13. Norman Myers, "Biodepletion," and "Tropical Deforestation." In *Conservation and Environmentalism: An Encyclopedia*, ed. Robert Paehlke (New York: Garland, 1995): 77–80, 642–45.

14. Robert Putnam, "Bowling Alone: America's Declining Social Capital." *Journal of Democracy* 6: 65–68.

15. Wackernagel and Rees, *Our Ecological Footprint*.

16. Robert Paehlke and Douglas Torgerson, *Managing Leviathan: Environmental Politics and the Administrative State* (Peterborough, Ontario: Broadview Press, 1990); William M. Lafferty, and James Meadowcroft, *Democracy and the Environment: Problems and Prospects* (Cheltenham, UK: Edward Elgar, 1996).

17. See Paehlke and Torgerson for details.

18. Michael Kidron, *Western Capitalism Since the War* (London: Penguin, 1970).

19. Richard Gwyn, "IMF Now De Facto Government for Millions." *Toronto Star* (December 19, 1997): A25.

20. See, for example, David Malin Roodman, *Paying the Piper: Subsidies, Politics, and the Environment* (Washington, DC: Worldwatch Institute, 1996); C. Jeanrenaud, ed. *Environmental Policy Between Regulation and Market* (Basel, Switzerland: Birkhäuser Verlag, 1997); and Robert Gale, Stephen Barg, and Alexander Gillies, *Green Budget Reform* (London: Earthscan, 1995).

21. Clarence J. Davies and Jan Mazurek, *Regulating Pollution: Does the U.S. System Work?* (Washington, DC: Resources for the Future, 1997).

22. On climate warning reforms, see for example Toronto Atmospheric Fund, *Realizing Toronto's Target for Greenhouse Gas Emission Reductions—Current Trends and Outlook* (Toronto, Canada: Torrie Smith Associates, 1997).

Notes to Chapter 6

1. Perhaps the clearest articulation of the claim that we already have overshot the carrying capacity of the planet is William R. Catton Jr., *Overshoot: The Ecological Basis of Revolutionary Change* (Urbana: University of Illinois Press, 1980): 52.

2. Freely adapted from *Rachel's Environment Health Weekly* (October 30, 1997), Environmental Research Foundation, P.O. Box 5036, Annapolis, MD, 21403, FAX (410) 263–8944; e-mail: erf@rachel.clark.net.

3. For a fuller development and critique of these assumptions, see my *Regarding Nature: Industrialism and Deep Ecology* (Albany: State University of New York Press, 1993).

4. See Raymond Dasmann, *Environmental Conservation*, 5th ed. (New York: Wiley, 1984).

5. "Ritual Regulation of Environmental Relations Among a New Guinea People," in Roy A. Rappaport, *Ecology, Meaning and Religion* (Berkeley, CA: North Atlantic Books, 1979): 28.

6. Robert Heilbroner notes that defining capitalism is a "profound and perplexing" problem to which he devoted his book, *The Nature and Logic of Capitalism* (New York: W.W. Norton, 1985).

7. The question of ownership in modern capitalism is complex, since many corporations are legally owned by stockholders who can exercise no effective control over the actions of the corporation. The classic study of this divorce of ownership and control is Adolf A. Berle and Gardiner C. Means, *The Modern Corporation and Private Property* (New York: Macmillan, 1922).

8. Fred Hirsch, *Social Limits to Growth* (Cambridge: Harvard University Press, 1976).

9. Paul Wachtel, *The Poverty of Affluence* (Philadelphia: New Society Publishers, 1989).

10. Of course, those who are regulated in this way tend to take control of the agencies of regulation. See Murray Edelman, *The Symbolic Uses of Politics* (Urbana: University of Illinois Press, 1964).

11. In this regard, see Jurgen Habermas, *Legitimation Crisis* (Boston: Beacon Press, 1975).

12. Hugh Stretton, *Capitalism, Socialism and the Environment* (New York: Cambridge University Press, 1976): 6.

13. For valuable ideas concerning such an economy, see *Economics, Ecology, Ethics: Essays Toward a Steady-State Economy*, ed. Herman E. Daly (San Francisco: Freeman and Co., 1980); and Herman E. Daly and John B. Cobb Jr., *For the Common Good: Redirecting the Economy Toward Community, the Environment, and a Sustainable Future* (Boston: Beacon Press, 1989).

14. Philip R. Pryde, "The 'Decade of the Environment' in the USSR," *Science* 220 (April 15, 1983): 275.

15. "The Puritan wanted to work in a calling; we are forced to do so. [The modern economic order] is now bound to the technical and economic conditions of ma-

chine production which today determine the lives of all individuals who are born into this mechanism, not only those directly concerned with economic acquisition, with irresistible force. Perhaps it will so determine them until the last ton of fossilized coal is burnt. In Baxter's view the care for external goods should lie on the shoulders of the 'saint like a light cloak, which can be thrown aside at any moment.' But fate decreed that the cloak should become an iron cage." Max Weber, *The Protestant Ethic and the Spirit of Capitalism*, trans. Talcott Parsons (New York: Scribner's, 1958): 181.

16. See the review of survey evidence within and between societies reported by Richard A. Easterlin, "Does Economic Growth Improve the Human Lot?" In *Nations and Households in Economic Growth*, eds. Paul A. David and Melvin W. Reder (Stanford, CA: Stanford University Press, 1972).

17. This phenomenon has been discussed from different perspectives at some length. For economic perspectives, see Tibor Scitovsky, *The Joyless Economy: An Inquiry into Human Satisfaction and Consumer Dissatisfaction* (New York: Oxford University Press, 1976); and Fred Hirsch, *Social Limits to Growth* (Cambridge: Harvard University Press, 1976). See Paul Wachtel, *The Poverty of Affluence* (Philadelphia: New Society Publishers, 1989) for a psychological perspective and Albert Borgmann, *Technology and the Character of Contemporary Life* (Chicago: University of Chicago Press, 1984), for a philosophical perspective on consumerism.

18. Marshall Sahlins, *Stone Age Economics* (Chicago: Aldine, 1972): 1–2.

19. See Sahlins and Colin Turnbull's lyrical description of the lives of rain forest pygmies in *The Forest People: A Study of the Pygmies of the Congo* (New York: Simon and Schuster, 1961).

20. Nafis Sadik, *The State of World Population* (New York: United Nations Population Fund, 1990): 12; emphasis in original.

21. The estimate is Michael Soulé's, "Conservation Biology and the 'Real World,'" in *Conservation Biology: The Science of Scarcity and Diversity*, ed. Michael E. Soulé (Sunderland, UK: Sinauer Associates, 1986): 4.

22. Neil Evernden, *The Natural Alien: Humankind and the Environment* (Toronto, Canada: University of Toronto Press, 1985): 11–12.

23. Full page advertisement on the back cover of *E: The Environmental Magazine*, 2, no. 3 (May/June 1991). It has run more than once.

24. Two anthologies are available that offer excellent introductions to deep ecology: George Sessions, ed. *Deep Ecology for the 21st Century* (Boston: Shambala, 1995); and Alan Drengson and Yuichi Inoue, eds. *The Deep Ecology Movement* (Berkeley, CA: North Atlantic Books, 1995).

25. The phrase is the title of Arthur Lovejoy's fertile study of the history of this notion in Western philosophy and literature. See his *Great Chain of Being: A Study of the History of an Idea* (Cambridge: Harvard University Press, 1936).

26. Ibid., 293; emphasis added.

27. See Colin Turnbull's *The Forest People*.

28. Herman E. Daly and John B. Cobb, *For the Common Good: Redirecting the Economy Toward Community, the Environment, and a Sustainable Future* (Boston: Beacon Press, 1989).

29. Bhikkhu Bodhi, "Foreword," *Buddhist Perspectives on the Ecocrisis*, Klaus Sandell, ed. (Kandy, Sri Lanka: Buddhist Publication Society, 1987): vi.

30. Arne Naess, *Ecology, Community and Lifestyle: Outline of an Ecosophy*, trans. David Rothenberg (New York: Cambridge University Press, 1989): 24.

31. Naess, *Ecology,* 91.

32. Robert C. Paehlke, *Environmentalism and the Future of Progressive Politics* (New Haven: Yale University Press, 1989): 168.

33. David M. Johns, "The Relevance of Deep Ecology to the Third World: Some Preliminary Comments," *Environmental Ethics* 12, no. 3 (1990): 242.

34. Karl Marx, "Economic and Philosophic Manuscripts," in Robert C. Tucker, *The Marx-Engels Reader* (New York: Norton, 1972): 80; emphasis in original. Interestingly, Marx also recognizes the process of the extension of identification when he claims that when workers unite in struggle, they acquire a new need for society: "The brotherhood of man is no mere phrase with them, but a fact of life," 100–101.

35. Naess, *Ecology, Community and Lifestyle*, 138.

Notes to Chapter 7

1. The term "green" in my title and throughout the text refers to a composite of the various social movements and political parties that go by that name across Europe, America, and Australasia. Although their emphases vary, all would share the core values enunciated by German greens in their 1983 election manifesto, "Our policy is a policy of active partnership with nature," ecological in its basic orientation, egalitarian in its social aspects, grassroots democratic politically, and committed to principles of nonviolence. See Die Grunen, *Programme of the German Green Party*, trans. Hans Fernbach (London: Heretic Books, 1983): 7.

2. Department of the Prime Minister and Cabinet, Commonwealth of Australia, *Ecologically Sustainable Development: A Commonwealth Discussion Paper* (Canberra: Australian Government Printing Service, June 1990).

3. John Passmore, *Man's Responsibility for Nature*, 2d ed. (London: Duckworth, 1980): 73.

4. P.S. Dasgupta and G.M. Heal, *Economic Theory and Exhaustible Resources* (Cambridge, UK: Cambridge University Press, 1979).

5. Some would say, with some justification, that the issues driving green politics are so different in different countries that it makes little sense to talk about green politics in general. But green ideas have proven sufficiently contagious, internationally, that there is an awfully lot in common between the canonical 1983 *Programme of the German Green Party*, and, for example, the U.S. green umbrella organization's statement of *Ten Key Values* (Kansas City, MO: Committees of Correspondence, 1986). See further Jonathon Porritt, *Seeing Green* (Oxford, UK: Blackwell, 1984); Charlene Spretnak and Fritjof Capra, *Green Politics*, rev. ed. (Santa Fe, NM: Bear & Co., 1986); and Arne Naess, *Ecology, Community and Lifestyle*, trans. David Rothenberg (Cambridge, UK: Cambridge University Press, 1989), especially chapter 6.

6. In the book I wrote from which this essay is drawn—*Green Political Theory* (Manchester, UK: Manchester University Press, 1991)—I further distinguish a green theory of agency (advocating decentralization, participatory democracy, and such). That, I there argue, is yet again distinct from (and, even within green political theory itself, lower in priority than) the green theory of value that gives unity to all the substantive green public policy proposals.

7. More established parties tend to be "catchall" parties, alliances of disparate factions with disparate interests. Being so naturally prevents them from offering programs displaying the clarity of moral vision of the greens.

8. That is not necessarily to say that we must always and everywhere accept green conclusions, if we ever accept them anywhere. But it is to say, purely as a matter of logic, that it simply is illegitimate for us to disregard for some purpose considerations that we take to be utterly compelling for others.

9. The larger project is carried forward in my book on *Green Political Theory*.

10. Compare, though, the differential weight given to each by, for example, W.D. Ross, *The Right and the Good* (Oxford, UK: Clarendon Press, 1930), and Richard B. Brandt, *Theory of the Good and the Right* (Oxford, UK: Clarendon Press, 1979).

11. As even Bernard Williams—himself no friend of consequentialism—is the first to admit. See his "A Critique of Utilitarianism," eds. J.J.C. Smart and Bernard Williams, in *Utilitarianism For and Against* (Cambridge, UK: Cambridge University Press, 1973): 75–150.

12. Officially, of course, there is a world of difference: The economic theory of value is supposed to be an empirical theory, whereas the philosophical theory of The Good is a normative theory. An economic theory of value, economists would want to insist, is just a predictive device in positive economics telling us the rate at which things exchange for one another. For all their positivistic pretensions, though, a theory of value is for economists as much as for philosophers a theory about what is and ought to be of value. That certainly is true of the main backers of the two theories of value, which I discuss below as being the principal competitors with my own. In their candid moments, neoclassical economists clearly concede that they regard consumer satisfaction as providing both the analytical source of market prices and the moral justification for allocating resources through a market relying upon them. Both Locke and, in his moralizing moments, Marx similarly regarded labor as both the source of exchange value and of moral entitlements.

13. It is not as if the standard economic theory of value does not have deeper philosophical underpinnings. In many respects the theory of The Good underlying neoclassical welfare economic theories of value amounts to little more than a stripped-down form of Bentham's hedonic calculus of human pleasure and its components. Economists are just rarely prepared to debate the merits of their theory of value when it is described in those terms.

14. See especially Naess, *Ecology, Community and Lifestyle*, chapter 5.

15. On these topics, see quite generally Frank H. Knight, "Value and Price," in *Encyclopedia of the Social Sciences, vol. 15*, ed. E.R.A. Seligman (New York: Macmillan, 1935): 218–25.

16. Knight's essay on "Value and Price" is a good guide to how economists traditionally have—and have not—addressed these issues. For recent philosophical accounts, see Brandt, *Theory of the Good and the Right*, and James Griffin, *Well-Being* (Oxford, UK: Clarendon Press, 1986), especially Part 1.

17. Fernando Vianello, "Labour Theory of Value," *The New Palgrave* 3 (1987): 107–13; Jon Elster, "The Labour Theory of Value," in *Making Sense of Marx* (Cambridge, UK: Cambridge University Press, 1985): 127–41.

18. "Disingenuously" because, as a long string of economists dating back beyond Adam Smith rightly complain, references to considerations like hardness are implicit appeals to the human purposes for which hard objects might be handy. And

when the implicit is made explicit, such theories of value cease to be natural re-source-based at all and instead become consumer-based. Naturally occurring prop-erties are then valuable really as amended in relation to, and indeed by virtue of, human purposes.

19. G. Weulersse, "Economics: History of Economic Thought: The Physiocrats," *Encyclopedia of the Social Sciences*, 5: 348–51.

20. Marxists reply to greens: Natural resources are of no use to anyone until they have been shaped by human hands to human purposes; in the classically Lockean version of this tale, even acorns must be picked up off the ground before they can be eaten. Neoclassical welfare economists reply to both Marxists and to greens: They may be right about *why* people value objects, but what it *is* for a thing to have value is intimately connected with the consumption act; at the end of the day, there can be no value without valuers: In Adam Smith's memorable example, if a man is dying of thirst diamonds are not nearly as valuable as water, whatever the productive histo-ries, intrinsic properties, or objective scarcities of the two commodities.

21. Distinguishing, for example, between what it means for something to have value, where that value comes from, how it is realized, and so on. By seeing all these competing theories of value as answers to slightly different questions about value, we might be able to concoct a composite theory that combines the strengths of all. Or we might not. In particular, the Marxist and green theories of value might be rather hard to reconcile, insofar as the one says that things have value by virtue of having been shaped by nature and the other by virtue of having been molded by the labor of humanity.

22. That is not to say that human creations have no value, merely that those man-made replicas have necessarily less value than the ones arising out of natural pro-cesses. For a homely example, recall that while natural pearls are considerably more valuable than cultured ones, the latter are not without value.

23. Although logically distinct, I shall here conflate these two types of theory—as they inevitably are conflated, wherever (as in the green theory of value, as well as in the other examples I shall discuss below) what matters about an object's history is the fact that certain processes figure in it.

24. See Robert Nozick, *Anarchy, State and Utopia* (Oxford, UK: Blackwell, 1974), especially chapter 7, where Nozick discusses this theory.

25. That perception, commonplace among political theorists, is equally common among ordinary citizens as well; see Tom R. Tyler, *Why People Obey the Law* (New Haven, CT: Yale University Press, 1990).

26. This theme is effectively elaborated by Mark Sagoff in "The Aesthetic Status of Forgeries," *Journal of Aesthetics and Art Criticism* 35 (1976): 169–80 and "On Restoring and Reproducing Art," *Journal of Philosophy* 75 (1978): 453–70. See also Colin Radford, "Fakes," *Mind* 87 (1978): 66–76, and more especially, the pa-pers collected in Denis Dutton, *The Forger's Art* (Berkeley: University of California Press, 1983).

27. The same is transparently true of historical landmarks, of course. Independence Hall is especially valuable because of the history of what happened there. Had it a different history—had the U.S. Constitution been drafted and signed elsewhere—that particular building would lose its significance and its peculiar value to us.

28. Martin H. Kriger, "What's Wrong with Plastic Trees?" *Science* 179 (1973): 446–55.

29. Legal philosophers who subsequently joined the debate inspired by Kriger's article show much more sophistication in this respect: Laurence H. Tribe, "Ways Not to Think About Plastic Trees: New Foundations for Environmental Law," *Yale Law Journal* 83 (1974): 1315–48; Mark Sagoff, "On Preserving the Natural Environment," *Yale Law Journal* 84 (1974): 205–67; and Laurence H. Tribe, "From Environmental Foundations to Constitutional Law: Learning from Nature's Future," *Yale Law Journal* 85 (1975): 545–56.

30. For an excellent discussion both of that particular case and of the larger issues it raises, see Robert Elliot, "Faking Nature," *Inquiry* 25 (1982): 81–93.

31. Ibid.

32. In the most powerful recent restatement of this theme, Bill McKibben, *The End of Nature* (New York: Random House, 1989) writes, "We have deprived nature of its independence, and that is fatal to its meaning. Nature's independence is its meaning; without it there is nothing but us" (58). And in consequence, "We can no longer imagine that we are part of something larger than ourselves—that is what all this boils down to" (83).

McKibben develops that theme particularly by reference to climatic change. "The greenhouse effect is a more apt name than those who coined it imagined. . . . We have built a greenhouse, a human creation, where once there bloomed a sweet and wild garden" (91). As he writes elsewhere, "By changing the weather, we make every spot on earth man-made and artificial. . . . A child born now will never know a natural summer, a natural autumn, winter, or spring. Summer is going extinct, replaced by something else that will be called 'summer.' This new summer will retain some of its relative characteristics—it will be hotter than the rest of the year, for instance, and the time of year when crops grow—but it will not be summer, just as even the post prosthesis is not a leg" (59).

33. Cynics might say that we could equally fix our place in the external world by adopting, as our life's project, the destroying or taming of things outside of and larger than ourselves. This theme is not unfamiliar: Frontiersmen talk in these terms of "taming the wilderness," Marxian economists of productive labor infusing value into intrinsically worthless raw materials. But insofar as the satisfaction in view is derived from the fact that you bring that which was originally outside of yourself, then to that extent this project is self-defeating. The more you succeed in bringing everything under your control, the less there is of a world that is outside of and larger than yourself in which you can set your life's work.

34. Some green writers experience no such reticence. For a spiritual twist to this tale, reflect, for example, upon talk of stewardship in the Judeo-Christian tradition, as discussed by John Passmore, *Man's Responsibility for Nature*, 28–42, and, among more explicitly green writers, Aldo Leopold, *A Sand County Almanac* (Oxford, UK: Oxford University Press, 1949); Charlene Spretnak, *The Spiritual Dimension of Green Politics* (Santa Fe, NM: Bear & Co., 1986); and McKibben, *The End of Nature*, 70–80. Or consider expressions, common within the deep ecology movement, like the "unity and diversity of life" and "wholeness," evoking as they do more Buddhist or Hindu echoes; see Naess, *Ecology, Community and Lifestyle*, chapter 7; and Richard Sylvan, "A Critique of Deep Ecology," *Radical Philosophy* 40 (Summer 1985): 2–12, and 41 (Autumn 1985): 10–22.

35. See, for example, Arne Naess, "The Shallow and the Deep, Long-Range Ecology Movements," *Inquiry* 16 (1973): 95–100, and *Ecology, Community and*

Lifestyle, especially chapters 1 and 7; Sylvan, "Critique of Deep Ecology"; and Bill Devall and George Sessions, *Deep Ecology: Living as if Nature Mattered* (Salt Lake City: Gibbs Smith, 1985).

36. Spretnak and Capra, *Green Politics*, chapter 2; Sylvan, "Critique"; Naess, *Ecology, Community, and Lifestyle*; Tim Luke, "Dreams of Deep Ecology," *Telos* 76 (1988): 65–92.

37. As Brian Barry, *Democracy, Power and Justice* (Oxford, UK: Clarendon Press, 1989): 303, complained of a similar rhetorical trick in Steven Lukes's "three-dimensional analysis of power," who would want a one- or two-dimensional analysis of anything when a three-dimensional analysis was on offer?

38. Richard Routley [Sylvan] and Val Routley [Plumwood], "Human Chauvinism and Environmental Ethics," in *Environmental Philosophy*, eds. D.S. Mannison, M.A. McRobbie, and R. Routley, 96–189 (Canberra: Australian National University, 1980), at 121–22; see also their "Against the Inevitability of Human Chauvinism," in *Ethics and Problems of the 21st Century*, eds. K.E. Goodpaster and K.M. Sayre (Notre Dame, IN: University of Notre Dame Press, 1979): 36–59.

39. Donald H. Regan, "Duties of Preservation," in Bryan G. Norton, ed. *The Preservation of Species* (Princeton, NJ: Princeton University Press, 1980), 203. Perhaps this is what is being urged, less clearly, by Holmes Rolston III, in "Values in Nature," *Environmental Ethics* 3 (1981): 113–28 and "Valuing Wildlands," *Environmental Ethics* 7 (1985): 23–48, expanded in his *Environmental Ethics* (Philadelphia, PA: Temple University Press, 1988).

40. See, for example, Routley and Routley, "Human Chauvinism."

41. Regan, "Duties of Preservation," 203.

42. J.S. Mill, "Nature," in *Collected Works Vol. 10*, ed. J.M. Robson, 373–402 (Toronto: University of Toronto Press, 1969).

43. Mill, "Nature," 380; Elliott Sober, "Philosophical Problems for Environmentalism," in *The Preservation of Species*, ed. Bryan G. Norton at 180 (Princeton, NJ: Princeton University Press, 1986). The quoted passage appears in italics in the original. For an evocative albeit unphilosophical retort, see McKibben, *End of Nature*, 64–68.

44. Indeed, if human creation is natural, too, then on this account stopping humans from destroying ancient monuments and historical landmarks that past humans have created is just part and parcel of preventing naturally created values from being naturally destroyed.

45. Notice that the self-defeatingness objection, canvassed in footnote 32 above, does not generalize as an objection to all destruction. The point there was merely that humanity is destroying its own source of satisfaction, insofar as satisfaction is derived from destroying things only if they have been created by nonhuman forces. If instead humanity could derive similar satisfaction from destruction per se (of human as of nonhuman creation, equally) then we really would have the basis for a perpetual motion satisfaction machine.

46. Mill, "Nature," 80–81.

47. Or, again, you might similarly set your own life in the context of the larger present projects of your group as a whole.

48. M.P. Golding and N.H. Golding, "Why Preserve Landmarks?" in *Ethics and Problems of the 21st Century*, eds. K.E. Goadpaster and K.M. Sayre (Notre Dame: Indiana University of Notre Dame Press, 1979): 175–90.

49. Which I think will generally, if not invariably, tend toward the same conclu-

sions. Not invariably, though, because many of the ancient monuments in question might be regarded as being every bit as much triumphs of the human will over natural barriers as is the city of Los Angeles.

50. John Passmore similarly contrasts models of "Man as Despot" with models of "Stewardship and Co-operation with Nature" in his seminal work, *Man's Responsibility for Nature*, chapters 1 and 2, respectively.

51. Marc Reisner, *Cadillac Desert: The American West and Its Disappearing Water* (New York: Viking Penguin, 1986).

52. It well may be more natural for nature to be perpetually out of balance, displaying wild cycles with great regularity.

53. Which may well be the case.

54. I am grateful for the comments of participants at the Annual Symposium of the Australian Academy of the Humanities, particularly Tony Coady, John Mulvaney, John Passmore, Philip Pettit, and Peter Singer. This essay summarizes and condenses work related to my book on *Green Political Theory*. For helpful discussions of those larger themes I am grateful to Richard Arneson, Brian Barry, David Copp, John Dryzek, Jon Elster, William Galston, Jean Hampton, Onora O'Neill, Philip Pettit, John Roemer, Richard Sylvan, and Albert Weale.

Notes to Chapter 8

1. See especially Robert Paehlke, *Environmentalism and the Future of Progressive Politics* (New Haven: Yale University Press, 1989).

2. See Thomas Fraser Homer-Dixon's essays, "On the Threshold: Environmental Changes as Causes of Acute Conflicts," *International Security* 16 (1991): 76–116, and "Environmental Scarcities and Violent Conflict," *International Security* 19 (1994): 5–40.

3. Michael E. Zimmerman, "Toward a Heideggerean *Ethos* for Radical Environmentalism," *Environmental Ethics* 5 (Summer 1983): 99–131; "The Thorn in Heidegger's Side: The Question of National Socialism," *The Philosophical Forum* 20 (Summer 1989): 326–65; "Rethinking the Heidegger—Deep Ecology Relationship," *Environmental Ethics* 15, no. 3 (Fall, 1993): 195–224.

4. Michael E. Zimmerman, "The Threat of Ecofascism," *Social Theory and Praxis* 21 (Summer 1995): 207–38.

5. Robert Pippin, "On the Notion of Technology as Ideology: Prospects," in *Technology, Pessimism, and Postmodernism*, eds. Yaron Ezrahi, Everett Mendelsohn, and Howard Segal (Dordrecht: Kluwer Academic Publishers, 1994): 93–113. Quotation is from p. 111.

6. Ibid., 108.

7. Reported by Glen Justice in "Group: Gas Leak Response Racist," *Times-Picayune*, New Orleans, October 29, 1995, B1.

8. Reported by Sara Shipley in "Cochran Fires Up Crowd for Bogalusa Class Action," *Times-Picayune*, New Orleans, November 10, 1995, A1, 16.

9. To give proper credit to Louisiana's petrochemical industry, I should point out that toxic emissions have declined dramatically during the past fifteen years.

10. In this regard, consider the role played both by the Great Awakening and by Masonic ideals in the theory and practice of the American Revolution.

11. For an excellent account of current theoretical challenges to the liberal doc-

trine of church-state separation, see C. Judd Owen, *Religion and the Decline of Liberal Rationalism* (Chicago: University of Chicago Press, 2001).

12. A distressing example is the unprecedented ecological catastrophe wreaked by the command economies of the former Soviet bloc. Indeed, anger about the public health and economic consequences of ecological destruction was a significant factor in the revolt by Eastern European countries against the Soviet Union. See Murray Feshbach and Alfred Friendly Jr., *Ecocide in the USSR: Health and Nature Under Seige* (New York: BasicBooks, 1992).

13. Michael E. Zimmerman, "A Strategic Direction for 21st Century Environmentalism: Free Market Environmentalism," *Strategies: Journal of Theory, Culture, and Politics* 13, no. 1 (May 2000): 89–110.

14. See Anna Bramwell, *Blood and Soil: Richard Walther Darre and Hitler's "Green Party"* (Bourne End, Buckinghamshire, UK: Kensal Press, 1985).

15. For a discussion of these disturbing right-wing political trends in Germany, see Janet Biehl, "'Ecology' and the Modernization of Fascism in the German Ultra-Right," in *Ecofascism: Lessons from the German Experience*, eds. Janet Biehl and Peter Staudenmaier (San Francisco: AK Press, 1995). For a critique of the antimodernist trends of some environmentalism, see Anna Bramwell, *Ecology in the Twentieth Century: A History* (New Haven, CT: Yale University Press, 1989).

16. Introduction to *Social Theory and the Global Environment*, eds. Michael Redclift and Ted Benton (London and New York: Routledge, 1994): 3.

17. See Jeffrey Herf, "Belated Pessimism: Technology and Twentieth Century German Conservative Intellectuals," in *Technology, Pessimism, and Postmodernism*, 115–36.

18. Max Horkheimer and Theodor W. Adorno, *Dialectic of Enlightenment* (New York: Continuum, 1976).

19. See Luc Ferry and Alain Renaut, *French Philosophy of the Sixties: An Essay in Antihumanism*, trans. Mary H.S. Cattani. (Amherst: University of Massachusetts Press, 1990).

20. See Donald Worster, "The Ecology of Order and Chaos," *Environmental Review* 14 (1990): 1–18.

21. For example, see: Bjorn Lomborg, *The Skeptical Environmentalist: Measuring the Real State of the World* (New York: Cambridge University Press, 2001); Joseph L. Bast, Peter J. Hill, and Richard C. Rue, *Eco-Sanity: A Common Sense Guide to Environmentalism* (Lanham, MD: Madison Books, 1996); Ronald Bailey, *Ecoscam: The False Prophecies of Ecological Calamity* (New York: St. Martin's Press, 1993); Wallace Kaufman, *No Turning Back: Dismantling the Fantasies of Environmental Thinking* (New York: Basic Books, 1994); Jacqueline Vaughn Switzer, *Green Backlash: The History and Politics of Environmental Opposition in the U.S.* (Boulder, CO: Lynne Rienner Publishers, 1997).

For opposing views, see Andrew Rowell, *Green Backlash: Global Subversion of the Environmental Movement* (New York: Routledge, 1996). But see also Michael Tobias, *World War III: Population and the Biosphere at the End of the Millennium* (Santa Fe, NM: Bear & Co., 1994); Paul R. Ehrlich and Anne H. Ehrlich, *Betrayal of Science and Reason: How Anti-Environment Rhetoric Threatens Our Future* (Washington, DC: Island Press, 1998).

22. Steven Vogel, *Against Nature: The Concept of Nature in Critical Theory* (New York: State University of New York Press, 1996).

214 NOTES TO CHAPTER 8

23. See Michael E. Soulé, "The Social Siege of Nature," in *Reinventing Nature? Responses to Postmodern Deconstruction*, eds. Michael E. Soulé and Gary Lease (Washington, DC: Island Press, 1995): 137–70. For a discussion of the issues raised in this book, see Michael E. Zimmerman, "The Postmodern Challenge to Environmentalism," *Terra Nova* 1 (1996): 129–38. See also Neil Evernden's insightful work, *The Social Creation of Nature* (Baltimore: Johns Hopkins University Press, 1992).

24. See Donna Haraway, *Simians, Cyborgs, and Women: The Reinvention of Nature* (New York: Routledge, 1991); N. Catherine Hayles, "Searching for Common Ground," in Soulé, *Reinventing Nature?*, 47–64.

25. See many of the essays in the excellent anthology, *Feminist Epistemologies*, eds. Linda Alcoff and Elizabeth Potter (New York: Routledge, 1993).

26. Neil Evernden, *The Natural Alien: Humankind and Environment* (Toronto: University of Toronto Press, 1985).

27. Arne Naess, *Ecology, Community, and Lifestyle*, trans. and ed. David Rothenberg (New York: Cambridge University Press, 1990).

28. Carolyn Merchant, *The Death of Nature* (New York: Harper & Row, 1980).

29. See Susan Bordo, "The Cartesian Masculinization of Thought," *Signs* 11 (1986): 439–56.

30. Karen J. Warren, "The Power and the Promise of Ecological Feminism," *Environmental Ethics* 12 (1990): 125–46. More recently, see Warren, *Ecofeminist Philosophy: A Western Perspective on What It Is and Why It Matters* (Lanham, MD: Rowman & Littlefield, 2000).

31. See my essay, "Deep Ecology and Ecofeminism: The Emerging Dialogue" in *Reweaving the World: The Emergence of Ecofeminism*, eds. Irene Diamond and Floria Feman Orenstein (San Francisco: Sierra Club Books, 1990).

32. Murray Bookchin, *The Ecology of Freedom* (Palo Alto, CA: Chesire Books, 1982).

33. Ken Wilber, *Sex, Ecology, Spirituality* (Boston: Shambhala, 1995). See also Wilber, *A Brief History of Everything* (Boston: Shambhala, 1996).

34. See my essay, "A Transpersonal Diagnosis of the Ecological Crisis," in *Ken Wilber in Dialogue*, eds. Donald Rothberg and Sean Kelly (Wheaton, Illinois: Quest Books, 1998).

35. Ken Wilber, *Up From Eden: A Transpersonal View of Human Evolution* (Boston: Shambhala, 1981).

36. See my essays, "Ken Wilber's Critique of Ecological Spirituality," in *Deep Ecology and World Religions*, eds., David Landis Barnhill and Roger S. Gottlieb (Albany: State University of New York Press, 2001); and "Possible Political Problems of Earth-Based Religiosity," in *Beneath the Surface: Critical Essays in the Philosophy of Deep Ecology*, eds. Eric Katz, Andrew Light, and David Rothenberg (Cambridge: MIT Press, 2000).

37. Gus diZerega, a political theorist and neopagan priest, maintains to the contrary that neopaganism is consistent with progressive views. Among his many essays, see "A Critique of Ken Wilber's Account of Deep Ecology and Nature Religions," *The Trumpeter* 13, no. 2 (Spring–Summer 1992): 52–71, and "Deep Ecology and Liberalism: The Greener Implications of Evolutionary Liberal Theory," *Review of Politics* 58, no. 4 (Fall 1996): 699–734. Despite earlier sharp disagreements with Wilber, diZerega is now a member of Wilber's Integral Institute.

38. Biehl, "'Ecology' and the Modernization of Fascism in the German Ultra-Right," 34.

39. Rosemary Radford Ruether, *Gaia and God* (Boston: Beacon Press, 1992), 4.

40. Ibid., 5.

41. See *Gentle Bridges: Conversations with the Dalai Lama on the Sciences of Mind*, by Bstan-Dzin-Rgya-Mtsho, eds. Francisco J. Varela, Jeremy W. Hayward (Boston: Shambhala, 2001).

Notes to Chapter 9

1. Glenn Tinder, *Political Thinking: The Perennial Questions*, 6th ed. (New York: Harper Collins, 1995): 9, 237, and 242.

2. See Tinder's discussion of this trait of political theory in the introduction and epilogue of ibid., 1–9, 237–50, respectively.

3. Ernest Nagel and James R. Newman, "Gödel's Proof," in *Contemporary Readings in Logical Theory*, eds. Irving M. Copi and James A. Gould (New York, Macmillan, 1967): 52.

4. Tinder, *Political Thinking*, 17, 18.

5. Milbrath, this volume, 37–38, emphasis in original. Also see Pirages's discussion of the third sociocultural revolution after the agricultural and industrial revolutions for an analysis of these issues regarding societal transformation.

6. See my contribution to "A Forum on the Role of Environmental Ethics in Restructuring Environmental Policy and Law for the Next Century," *Policy Currents* 7, no. 2 (June 1997): 3–5.

7. See Executive Committee of the Club of Rome, "Commentary," in Donella H. Meadows, Dennis L. Meadows, Jorgen Randers, and William W. Behrens III, *The Limits to Growth: A Report to the Club of Rome's Project on the Predicament of Mankind*, 2d. ed. (New York: New American Library, 1975): 197; Rachel Carson, *Silent Spring* (Boston: Houghton Mifflin, 1962).

8. For two examples of criticism of the environmental limits to growth position, see Wilfred Beckerman, *Two Cheers for the Affluent Society: A Spirited Defense of Economic Growth* (New York: St. Martin's Press, 1975), and Peter Passell and Leonard Ross, *The Retreat From Riches: Affluence and Its Enemies* (New York: Viking Press, 1974).

9. M.E. Zimmerman, this volume.

10. See the essay with that title, "Consumption as a Way of Life," in *Channels of Desire: Mass Images and the Shaping of American Consciousness*, eds. Stuart Ewen and Elizabeth Ewen (Minneapolis: University of Minnesota Press, 1992, 23–51.

11. M.E. Zimmerman, this volume, 176, emphasis in original.

12. See the important article by Richard A. Easterlin, "Does Economic Growth Improve the Human Lot? Some Empirical Evidence," in *Nations and Households in Economic Growth: Essays in Honor of Moses Abramovitz*, eds. Paul A. David and Melvin W. Reder (New York: Academic Press, 1974): 89–115; and Robert E. Lane, *The Loss of Happiness in Market Democracies* (New Haven: Yale University Press, 2000).

13. See my discussion of Hobbes's political theory and its importance to modernity and the environmental crisis, in addition to my essay above, in *The Death of Industrial Civilization*, chapter 8.

14. Daniel Bell, *The Cultural Contradictions of Capitalism* (New York: Basic Books, 1976): 49–50.

15. For a presentation of this criticism of environmentalism and the resulting limits to growth controversy, see my *Death of Industrial Civilization*, chapter 1.

16. See Goodin's contribution to this book; also see Milbrath's description of an alternative sustainable society and its nonmaterial values, and McLaughlin's description of deep ecology, and Pirages' discussion of the need for a third sociocultural revolution, in this volume.

17. Milbrath, this volume, 51.

18. See Daniel Bell, "The Return of the Sacred: The Argument About the Future of Religion," in *Progress and Its Discontents*, eds. Gabriel A. Almond, Marvin Chodorow, and Roy Harvey Pearce (Berkeley: University of California Press, 1982): 523, for the last two lines of this quotation. No citation is given by Bell. The passage is from the *Ethics of the Fathers*, and is as follows: "He [Rabbi Tarfon] used to say: You are not called upon to complete the work [of Torah study], yet you are not free to evade it." See Philip Birnbaum, translator and annotator, *Ethics of the Fathers* (New York: Hebrew Publishing, 1949), chapter 2, verses 20 and 21: 16. The words in brackets in both the text and note were provided from this edition of the *Ethics of the Fathers*.

19. Kassiola, *The Death of Industrial Civilization*, 217.

Notes to Afterword

1. The American Heritage Dictionary of the English Language, 3d ed. (Boston: Houghton Mifflin, 1992): 507.

2. See Joel Jay Kassiola, *The Death of Industrial Civilization*, (Albany: State University of New York Press, 1990): 6–11.

3. Woody Allen quoted in Robert Byrne, *The 637 Best Things Anybody Ever Said* (New York: Atheneum, 1982): 79, #386.

4. Alexander Lowen quoted in Philip Slater, *Earthwalk* (Garden City, NY: Anchor Books, 1974): 2.

5. Slater, Earthwalk, 2.

6. Erich Fromm, *To Have or To Be?* (New York: Harper and Row, 1975): 40.

7. Alvin Toffler, *The Eco-Spasm Report* (New York: Bantam Books, 1975): 105.

Recommended Additional Reading

Although the number of valuable readings in the many themes relevant to environmental political theory is immense, I have tried in this section to provide a useful and comprehensive list for both students and scholars of the environment. Any classificatory scheme will include overlaps and some arbitrariness but the aim of this section is to provide some guidance to the readings for selected topics. Items with an asterisk indicate an especially noteworthy work in the judgment of the editor.

Ecology, Environmental Limits to Economic Growth, and the Environmental Crisis

Ashworth, William. *The Economy of Nature: Rethinking the Connections Between Ecology and Economics.* Boston: Houghton Mifflin, 1995.

Athanasiou, Tom. *Divided Planet: The Ecology of Rich and Poor.* Boston: Little, Brown, 1996.

Baxter, Brian. *Ecologism: An Introduction.* Washington, DC: Georgetown University Press, 1999.

Barney, Gerald O., Study Director. *The Global 2000 Report to the President: Entering the Twenty-First Century.* Charlottesville, VA: Blue Angel, 1981.

Bookchin, Murray. *Toward an Ecological Society.* Montreal: Black Rose Books, 1980.

———. *The Modern Crisis.* Philadelphia, PA: New Society.

Botkin, James W.; Mahdi Elmandjra; and Mircea Malitza. *No Limits to Learning: Bridging the Human Gap: A Report to the Club of Rome.* Oxford, UK: Pergamon Press, 1981.

Brown, Lester R. *The Twenty-Ninth Day: Accommodating Human Needs and Numbers to the Earth's Resources.* New York: W.W. Norton, 1978.

Brown, Lester R., Christopher Flavin, and Sandra Postel. *Saving the Planet: How to Shape an Environmentally Sustainable Global Economy.* New York: W.W. Norton, 1991.

Brown, Lester R. et al., eds. *State of the World* Annuals. New York: W.W. Norton, 1984–Present.

———. *Vital Signs: The Trends That Are Shaping Our Future* Annals. New York: W.W. Norton.

Buchholz, Rogene A. *Principles of Environmental Management: The Greening of Business.* Englewood Cliffs, NJ: Prentice-Hall, 1993.

Cahn, Matthew Alan, and Rory O'Brien, eds. *Thinking About the Environment: Readings on Politics, Property and the Physical World.* Armonk, NY: M.E. Sharpe, 1996.

Cahn, Robert. *Footprints on the Planet: A Search for an Environmental Ethic.* New York: Universe Books, 1978.

*Catton Jr., William R. *Overshoot: The Ecological Basis of Revolutionary Change.* Urbana, IL: University of Illinois Press, 1982.

*Daly, Herman E., ed. *Toward a Steady State Economy.* San Francisco: W.H. Freeman, 1973.

*———, ed. *Economics, Ecology, Ethics: Essays Toward a Steady-State Economy.* San Francisco: Freeman, 1980.

———. *Beyond Growth: The Economics of Sustainable Development.* Boston: Beacon Press, 1996.

Daly, Herman E., and Townsend, Kenneth N., eds. *Valuing the Earth: Economics, Ecology, Ethics.* Cambridge, MA: MIT Press, 1993.

*Davis, W. Jackson. *The Seventh Year: Industrial Civilization in Transition.* New York: W.W. Norton, 1979.

Ehrlich, Paul R., and Anne H. Ehrlich. *The End of Affluence: A Blueprint for Your Future.* New York: Ballantine Books, 1974.

Ehrlich, Paul R.; Anne H. Ehrlich; and John P. Holdren. *Ecoscience: Population, Resources, Environment.* San Francisco: W.H. Freeman, 1977.

Ehrlich, Paul R.; Anne H. Ehrlich; and John P. Holdren, eds. *The Cassandra Conference: Resources and the Human Predicament.* College Station: Texas A&M University Press, 1988.

Executive Committee of the Club of Rome. "Commentary," in *The Limits to Growth: A Report to the Club of Rome's Project on the Predicament of Mankind,* 2d ed., pp. 189–200, edited by Donella H. Meadows, Dennis L. Meadows, Jorgen Randers, and William W. Behrens III. New York: New American Library, 1975.

Finnin, William M., Jr., and Smith, Gerald Alonzo, eds. *The Morality of Scarcity: Limited Resources and Social Policy.* Baton Rouge: Louisiana State University Press, 1979.

Galtung, John. "The Limits to Growth," and "Class Politics." *Journal of Peace Research* 1–2 (1973): 101–14.

*Gare, Arran E. *Postmodernism and the Environmental Crisis.* London: Routledge, 1995.

Glotfelty, Cheryll, and Harold. L. Fromm, eds. *The Ecocriticism Reader: Landmarks in Literary Ecology.* Athens: University of Georgia Press, 1996.

Goldsmith, Edward. *The Way: An Ecological World-View.* Boston: Shambhala, 1993.

———. *The Great U-Turn De-Industrializing Society.* Devon, UK: Green Books, 1988.

Goldsmith, Edward; Robert Allen; Michael Allaby; John Davoll; and Sam Lawrence. *Blueprint for Survival.* New York: New American Library, 1972.

*Hardin, Garrett. "The Tragedy of the Commons," in *Economics, Ecology, Ethics: Essays Toward a Steady-State Economy*, edited by Herman E. Daly, pp. 100–14. San Francisco: Freeman, 1980.

Harrison, Paul. *The Third Revolution: Population, Environment and a Sustainable World.* London: Penguin Books, 1993.

Heilbroner, Robert. *An Inquiry into the Human Prospect.* New York: W.W. Norton, 1975.

*Humphrey, Craig, R.; Tammy L. Lewis; and Frederick H. Buttel. *Environment, Energy and Society: A New Synthesis.* Belmont, CA: Wadsworth/Thompson Learning, 2002.

Krishan, Rajaram; Jonathan M. Harris; and Neva R. Goodwin. *A Survey of Ecological Economics.* Washington, DC: Island Press, 1995.

Macauley, David, ed. *Minding Nature: The Philosophers of Ecology.* New York: Guilford Press, 1996.

Manes, Christopher. *Green Rage: Radical Environmentalism and the Unmaking of Civilization.* Boston: Little, Brown, 1990.

McKibben, Bill. *The End of Nature.* New York: Random House, 1989.

*McMichael, A.J. *Planetary Overload: Global Environmental Change and the Health of the Human Species.* Cambridge, UK: Cambridge University Press, 1993.

Meadows, Dennis L., ed. *Alternative to Growth I: A Search for Sustainable Futures.* Cambridge, MA: Ballinger, 1977.

*Meadows, Donella H.; Dennis L. Meadows; and Jorgen Randers. *Beyond the Limits: Confronting Global Collapse, Envisioning A Sustainable Future.* Post Mills, VT: Chelsea Green, 1992.

*Meadows, Donella H.; Dennis L. Meadows; Jorgen Randers; and William W. Behrens III. *The Limits to Growth: A Report to the Club of Rome's Project on the Predicament of Mankind*, 2d ed. New York: New American Library, 1975.

Mesarovic, Mihajlo, and Edouard Pestel. *Mankind at a Turning Point: The Second Report to the Club of Rome.* New York: E.P. Dutton, 1974.

Milbrath, Lester W. *Learning to Think Environmentally While There Is Still Time.* Albany: State University of New York Press, 1996.

Mishan, E.J. *Technology and Growth: The Price We Pay.* New York: Praeger, 1970.

———. *The Economic Growth Debate: An Assessment.* London: George Allen and Unwin, 1977.

Naess, Arne. *Ecology, Community and Lifestyle: Outline of an Ecosophy*, translated by David Rothenberg. New York: Cambridge University Press, 1991.

Norton, Bryan G. *Toward Unity Among Environmentalists.* New York: Oxford University Press, 1991.

Oates, David. *Earth Rising: Ecological Belief in an Age of Science.* Corvallis: Oregon State University Press, 1989.

Orr, David W., and Marvin S. Soroos, eds. *The Global Predicament: Ecological Perspectives on World Order.* Chapel Hill: University of North Carolina Press, 1979.

Peccei, Aurelio. *One Hundred Pages for the Future: Reflections of the President of the Club of Rome.* New York: New American Library, 1982.

Pirages, Dennis, ed. *Building Sustainable Societies: A Blueprint for a Post-Industrial World.* Armonk, NY: M.E. Sharpe, 1996.

———. *The Sustainable Society: Implications for Limited Growth.* New York: Praeger, 1977.

Pirages, Dennis, and Paul Ehrlich. *Ark II: Social Response to Environmental Imperatives.* New York: Viking Press, 1974.

Ponting, Clive. *A Green History of the World: The Environment and the Collapse of Great Civilizations.* New York: Penguin Books, 1992.

Rifkin, Jeremy. *Biosphere Politics: A New Consciousness for a New Century.* New York: Crown, 1991.

Sagoff, Mark. *The Economy of the Earth: Philosophy, Law, and the Environment.* Cambridge, UK: Cambridge University Press, 1989.

Sale, Kirkpatrick. *Human Scale.* New York: G. P. Putnam's Sons, 1982.

*Schumacher, E.F. *Small Is Beautiful: Economics as if People Mattered.* New York: Harper and Row, 1975.

Schurr, Sam H., ed. *Energy, Economic Growth and the Environment.* Baltimore: Johns Hopkins University Press, 1973.

Smith, Gerald Alonzo. "Epilogue: Malthusian Concerns from 1800–1962." In *The Morality of Scarcity: Limited Resources and Social Policy,* edited by William M. Finnin, Jr., and Gerald Alonzo Smith. Baton Rouge: Louisiana State University Press, 1979.

Smith, Mark J. *Ecologism: Towards Ecological Citizenship.* Minneapolis: University of Minnesota Press, 1998.

Smith, V. Kerry, ed. *Scarcity and Growth Reconsidered.* Baltimore: Johns Hopkins University Press, 1979.

Southwick, Charles H., ed. *Global Ecology.* Sunderland, MA: Sinauer Associates, 1985.

*Sprout, Harold, and Margaret Sprout. *The Ecological Perspective in Human Affairs with Special Reference to International Politics.* Princeton, NJ: Princeton University Press, 1965.

*Stavrianos, L.S. *The Promise of the Coming Dark Age.* San Francisco: W.H. Freeman, 1976.

Stivers, Robert L. *The Sustainable Society: Ethics and Economic Growth.* Philadelphia, PA: Westminster Press, 1976.

Stott, Philip, and Sian Sullivan, eds. *Political Ecology: Science, Myth and Power.* New York: Oxford University Press, 2000.

Tinbergen, Jan, coordinator. *Rio: Reshaping the International Order: A Report to the Club of Rome.* New York: New American Library, 1976.

Toffler, Alvin. *The Eco-Spasm Report.* New York: Bantam Books, 1975.

*The World Commission on Environment and Development. *Our Common Future.* Oxford, UK: Oxford University Press, 1987.

*The World Resources Institute, the United Nations Environment Programme, and the United Nations Development Programme. *World Resources: A Guide to the Global Environment.* Biannual Series. New York: Oxford University Press, 1984–present.

Worster, Donald. *Nature's Economy: A History of Ecological Ideas.* 2d ed. Cambridge, UK: Cambridge University Press, 1995.

———. *The Wealth of Nature: Environmental History and the Ecological Imagination.* New York: Oxford University Press, 1993.

Yearly, Steven. *The Green Case: A Sociology of Environmental Issues, Arguments and Politics.* London: HarperCollins, 1991.

The Critique of Environmental Limits-to-Growth Position and Environmentalism

Bailey, Ronald. *Eco-Scam: The False Prophets of Ecological Apocalypse.* New York: St. Martin's Press, 1994.

*Beckerman, Wilfred. *Two Cheers for the Affluent Society: A Spirited Defense of Economic Growth.* New York: St. Martin's Press, 1975.

Bramwell, Anna. *Ecology in the 20th Century: A History.* New Haven, CT: Yale University Press, 1989.

Bruce-Biggs, B. "Against the Neo-Malthusians." *Commentary* 58, no. 1 (July 1974): 25–29.

Cole, H. S. D.; Christopher Freeman; Marie Jahoda; and K.L.R. Pavitt. *Models of Doom: A Critique of the Limits to Growth.* New York: Universe Books, 1975.

Ferry, Luc. *The New Ecological Order*, translated by Carol Volk. Chicago: University of Chicago Press, 1995.

Kahn, Herman. *World Economy Development: 1979 and Beyond.* New York: William Morrow, 1979.

Kahn, Herman; William Brown; and Leon Martel. *The Next 200 Years: A Scenario for America and the World.* New York: William Morrow, 1976.

Klein, Rudolph. "Growth and Its Enemies." *Commentary* 53, no. 6 (June 1972): 37–44.

*Lewis, Martin W. *Green Delusions: An Environmentalist Critique of Radical Environmentalism.* Durham, NC: Duke University Press, 1992.

Maddox, John. *The Doomsday Syndrome.* London: Macmillan, 1972.

Maurice, Charles, and Charles W. Smithson. *The Doomsday Myth: 10,000 Years of Economic Crises.* Stanford, CA: Hoover Institution Press, 1984.

Neuhaus, Richard. *In Defense of People: Ecology and the Seduction of Radicalism.* New York: Macmillan, 1971.

Olson, Mancur. "Introduction," In *The No-Growth Society*, edited by Olson Mancur and Hans H. Landsberg, pp. 1–13. New York: W.W. Norton, 1973.

Mancur, Olson, and Hans H. Landsberg. "Epilogue," in *The No-Growth Society*, edited by Olson Mancur and Hans H. Landsberg, pp. 229–41. New York: W.W. Norton, 1973.

*Mancur, Olson, and Hans H. Landsberg, eds. *The No Growth Society.* New York: W.W. Norton, 1973.

*Passell, Peter, and Leonard Ross. *The Retreat From Riches: Affluence and Its Enemies.* New York: Viking Press, 1974.

Pavitt, K.L.R. "Malthus and Other Economists: Some Doomsdays Revisited," in *Models of Doom: A Critique of the Limits to Growth*, edited by H.S.D. Cole et al. New York: Universe Books, 1975.

Rubin, Charles T. *The Green Crusade: Rethinking the Roots of Environmentalism.* New York: Free Press, 1994.

*Simon, Julian I. *The Ultimate Resource.* Princeton, NJ: Princeton University Press, 1981.

*Simon, Julian I., and Herman Kahn, eds. *The Resourceful Earth: A Response to Global 2000.* New York: Basil Blackwell, 1984.

Singer, Max. *Passage to a Human World: The Dynamics of Creating Global Wealth.* New Brunswick, NJ: Transaction Publishers, 1989.

Thurow, Lester C. *The Zero-Sum Society: Distribution and the Possibilities for Economic Change.* New York: Basic Books, 1980.

*Wallich, Henry C. "Zero Growth." *Newsweek*, January 24, 1972, p. 62.

*————. "More on Growth." *Newsweek*, March 13, 1972, p. 86.

Walter, Edward. *The Immorality of Limiting Growth.* Albany: State University of New York, 1981.

Environmental Political Theory

Conley, Verena Andermatt. *Ecopolitics: The Environment in Poststructuralist Thought.* London: Routledge, 1997.

*Daly, Herman E., and John B. Cobb Jr. *For the Common Good: Redirecting the Economy Toward Community, the Environment, and a Sustainable Future.* Boston: Beacon Press, 1989.

*De-Shalit, Avner. *The Environment: Between Theory and Practice.* Oxford: Oxford University Press, 2000.

Devall, Bill. *Living Richly in an Age of Limits.* Salt Lake City: Gibbs Smith, 1993.

————. *Simple in Means, Rich in Ends: Practicing Deep Ecology.* Salt Lake City: Gibbs Smith, 1988.

Devall, Bill, and George Sessions. *Deep Ecology: Living as if Nature Mattered.* Salt Lake City: Gibbs Smith, 1985.

*Dobson, Andrew. *Green Political Thought: An Introduction.* New York: HarperCollins, 1990.

————. *Justice and the Environment: Conceptions of Environmental Sustainability and Dimensions of Social Justice.* Oxford, UK: Oxford University Press, 1998.

————, ed. *The Green Reader: Essays Toward a Sustainable Society.* San Francisco: Mercury House, 1991.

Dobson, Andrew, and Paul Licardie, eds. *The Politics of Nature: Explorations in Green Political Theory.* London: Routledge, 1995.

Doherty, Brian, and Marius de Geus, eds. *Democracy and Green Political Thought: Sustainability, Rights and Citizenship.* London: Routledge, 1996.

*Douthwaite, Richard. *The Growth Illusion: How Economic Growth Has Enriched the Few, Impoverished the Many, and Endangered the Planet.* Tulsa: Council Oaks Books, 1993.

Dryzek, John S. *The Politics of the Earth: Environmental Discourses.* Oxford, UK: Oxford University Press, 1997.

————. *Rational Ecology: Environment and Political Economy.* Oxford: Blackwell, 1987.

*Eckersley, Robyn. *Environmentalism and Political Theory: Toward an Ecocentric Approach.* Albany: State University of New York Press, 1992.

Environmental Values. Quarterly Journal. Cambridge, UK: White Horse Press.

*Goodin, Robert E. *Green Political Theory.* Cambridge, UK: Polity Press, 1992.

Gorz, Andre. *Ecology as Politics*, translated by Patsy Vigderman and Jonathan Cloud. Boston: South End Press, 1980.

*Gottlieb, Roger S., ed. *The Ecological Community: Environmental Challenges for Philosophy, Politics and Morality.* New York: Routledge, 1997.

Hayward, Tim. *Political Theory and Ecological Values.* New York: St. Martin's Press, 1998.

Kassiola, Joel Jay. "The Limits to Economic Growth: Politicizing Advanced Industrial Society," *Philosophy and Social Criticism* 8 (Spring 1981): 87–113.

———. *The Death of Industrial Civilization: The Limits to Economic Growth and the Repoliticization of Advanced Industrial Society.* Albany: State University of New York Press, 1990.

Low, Nicholas, and Gleeson, Brendan. *Justice, Society and Nature: An Exploration of Political Ecology.* London: Routledge, 1998.

Luke, Timothy W. *Ecocritique: Contesting the Politics of Nature, Economy and Culture.* Minneapolis: University of Minnesota Press, 1997.

*McLaughlin, Andrew. *Regarding Nature: Industrialism and Deep Ecology.* Albany: State University of New York Press, 1990.

*Merchant, Carolyn. *Radical Ecology: The Search for a Living World.* New York: Routledge, 1992.

Meyer, John. *Political Nature: Environmentalism and the Interpretation of Western Thought.* Cambridge: MIT Press, 2001.

*Milbrath, Lester W. *Envisioning a Sustainable Society: Learning Our Way Out.* Albany: State University of New York Press, 1989.

O'Connor, James. *Natural Causes: Essays in Ecological Marxism.* New York: Guilford Press, 1998.

O'Connor, Martin, ed. *Is Capitalism Sustainable? Political Economy and the Politics of Ecology.* New York: Guilford Press, 1994.

Ophuls, W. *Ecology and the Politics of Scarcity: A Prologue to a Political Theory of the Steady State.* San Francisco: W. Freeman, 1977.

———. "The Politics of a Sustainable Society," in *The Sustainable Society*, edited by Dennis Pirages, pp. 157–72. New York: Praeger.

*Ophuls, W., and Stephen Boyan, Jr. *Ecology and the Politics Revisited: The Unraveling of the American Dream.* New York: W.H. Freeman, 1992.

*Paehlke, Robert. *Environmentalism and the Future of Progressive Politics.* New Haven, CT: Yale University Press, 1989.

*Pepper, David. *Modern Environmentalism: An Introduction.* London: Routledge, 1996.

Pirages, Dennis. *The New Context for International Relations: Global Ecopolitics.* North Scituate, MA: Duxbury Press, 1978.

Porritt, Jonathon. *Seeing Green: The Politics of Ecology Explained.* New York: Basil Blackwell, 1985.

*Schnaiberg, Allan, and Kenneth Alan Gould. *Environmental Society: The Enduring Conflict.* New York: St. Martin's Press, 1994.

*Zimmerman, Michael E. *Contesting Earth's Future: Radical Ecology and Postmodernity.* Berkeley, CA: University of California Press, 1994.

Works in the Tradition of Political Theory Relevant to the Environmental Crisis

Arendt, Hannah. *The Human Condition: A Study of the Central Dilemmas Facing Modern Man.* Garden City, NY: Doubleday/Anchor Books, 1959.

Baier, Kurt, and Nicholas Rescher, eds. *Values and the Future: The Impact of Technological Change on American Values.* New York: Free Press, 1971.

Bellah, Robert N.; Richard Madsen; William Sullivan; Ann Swidler; and Steven M.

Tipton. *Habits of the Heart: Individualism and Commitment in American Life.* Berkeley: University of California Press, 1985.

Berger, Peter L., and Thomas Luckmann. *The Social Construction of Reality: A Treatise in the Sociology of Knowledge.* Garden City, NY: Doubleday, 1966.

Boulding, Kenneth E. "New Goals for Society?" in *Energy, Economic Growth, and the Environment,* edited by Sam H. Schurr, pp. 139–51. Baltimore: Johns Hopkins University Press, 1973.

Camus, Albert. *The Myth of Sisyphus and Other Essays,* translated by Justin O'Brien. New York: Alfred Knopf, 1955.

Cooper, David E., and Joy Palmer, eds. *Just Environments: Intergenerational, International and Interspecies Issues.* London: Routledge, 1995.

*Daly, Herman E. *Steady-State Economics: The Economics of Biophysical Equilibrium and Moral Growth.* San Francisco: W.H. Freeman, 1977.

*Dumont, Louis. *From Mandeville to Marx: The Genesis and Triumph of Economic Ideology.* Chicago: University of Chicago Press, 1977.

*Fromm, Erich. *To Have or To Be?* New York: Harper & Row, 1976.

Gilroy, John Martin. *Justice and Nature: Kantian Philosophy, Environmental Policy, and the Law.* Washington, DC: Georgetown University Press, 2000.

Gottlieb, Roger S. *The Ecological Community: Environmental Challenges for Philosophy, Politics, and Morality.* New York: Routledge, 1997.

Harrison, Paul R. *The Disenchantment of Reason: The Problem of Socrates in Modernity.* Albany: State University of New York Press, 1994.

*Hirsch, Fred. *Social Limits to Growth.* Cambridge, MA: Harvard University Press, 1976.

*Hirschman, Albert O. *Shifting Involvements: Private Interest and Public Policy.* Princeton: Princeton University Press, 1982.

Hobbes, Thomas. *Leviathan,* edited and annotated by Richard E. Flathman and David Johnston. New York: W.W. Norton, 1997.

Horne, Thomas A. *The Social Theory of Bernard Mandeville: Virtue and Commerce in Early Eighteenth Century England.* New York: Columbia University Press, 1978.

———. "Envy and Commercial Society: Mandeville and Smith on Private Vice, Public Benefits." *Political Theory* 9 (November 1981): 551–69.

Lasch, Christopher. *The True and Only Heaven: Progress and Its Critics.* New York: W.W. Norton, 1991.

*Leiss, William. *The Domination of Nature.* Boston: Beacon Press, 1974.

*Macpherson, C.B. *The Political Theory of Possessive Individualism: Hobbes to Locke.* Oxford, UK: Oxford University Press, 1965.

Marcuse, Herbert. *One-Dimensional Man: Studies in the Ideology of Advanced Industrial Society.* Boston: Beacon Press, 1978.

Marietta Jr., Don E., and Lester Embree, eds. *Environmental Philosophy and Environmental Activism.* Lanham, MD: Rowman and Littlefield, 1995.

*Merchant, Carolyn. *The Death of Nature: Women, Ecology and the Scientific Revolution.* New York: HarperCollins, 1990.

Milton, Kay. *Environmentalism and Cultural Theory: Explaining the Role of Anthropology in Environmental Discourse.* London: Routledge, 1996.

Oelschlaeger, Max, ed. *Postmodern Environmental Ethics.* Albany: State University of New York Press, 1995.

Rengger, N.J. *Political Theory, Modernity and Postmodernity: Beyond Enlighten-ment and Critique.* Oxford: Blackwell, 1995.

Rescher, Nicholas. "What is Value Change? A Framework for Research," in *Values and the Future: The Impact of Technological Change on American Values*, edited by Kurt Baier and Nicholas Rescher, pp. 68–109. New York: Free Press, 1971.

Rolston III, Holmes. *Philosophy Gone Wild: Environmental Ethics.* Buffalo, NY: Prometheus, 1989.

Sekora, John. *Luxury: The Concept in Western Thought: Eden to Smollet.* Balti-more: Johns Hopkins University Press, 1977.

Shi, David E. *The Simple Life: Plain Living and High Thinking in American Cul-ture.* New York: Oxford University Press, 1986.

Springborg, Patricia. *The Problem of Human Needs and the Critique of Civilization.* London: George Allen and Unwin, 1981.

Stone, Christopher D. *Earth and Other Ethics: The Case for Moral Pluralism.* New York: Harper & Row, 1987.

Sylvan, Richard, and David Bennett. *The Greening of Ethics: From Anthropocentrism to Deep-Green Theory.* Cambridge, UK: White Horse Press, 1994.

Taylor, Paul W. *Respect for Nature: A Theory of Environmental Ethics.* Princeton, NJ: Princeton University Press, 1986.

*Tinder, Glenn. *Political Thinking: The Perennial Questions.* 6th ed. New York: HarperCollins, 1995.

Van de Veer, Donald, and Christine Pierce, eds. *The Environmental Ethics and Policy Book: Philosophy, Ecology, Economics.* 2d ed. Belmont, CA: Wadsworth, 1998.

Vaughan, Frederick. *The Tradition of Political Hedonism: From Hobbes to J.S. Mill.* New York: Fordham University Press, 1984.

Wenz, Peter S. *Environmental Justice.* Albany: State University of New York Press, 1988.

*Xenos, Nicholas. *Scarcity and Modernity.* London: Routledge, 1989.

———. "Liberalism and the Postulate of Scarcity." *Political Theory* 15, no. 2 (May 1987): 225–43.

Economics, Politics, and Capitalism

Ackerman, Frank; David Kiron; Neva R. Goodwin; Jonathan M. Harris; and Kevin Gallagher, eds. *Human Well-Being and Economic Goals.* Washington, DC: Is-land Press, 1997.

Applebaum, Eileen. "Radical Economics," in *Modern Economic Thought*, edited by Sidney Weintraub, pp. 559–74. Philadelphia: University of Pennsylvania Press, 1977.

Arndt, H.W. *The Rise and Fall of Economic Growth: A Study in Contemporary Thought.* Chicago: University of Chicago Press, 1978.

Barber, William J. *A History of Economic Thought.* New York: Penguin Books, 1977.

Bell, Daniel. "Models and Reality in Economic Discourse," in *The Crisis in Eco-nomic Theory*, edited by Daniel Bell and Irving Kristol, pp. 46–80. New York: Basic Books, 1981.

Capitalism, Nature, Socialism: A Journal of Socialist Ecology. New York: Guilford Press, Quarterly Journal.

David, Paul A., and Melvin W. Reder, eds. *Nations and Households in Economic*

Growth: Essays in Honor of Moses Abramovitz. New York: Academic Press, 1974.

*Dobb, Maurice. *Theories of Value and Distribution Since Adam Smith: Ideology and Economic Theory.* Cambridge, UK: Cambridge University Press, 1973.

*Easterlin, Richard A. "Does Economic Growth Improve the Human Lot? Some Empirical Evidence," in *Nations and Households in Economic Growth: Essays in Honor of Moses Abramovitz,* edited by Paul A. David, and Melvin W. Reder, pp. 89–115. New York: Academic Press, 1974.

*Edwards, Richard C. "The Logic of Capital Accumulation," in *The Capitalist System: A Radical Analysis of American Society,* edited by Richard C. Edwards, Michael Reich, and Thomas E. Weisskopf, 2d ed., pp. 99–105. Englewood Cliffs, NJ: Prentice-Hall, 1978.

*Edwards, Richard, C.; Michael Reich; and Thomas E. Weisskopf, eds. *The Capitalist System: A Radical Analysis of American Society.* 2d ed. Englewood Cliffs, NJ: Prentice-Hall, 1978.

Ekins, Paul, ed. *The Living Economy: A New Economics in the Making.* London: Routledge and Kegan Paul, 1986.

Froman, Creel. *The Two American Political Systems: Society, Economics, and Politics.* Englewood Cliffs, NJ: Prentice-Hall, 1984.

*Galbraith, John Kenneth. *The New Industrial State.* 2d ed. rev. New York: New American Library, 1972.

Gappert, Gary. *Post-Affluent American: The Social Economy of the Future.* New York: Franklin Watts, 1979.

*Harrington, Michael. *The Twilight of Capitalism.* New York: Simon and Schuster, 1976.

*Heilbroner, Robert L. *The Limits of American Capitalism.* New York: Harper & Row, 1967.

*Henderson, Hazel. *The Politics of the Solar Age: Alternatives to Economics.* Garden City, NY: Anchor Press/Doubleday, 1981.

————. *Beyond Globalization: Shaping a Sustainable Global Economy.* West Hartford, CT: Kumarian Press, 1999.

Hirsch, Fred, and John H. Goldthorpe, eds. *The Political Economy of Inflation.* Cambridge, MA: Harvard University Press, 1979.

*Hirschman, Albert O. *The Passions and the Interests: Political Arguments for Capitalism Before Its Triumph.* Princeton, NJ: Princeton University Press, 1978.

————. *Essays in Trespassing: Economics to Politics and Beyond.* Cambridge, UK: Cambridge University Press, 1981.

————. "Rival Interpretations of Market Society: Civilizing, Destructive and Feeble?" *Journal of Economic Literature* 20 (December 1982): 1463–84.

Hook, Sidney, ed. *Human Values and Economic Policy: A Symposium.* New York: New York University Press, 1967.

Hunt, E.K. "The Transition from Feudalism to Capitalism," in *The Capitalist System: A Radical Analysis of American Society,* edited by Richard C. Edwards, Michael Reich, and Thomas E. Weisskopf. 2d ed., pp. 55–64. Englewood Cliffs, NJ: Prentice-Hall, 1978.

*Keynes, John Maynard. "Economic Possibilities for our Grandchildren," in *Essays in Persuasion,* edited by John Maynard Keynes, pp. 358–73. New York: W.W. Norton, 1963.

Krishnan, Rajaram; Jonathan M. Harris; and Neva R. Goodwin, eds. *A Survey of Ecological Economics*. Washington, DC: Island Press, 1995.

*Lane, Robert E. "Markets and the Satisfaction of Human Wants." *Journal of Economic Issues* 12 (December 1978): 799–827.

Lowe, Adolphe. *On Economic Knowledge: Toward A Science of Political Economy*, enlarged ed. Armonk, NY: M.E. Sharpe, 1983.

*Lutz, Mark A., and Kenneth Lux. *The Challenge of Humanistic Economics*. Menlo Park, CA: Benjamin Cummings, 1979.

*———. *Humanistic Economics: The New Challenge*. New York: Bootstrap Press, 1988.

*McCloskey, Donald N. *The Rhetoric of Economics*. Madison: University of Wisconsin Press, 1985.

Mermelstein, David, ed. *Economics: Mainstream Readings and Radical Critiques*. 2d ed. New York: Random House, 1973.

Miles Jr., Rufus E. *Awakening From the American Dream: The Social and Political Limits to Growth*. New York: Universe Books, 1976.

Moore Jr., Barrington. *Moral Aspects of Economic Growth and Other Essays*. Ithaca, NY: Cornell University Press, 1998.

O'Connor, James. *Natural Causes: Essays in Ecological Marxism*. New York: Guilford Press, 1998.

O'Connor, Martin, ed. *Is Capitalism Sustainable? Political Economy and the Politics of Ecology*. New York: Guilford Press, 1994.

*Rosenberg, Alexander. *Economics—Mathematical Politics or Science of Diminishing Returns*. Chicago: University of Chicago Press, 1992.

Samuels, Warren J. "Ideology in Economics," in *Modern Economic Thought*, edited by Sidney Weintraub, pp. 467–84. Philadelphia: University of Pennsylvania Press, 1977.

Schumpeter, Joseph A. *Capitalism, Socialism and Democracy*. 3d ed. New York: Harper & Row, 1962.

*Scitovsky, Tibor. *Human Desire and Economic Satisfaction: Essays on the Frontier of Economics*. Washington Square: New York University Press, 1989.

*———. *The Joyless Economy: An Inquiry Into Human Satisfaction and Consumer Dissatisfaction*. New York: Oxford University Press, 1976.

Sennett, Richard. *The Fall of Public Man: On the Social Psychology of Capitalism*. New York: Random House, 1978.

Smith, Adam. *An Inquiry into the Nature and Causes of the Wealth of Nations*, edited by Richard F. Teichbraeber III. New York: Random House, 1985.

Smith, Gerald Alonzo. "The Teleological View of Wealth: A Historical Analysis." In *Economics, Ecology, Ethics: Essays Toward a Steady-State Economy*, edited by Herman E. Daly, pp. 215–37. San Francisco: Freeman, 1980.

*Schmookler, Andrew Bard. *The Illusion of Choice: How the Market Economy Shapes Our Destiny*. Albany: State University of New York Press, 1993.

*Tawney, R.H. *Religion and the Rise of Capitalism*. New York: New American Library, 1961.

Teune, Henry. *Growth*. Newbury Park, CA: Sage Publications, 1988.

Vickers, Douglas. *Economics and Ethics: An Introduction to Theory, Institutions, and Policy*. Westport, CT: Prager, 1997.

Weber, Max. *The Protestant Ethic and the Spirit of Capitalism*, translated by Talcott Parson. London: HarperCollins, 1991.

Weintraub, Sidney, ed. *Modern Economic Thought*. Philadelphia: University of Pennsylvania Press, 1977.

*Weisskopf, Thomas E. "The Irrationality of Capitalist Economic Growth," in *The Capitalist System: A Radical Analysis of American Society*, 2d ed., edited by Richard C. Edwards, Michael Reich, and Thomas E. Weisskopf, pp. 395–409. Englewood Cliffs, NJ: Prentice-Hall, 1978.

*———. "Economic Growth Versus Existential Balance," in *Toward a Steady State Economy*, edited by Herman E. Daly, pp. 240–51. San Francisco: W.H. Freeman, 1973.

*Weisskopf, Walter A. *Alienation and Economics*. New York: Dell, 1971.

Wolfe, Alan. *America's Impasse: The Rise and Fall of the Politics of Growth*. New York: Pantheon, 1981.

———. *The Limits of Legitimacy: Political Contradictions of Contemporary Capitalism*. New York: Free Press, 1977.

The Modern Consumer Society and Its Alternatives

Appadurai, Arjun, ed. *The Social Life of Things: Commodities in Cultural Perspective*. Cambridge: Cambridge University Press, 1999.

*Baudrillard, Jean. *The System of Objects*, translated by James Benedict. London: Verso, 1997.

———. *The Consumer Society: Myths and Structures*. London: Sage, 1998.

———. *Symbolic Exchange and Death*, translated by Iain Hamilton Grant. London: Sage, 1998.

*Bocock, Robert. *Consumption*. London: Routledge, 1995.

Campbell, Colin. *The Romantic Ethic and the Spirit of Modern Consumerism*. Oxford: Basil Blackwell, 1989.

*Crocker, David A., and Toby Linden, eds. *Ethics of Consumption: The Good Life, Justice, and Global Stewardship*. Lanham, MD: Rowman and Littlefield, 1998.

*Daly, Herman E., ed. *Economics, Ecology, Ethics: Essays Toward a Steady-State Economy*. San Francisco: Freeman, 1980.

Davis, Fred. *Fashion, Culture, and Identity*. Chicago: University of Chicago Press, 1992.

*Douglas, Mary, and Baron Isherwood. *The World of Goods: Towards an Anthropology of Consumption*. New York: W.W. Norton, 1979.

*Durning, Alan Thein. *How Much Is Enough? The Consumer Society and the Future of the Earth*. New York: W.W. Norton, 1992.

Fine, Ben, and Ellen Leopold. *The World of Consumption*. London: Routledge, 1993.

Ehrenreich, Barbara. *Fear of Falling: The Inner Life of the Middle Class*. New York: HarperCollins, 1990.

*Elgin, Duane. *Voluntary Simplicity: Toward a Way of Life That Is Outwardly Simple and Inwardly Rich*. New York: William Morrow, 1981.

*Ewen, Stuart. *All Consuming Images: The Politics of Style in Contemporary Culture*. New York: Basic Books, 1988.

*———. *Captains of Consciousness: Advertising and the Social Roots of the Consumer Culture*. Minneapolis: University of Minnesota Press, 1992.

Ewen, Stuart, and Elizabeth Ewen. *Channels of Desire: Mass Images and the Shaping of American Consciousness.* Minneapolis: University of Minnesota Press, 1992.

Frank, Robert H. *Choosing the Right Pond: Human Behavior and the Quest for Status.* New York: Oxford University Press, 1986.

*———. *Luxury Fever: Why Money Fails to Satisfy in an Era of Excess.* New York: Free Press, 1999.

*Frank, Robert H., and Philip J. Cook. *The Winner-Take-All Society: Why the Few at the Top Get So Much More Than the Rest of Us.* New York: Penguin Books, 1996.

Frank, Thomas. *The Conquest of Cool: Business Culture, Counterculture, and the Rise of Hip Consumerism.* Chicago: University of Chicago Press, 1997.

Frank, Thomas, and Matt Weiland, ed. *Commodify Your Dissent: Salvos from the Baffler.* New York: W.W. Norton, 1997.

*Gagnier, Regina. *The Insatiability of Human Wants: Economics and Aesthetics in Market Society.* Chicago: University of Chicago Press, 2000.

Global Environmental Politics. Issue on Consumption 1, no. 3 (August 2001). MIT Press. Quarterly Journal.

*Goodwin, Neva R.; Frank Ackerman; and David Kiron, eds. *The Consumer Society.* Washington, DC: Island Press, 1997.

Heilbroner, Robert L. *Business Civilization in Decline.* New York: W.W. Norton, 1976.

Kellner, Douglas, ed. *Baudrillard: A Critical Reader.* Cambridge, UK: Blackwell, 1994.

———. *Jean Baudrillard: From Marxism to Postmodernism and Beyond.* Stanford, CA: Stanford University Press, 1989.

*Kohn, Alfie. *No Contest: The Case Against Competition.* Boston: Houghton-Mifflin, 1986.

Key, Wilson Bryan. *Subliminal Seduction: Ad Media's Manipulation of a Not So Innocent America.* New York: New American Library, 1974.

Kristol, Irving. "Rationalism in Economics," in *The Crisis in Economic Theory,* edited by Daniel Bell and Irving Kristol, pp. 201–18. New York: Basic Books, 1981.

*Lane, Robert E. *The Market Experience.* Cambridge: Cambridge University Press, 1995.

*———. *The Loss of Happiness in Market Democracies.* New Haven: Yale University Press, 2000.

Lasch, Christopher. *The Culture of Narcissism: American Life in an Age of Diminishing Expectations.* New York: Warner Books, 1979.

*Lee, Martyn J. *Consumer Culture Reborn: The Cultural Politics of Consumption.* London: Routledge, 1993.

Leiss, William. *The Limits to Satisfaction: An Essay on the Politics of Needs and Commodities.* Toronto: University of Toronto Press, 1976.

Leonard, George. "Winning Isn't Everything, It's Nothing." *Intellectual Digest,* (October 1973): 45–47.

Linder, Staffan Burenstam. *The Harried Leisure Class.* New York: Columbia University Press, 1970.

McCracken, Grant. *Culture and Consumption: New Approaches to the Symbolic Character of Consumer Goods and Activities.* Bloomington: Indiana University Press, 1990.

*McKendrick, Neil; John Brewer; and J.H. Plumb. *The Birth of Consumer Society: The Commercialization of Eighteenth-Century England.* Bloomington: Indiana University Press, 1985.

Miller, Daniel. *A Theory of Shopping.* Ithaca, NY: Cornell University Press, 1998.

———, ed. *Material Cultures: Why Some Things Matter.* Chicago: University of Chicago Press, 1998.

Mintz, Sidney W. *Tasting Food, Tasting Freedom: Excursions Into Eating, Culture and the Past.* Boston: Beacon Press, 1996.

Myers, David G. *The American Paradox: Spiritual Hunger in an Age of Plenty.* New Haven, CT: Yale University Press, 2000.

*Newman, Katherine S. *Declining Fortunes: The Withering of the American Dream.* New York: Basic Books, 1993.

———. *Falling From Grace: The Experience of Downward Mobility on the American Middle Class.* New York: Free Press, 1988.

Poster, Mark, ed. *Jean Baudrillard: Selected Writings.* Stanford, CA: Stanford University Press, 1988.

*Preteceille, Edmond, and Jean-Pierre Terrail. *Capitalism, Consumption and Needs,* translated by Sarah Matthews. Oxford, UK: Basil Blackwell, 1986.

Ritzer, George. *The McDonaldization Thesis: Explorations and Extensions.* London: Sage, 1998.

*———. *Enchanting a Disenchanted World: Revolutionizing the Means of Consumption.* Thousand Oaks, CA.: Pine Forge Press, 1999.

Rosenblatt, Roger, ed. *Consuming Desires: Consumption, Culture, and the Pursuit of Happiness.* Washington, DC: Island Press, 1999.

Schmidt, Leigh Eric. *Consumer Rites: The Buying and Selling of American Holidays.* Princeton, NJ: Princeton University Press, 1995.

*Schor, Juliet. *Do Americans Shop Too Much?*, edited by Joshua Cohen and Joel Rogers. Boston: Beacon Press, 2000.

*———. *The Overspent American: Upscaling, Downshifting, and the New Consumer.* New York: Basic Books, 1998.

———. *The Overworked American: The Unexpected Decline of Leisure.* New York: Basic Books, 1991.

Slater, Don. *Consumer Culture and Modernity.* Cambridge, UK: Polity Press, 1997.

*Slater, Philip. *Wealth Addiction.* New York: E.P. Dutton, 1980.

*———. *Earthwalk.* Garden City, NY: Anchor Books, 1974.

Strasser, Susan; Charles McGovern; and Matthias Judt, eds. *Getting and Spending: European and American Societies in the Twentieth Century.* Cambridge, UK: Cambridge University Press, 1998.

*Tawney, R.H. *The Acquisitive Society.* New York: Harcourt, Brace and World, 1948.

Valaskakis, Kimon; Peter S. Sindell; J. Graham Smith; and Iris Fitzpatrick-Martin. *The Conserver Society: A Workable Alternative for the Future.* New York: Harper & Row, 1979.

Vanden Broeck, Goldian, ed. *Less is More: The Art of Voluntary Poverty.* New York: Harper & Row, 1978.

*Veblen, Thorstein. *The Theory of the Leisure Class: An Economic Study of Institutions.* New York: New American Library, 1963.

Wagner, Philip L. *Showing Off: The Geltung Hypothesis*. Austin: University of Texas Press, 1996.

Weiss, Richard. *The American Myth of Success: From Horatio Alger to Norman Vincent Peale*. Urbana: University of Illinois Press, 1988.

Westra, Laura, and Particia H. Wehane, eds. *The Business of Consumption: Environmental Ethics and the Global Economy*. Lanham, MD: Rowman and Littlefield, 1998.

Modernity, Postmodernity, and Social Change Theory

Almond, Gabriel A.; Marvin Chodorow; and Roy Harvey Pearce, eds. *Progress and Its Discontents*. Berkeley: University of California Press, 1982.

Amin, Samir; Giovanni Arrighi; Andre Gunder Frank; and Immanuel Wallerstein, eds. *Dynamics of Global Crisis*. New York: Monthly Review Press, 1982.

*Baudrillard, Jean. *Selected Writings*, edited by Mark Poster and translated by Jacques Mourrain. Stanford, CA: Stanford University Press, 1992.

*Bauman, Zygmunt. *Intimations of Postmodernity*. London: Routledge, 1992.

Bell, Daniel. *The Coming of Post-Industrial Society: A Venture in Social Forecasting*. New York: Basic Books, 1976.

————. *The Cultural Contradictions of Capitalism*. New York: Basic Books, 1976.

————. "The Return of the Sacred: The Argument About the Future of Religion," in *Progress and Its Discontents*, edited by Gabriel A. Almond, Marvin Chodorow, and Roy Harvey Pearce, pp. 501–23. Berkeley: University of California Press, 1982.

Berger, Peter L.; Brigette Berger; and Hansfried Kellner. *The Homeless Mind: Modernization and Consciousness*. New York: Random House, 1973.

*Bernstein, Richard J. *The New Constellation: The Ethical-Political Horizons of Modernity/Postmodernity*. Cambridge, MA: MIT Press, 1992.

*Best, Steven, and Steven Kellner. *Postmodern Theory: Critical Interrogations*. New York: Guilford Press, 1991.

*Birnbaum, Norman. *The Crisis of Industrial Society*. New York: Oxford University Press, 1969.

————, ed. *Beyond the Crisis*. New York: Oxford University Press, 1977.

Bookchin, Murray. *Remaking Society*. Montreal: Black Rose Books, 1989.

Boulding, Kenneth E. *The Meaning of the Twentieth Century: The Great Transition*. New York: Harper & Row, 1964.

*Bourdieu, Pierre. *Distinction: A Social Critique of the Judgment of Taste*, translated by Richard Nice. Cambridge, MA: Harvard University Press, 1984.

Bowers, C.A. *Educating for an Ecologically Sustainable Culture: Rethinking Moral Education, Creativity, Intelligence and Other Modern Orthodoxies*. Albany: State University of New York Press, 1994.

*Braudel, Fernand. *Civilization and Capitalism, 15th–18th Centuries: Vol. 3: The Perspective of the World*. New York: Harper & Row, 1984.

*Camilleri, Joseph A. *Civilization in Crisis: Human Prospects in a Changing World*. Cambridge, UK: Cambridge University Press, 1976.

*Camus, Albert. *The Rebel: An Essay on Man in Revolt*, translated by Anthony Bower. New York: Alfred A. Knopf, 1956.

Clark, Mary E. *Ariadne's Thread: The Search for New Modes of Thinking*. New York: St. Martin's Press, 1989.

Cohan, A.S. *Theories of Revolution: An Introduction.* New York: John Wiley, 1975.

Cohen, Joshua, and Joel Rogers. *On Democracy: Toward a Transformation of American Society.* New York: Penguin Books, 1983.

Davies, James C. *When Men Revolt and Why.* New York: Free Press, 1971.

Davies, Joan, and Samuel Mauch. "Strategies for Societal Development," in *Alternative to Growth I: A Search for Sustainable Futures,* edited by Dennis L. Meadows, pp. 217–42. Cambridge, MA: Ballinger, 1977.

Debord, Guy. *The Society of the Spectacle,* translated by Donald Nicholson-Smith. New York: Zone Books, 1995.

Dickens, David R., and Andrea Fontana, eds. *Postmodernism and Social Inquiry.* New York: Guilford, 1994.

Dreitzel, Hans Peter. "On the Political Meaning of Culture," in *Beyond the Crisis,* edited by Norman Birnbaum, pp. 83–129. New York: Oxford University Press, 1977.

Dupre, Louis. *Passage to Modernity: An Essay in the Hermeneutics of Nature and Culture.* New Haven, CT: Yale University Press, 1993.

*Ehrenfeld, David. *The Arrogance of Humanism.* New York: Oxford University Press, 1981.

*Ellis, Adrian, and Krishan Kumar, eds. *Dilemmas of Liberal Democracies: Studies on Fred Hirsch's Social Limits to Growth.* London: Tavistock Publications, 1983.

Engel, J. Ronald, and Joan Gibb Engel, eds. *Ethics of Environmental Development: Global Challenge, International Response.* Tucson: University of Arizona Press, 1990.

Frank, Andre Gunder. "Crisis of Ideology and Ideology of Crisis," in *Dynamics of Global Crisis,* edited by Samir Amin, Giovanni Arrighi, Andre Gunder Frank, and Immanuel Wallerstein, pp. 109–65. New York: Monthly Review Press, 1982.

Frankel, Boris. *The Post-Industrial Utopias.* Madison: University of Wisconsin Press, 1987.

Friedman, John. *The Good Society: A Personal Account of Its Struggle with the World of Social Planning and a Dialectical Inquiry into the Roots of Radical Practice.* Cambridge, MA: MIT Press, 1982.

Frisby, David. *Fragments of Modernity: Theories of Modernity in the Work of Simmel, Kracauer and Benjamin.* Cambridge, MA: MIT Press, 1988.

*Giddens, Anthony. *Modernity and Self-Identity: Self and Society in the Late Modern Age.* Stanford, CA: Stanford University Press, 1991.

Gleick, James. *Faster: The Acceleration of Just About Everything.* New York: Pantheon Books, 1999.

Gurr, Ted Robert. *Why Men Rebel.* Princeton, NJ: Princeton University Press, 1972.

Habermas, Jürgen. *A Philosophical Discourse of Modernity,* translated by Frederick G. Lawrence. Cambridge, MA: MIT Press, 1992.

———. *Legitimation Crisis,* translated by Thomas McCarthy. Boston: Beacon Press, 1975.

Hagopian, Mark N. *The Phenomenon of Revolution.* New York: Dodd, Mead, 1974.

Harmon, Willis N. *An Incomplete Guide to the Future.* New York: W.W. Norton, 1979.

Harrison, Paul R. *The Disenchantment of Reason: The Problem of Socrates in Modernity.* Albany: State University of New York Press, 1994.

*Harvey, David. *The Condition of Postmodernity: An Enquiry into the Origins of Cultural Change.* Oxford, UK: Basil Blackwell, 1990.

Himmelfarb, Gertrude. *The De-Moralization of Society: From Victorian Virtues to Modern Values.* New York: Vintage Books, 1996.

*Honig, Bonnie. *Political Theory and the Displacement of Politics.* Ithaca, NY: Cornell University Press, 1993.

*Inglehart, Ronald. *Modernization and Postmodernization: Cultural, Economic, and Political Change in 43 Societies.* Princeton, NJ: Princeton University Press, 1997.

*————. *Cultural Shift in Advanced Industrial Society.* Princeton, NJ: Princeton University Press, 1990.

*————. *The Silent Revolution: Changing Values and Political Styles Among Western Publics.* Princeton, NJ: Princeton University Press, 1977.

*Jameson, Frederic. *Postmodernism, or the Cultural Logic of Late Capitalism.* Durham, NC: Duke University Press, 1995.

*Kellner, Douglas. *Jean Baudrillard: From Marxism to Postmodernism and Beyond.* Stanford, CA: Stanford University Press, 1989.

————. *Baudrillard: A Critical Reader.* Oxford, UK: Basil Blackwell, 1994.

Kraft, Michael E. "Political Change and the Sustainable Society," in *The Sustainable Society: Implications for Limited Growth*, edited by Dennis Pirages, pp. 173–96. New York: Praeger, 1977.

Kumar, Krishan. *From Post–Industrial to Post–Modern Society: New Theories of the Contemporary World.* Oxford, UK: Basil Blackwell, 1996.

Laclau, Ernesto, and Chantal Mouffe. *Hegemony and Socialist Strategy: Towards a Radical Democratic Politics.* London: Verso, 1996.

Lakey, George. *Strategy for a Living Revolution.* San Francisco: W.H. Freeman, 1973.

Larmore, Charles. *The Morals of Modernity.* Cambridge, UK: Cambridge University Press, 1996.

Laslett, Peter. *The World We Have Lost: England Before the Industrial Age.* 2d ed. New York: Charles Scribner's Sons, 1973.

Laszlo, Ervin et al. *Goals for Mankind: A Report to the Club of Rome on the New Horizons of Global Community.* New York: New American Library, 1978.

*Lyotard, Jean-Francois. *The Postmodern Condition: A Report on Knowledge*, translated by Geoff Bennington and Brian Massumi. Minneapolis: University of Minnesota Press, 1985.

*Mumford, Lewis. *The Myth of the Machine.* 2 vols. New York: Harcourt, Brace, Jovanovich, 1967, 1970.

*Ophuls, William. *Requiem for Modern Politics: The Tragedy of the Enlightenment and the Challenge of the New Millennium.* Boulder, CO: Westview Press, 1997.

*Polyanyi, Karl. *The Great Transformation: The Political and Economic Origins of Our Time.* Boston: Beacon Press, 1957.

Rorty, Richard. *Contingency, Irony, and Solidarity.* Cambridge, UK: Cambridge University Press, 1999.

*Rosenau, Pauline Marie. *Post-Modernism and the Social Sciences: Insights, Inroads and Intrusions.* Princeton, NJ: Princeton University Press, 1992.

Smart, Barry. *Modern Conditions, Postmodern Controversies.* London: Routledge, 1992.

Smith, Preserved. "A History of Modern Culture." Volume 1 of *Origins of Modern Culture: 1543–1687*. New York: Collier Books, 1962.
*Tarrow, Sidney. *Power in Movement: Social Movements, Collective Action and Politics*. Cambridge, UK: Cambridge University Press, 1996.
*Touraine, Alain. *Critique of Modernity*, translated by David Macey. Oxford, UK: Basil Blackwell, 1995.
Wallerstein, Immanuel. "Crisis as Transition," in *Dynamics of Global Crisis*, edited by Samir Amin, Giovanni Arrighi, Andre Gunder Frank, and Immanuel Wallerstein, pp. 11–54. New York: Monthly Review Press, 1982.
White, Stephen K. *Political Theory and Postmodernism*. Cambridge, UK: Cambridge University Press, 1996.
*Wiener, Martin J. *English Culture and the Decline of the Industrial State: 1850–1980*. Cambridge, UK: Cambridge University Press, 1981.
Yack, Bernard. *The Fetishism of Modernities: Epochal Self-Consciousness in Contemporary Social and Political Thought*. Notre Dame, IN: University of Notre Dame Press, 1997.

Green and Ecofeminist Social Change Movements

Bahro, R. *Building the Green Movement*, translated by Mary Tyler. Philadelphia: New Society, 1986.
*Boggs, Carl. *Social Movements and Political Power: Emerging Forms of Radicalism in the West*. Philadelphia, PA: Temple University Press.
*Brecher, Jeremy; Tim Costello; and Brendan Smith. *Globalization from Below: The Power of Solidarity*. Cambridge, MA: South End Press, 2000.
Brulle, Robert J. *Agency, Democracy, and Nature: The U.S. Environmental Movement from a Critical Theory Perspective*. Cambridge, MA: MIT Press, 2000.
*Bryant, Bunyan, ed. *Environmental Justice Issues, Policies and Solutions*. Washington, DC: Island Press, 1995.
Bryner, Gary C. *Gaia's Wager: Environmental Movements and the Challenge of Sustainability*. London: Rowman and Littlefield, 2001.
*Bullard, Robert D., ed. *Confronting Environmental Racism: Voices from the Grassroots*. Boston: South End Press, 1993.
*Cable, Sherry, and Charles Cable. *Environmental Problems, Grassroots Solutions: The Politics of Grassroots Environmental Conflict*. New York: St. Martin's Press, 1995.
*Cohen, Jean L., ed. "Social Movements." *Social Research*, Special Issue, 52 (Winter, 1985).
Dalton, Russell, J. *The Green Rainbow: Environmental Groups in Western Europe*. New Haven, CT: Yale University Press, 1994.
*Diamond, Irene, and Floria Feman Orenstein, eds. *Reweaving the World: The Emergence of Ecofeminism*. San Francisco: Sierra Club Books, 1990.
*Dowie, Mark. *Losing Ground: American Environmentalism and the Close of the Twentieth Century*. Cambridge, MA: MIT Press, 1997.
Dunlap, Riley E., and Angela G. Mertig, eds. *American Environmentalism: The U.S. Environmental Movement, 1970–1990*. New York: Taylor and Francis, 1992.

Eder, Klaus. "The New Social Movements: Moral Crusades, Political Pressure Groups or Social Movements." *Social Research* 52 (Winter, 1985): 869–90.

Ekins, Paul. *A New World Order: Grassroots for Global Change.* London: Routledge, 1992.

*Eyerman, Ron, and Andrew Jamison. *Social Movements: A Cognitive Approach.* University Park: Pennsylvania State University Press, 1991.

*Gaard, Greta, ed. *Ecofeminism: Women, Animals, Nature.* Philadelphia: Temple University Press, 1993.

*Gottlieb, Robert. *Forcing the Spring: The Transformation of the American Environmental Movement.* Washington, DC: Island Press, 1993.

*———. *Environmentalism Unbound: Exploring New Pathways for Change.* Cambridge, MA: MIT Press, 2001.

Gowan, Susanne; George Lakey; William Mayer; and Richard Taylor. *Moving Toward a New Society.* Philadelphia: New Society Press, 1976.

Hampson, Fen Osler, and Judith Reppey, eds. *Earthly Goods: Environmental Change and Social Justice.* Ithaca, NY: Cornell University Press, 1996.

*Homer-Dixon, Thomas F. *Environment, Scarcity, and Violence.* Princeton, NJ: Princeton University Press, 1999.

Homer-Dixon, Thomas F., and Jesssica Blitt, eds. *Ecoviolence: Links Among Environment, Population, and Security.* Lanham, MD: Rowman and Littlefield, 1998.

Hulsberg, Werner. *The German Greens: A Social and Political Profile.* London: Verso, 1988.

Kelly, Petra. *Fighting for Hope*, translated by Marianne Howarth. Boston: South End Press, 1984.

Kolinsky, Eva, ed. *The Greens in West Germany: Organization and Policy Making.* Oxford, UK: Berg, 1989.

*List, Peter C., ed. *Radical Environmentalism: Philosophy and Tactics.* Belmont, CA: Wadsworth, 1993.

McCormick, John. *Reclaiming Paradise: The Global Environmental Movement.* Bloomington: Indiana University Press, 1989.

Milbrath, Lester W. *Environmentalists: Vanguard for a New Society.* Albany: State University of New York Press, 1984.

*Morris, Aldon D., and Carol McClurg Mueller, eds. *Frontiers in Social Movement Theory.* New Haven, CT: Yale University Press, 1992.

*Offe, Claus. "New Social Movements: Challenging the Boundaries of Institutional Politics." *Social Research* 52 (Winter 1985): 817–68.

Orr, David W. *Ecological Literacy: Education and the Transition to a Postmodern World.* Albany: State University of New York Press, 1992.

Press, Daniel. *Democratic Dilemmas in the Age of Ecology: Trees and Toxics in the American West.* Durham, NC: Duke University Press, 1994.

*Rensenbrink, John. *The Greens and the Politics of Transformation.* San Pedro, CA: R. and E. Miles, 1992.

*Scarce, Rik. *Eco-Warriors: Understanding the Radical Environmental Movement.* Chicago: Noble Press, 1990.

Schlosberg, David. *Environmental Justice and the New Pluralism.* Oxford, UK: Oxford University Press, 1999.

Shabecoff, Philip. *Earth Rising: American Environmentalism in the 21st Century.* Washington, DC: Island Press, 2001.

*Shiva, Vandana. *Staying Alive: Women, Ecology, and Development.* London: Zed Books, 1989.

Smith, Gregory A. *Education and the Environment: Learning to Live with Limits.* Albany: State University of New York Press, 1992.

Spretnak, Spretnak, and Fritjof Capra. *Green Politics*, rev. ed. Santa Fe, NM: Bear & Co., 1986.

*Tarrow, Sidney. *Power in Movement: Social Movements, Collective Action and Politics.* Cambridge, MA: Cambridge University Press, 1996.

*Taylor, Bron Raymond, ed. *Ecological Resistance Movements: The Global Emergence of Radical and Popular Environmentalism.* Albany: State University of New York Press, 1995.

*Tokar, Brian. *Earth for Sale: Reclaiming Ecology in the Age of Corporate Greenwash.* Boston: South End Press, 1997.

Warren, Karen J. *Ecofeminist Philosophy: A Western Perspective on What It Is and Why It Matters.* Lanham, MD: Rowman and Littlefield, 2000.

Environmental Public Policy Process and Analysis

Brown, Peter G., and Henry Shue, eds. *Food Policy: The Responsibility of the United States in the Life and Death Choices.* New York: Free Press, 1977.

Davis, Charles E. *The Politics of Hazardous Waste.* Englewood Cliffs, NJ: Prentice-Hall, 1993.

Enthoven, Alain C., and A. Myrick Freeman III, eds. *Pollution, Resources and the Environment.* New York: W.W. Norton, 1973.

*Ferre, Frederick, and Peter Hartel, eds. *Ethics and Environmental Policy: Theory Meets Practice.* Athens: University Georgia Press, 1994.

Gamman, John K. *Overcoming Obstacles in Environmental Policymaking: Creating Partnerships Through Mediation.* Albany: State University of New York Press, 1994.

Hannigan, John A. *Environmental Sociology: A Social Constructionist Perspective.* London: Routledge, 1995.

Kamieniecki, Sheldon; Robert O'Brien; and Michael Clarke, eds. *Controversies in Environmental Policy.* Albany: State University of New York, 1986.

*Kraft, Michael E. *Environmental Policy and Politics: Toward the Twenty-first Century.* New York: HarperCollins, 1996.

Lester, James P., ed. *Environmental Politics and Policy: Theories and Evidence.* Durham, NC: Duke University Press, 1989.

Paulsen, David F., and Robert B. Denhardt, eds. *Pollution and Public Policy: A Book of Readings.* New York: Dodd, Mead, 1973.

Peet, John. *Energy and the Ecological Economics of Sustainability.* Washington, DC: Island Press, 1992.

Rosenbaum, Walter A. *Environmental Politics and Policy.* 5th ed. Washington, DC: CQ Press, 2002.

Sprout, Harold, and Margaret Sprout. *The Context of Environmental Politics: Unfinished Business for America's Third Century.* Lexington: University of Kentucky Press, 1978.

Vig, Norman J. and Michael E. Kraft, eds. *Environmental Policy.* 4th ed. Washington, DC: CQ Press, 2000.

———, eds. *Environmental Policy in the 1900s: Toward a New Agenda.* Washington, DC: Congressional Quarterly Press, 1990.

———, eds. *Environmental Policy in the 1980's: Reagan's New Agenda.* Washington, DC: Congressional Quarterly Press, 1984.

Verburg, Carol J., ed. *The Environmental Predicament: Four Issues for Critical Analysis.* Boston: Bedford Books, 1995.

Wells, Donald T. *Environmental Policy: A Global Perspective for the Twenty-first Century.* Englewood Cliffs, NJ: Prentice-Hall, 1996.

About the Editor and Contributors

Andrew Dobson
Department of Government Politics, Open University, United Kingdom.

Robert E. Goodin
Philosophy Program, Research School of Social Sciences, Australian National University, Canberra, Australia

Joel Jay Kassiola
Dean of the College of Behavioral and Social Sciences, San Francisco State University, San Francisco, California

Andrew McLaughlin
Department of Philosophy, Herbert H. Lehman College of the City University of New York, Bronx, New York

Lester W. Milbrath
Director Emeritus, Research Program in Environment and Society, State University of New York at Buffalo, Buffalo, New York

Robert C. Paehlke
Department of Political Science, Trent University, Peterborough, Ontario, Canada

Dennis Pirages
Department of Political Science, University of Maryland, College Park, Maryland

Michael Zimmerman
Department of Philosophy, Tulane University, New Orleans, Louisiana

Index